Paul Kelsey, MLIS
Sigrid Kelsey, MLIS
Editors

Outreach Services in Academic and Special Libraries

Outreach Services in Academic and Special Libraries has been co-published simultaneously as *The Reference Librarian*, Volume 39, Number 82 2003.

Pre-publication
REVIEWS,
COMMENTARIES,
EVALUATIONS . . .

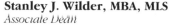

"THIS IS LIBRARY LITERATURE AT ITS BEST! The unusually strong contributions in this book offer creative approaches to a variety of outreach contexts, together with solid quantitative analysis and proven results."

Stanley J. Wilder, MBA, MLS
Associate Dean
River Campus Libraries
University of Rochester

More pre-publication
REVIEWS, COMMENTARIES, EVALUATIONS . . .

"TIMELY. . . . OF COMPELLING INTEREST. . . . PACKED FULL OF PRACTICAL IDEAS AND TECHNIQUES to extend library services and to engage patrons. The authors describe, for example, how to create outreach programs at traditional residential academic institutions, how outreach to faculty can promote both curricular and library programs with equal effectiveness, how the information needs of firefighters can be met, how Internet access for members of African-American churches can reduce the disparity in health care. Bibliographies are appended to each chapter so additional information can be sought quite easily. Buy the book; read the essays; consider the numerous ways by which you can extend your services and help your patrons; reach out!"

Henry M. Yaple, MLS
College Librarian
Penrose Library
Whitman College

"A FRESH LOOK AT OUTREACH ROLES FOR LIBRARIANS from contributors in academic and special libraries. . . . Demonstrates initiatives targeting diverse populations, and showcases extraordinary resources reaching beyond institution boundaries. Some highlighted programs include using partnerships to address the information needs of farming communities, recruiting minority high school students as future librarians, creating bilingual resources, and employing Web-based outreach for environmentalists and scientists. AFTER READING THIS BOOK, READERS WILL GAIN NEW IDEAS TO REACH UNDERSERVED POPULATIONS WITH SPECIFIC INFORMATION NEEDS."

Abby Holt, MLIS
Campus Outreach Librarian
University of Arkansas
for Medical Sciences

The Haworth Information Press
An Imprint of The Haworth Press, Inc.

Outreach Services in Academic and Special Libraries

Outreach Services in Academic and Special Libraries has been co-published simultaneously as *The Reference Librarian*, Number 82 2003.

COLORADO COLLEGE LIBRARY
COLORADO SPRINGS
· COLORADO

The Reference Librarian Monographic "Separates"

Below is a list of "separates," which in serials librarianship means a special issue simultaneously published as a special journal issue or double-issue *and* as a "separate" hardbound monograph. (This is a format which we also call a "DocuSerial.")

"Separates" are published because specialized libraries or professionals may wish to purchase a specific thematic issue by itself in a format which can be separately cataloged and shelved, as opposed to purchasing the journal on an on-going basis. Faculty members may also more easily consider a "separate" for classroom adoption.

"Separates" are carefully classified separately with the major book jobbers so that the journal tie-in can be noted on new book order slips to avoid duplicate purchasing.

You may wish to visit Haworth's Website at . . .

http://www.HaworthPress.com

. . . to search our online catalog for complete tables of contents of these separates and related publications.

You may also call 1-800-HAWORTH (outside US/Canada: 607-722-5857), or Fax 1-800-895-0582 (outside US/Canada: 607-771-0012), or e-mail at:

docdelivery@haworthpress.com

Outreach Services in Academic and Special Libraries, edited by Paul Kelsey, MLIS, and Sigrid Kelsey, MLIS (No. 82, 2003). *Presents an array of models and case studies for creating and implementing outreach services in academic and special library settings.*

Managing the Twenty-First Century Reference Department: Challenges and Prospects, edited by Kwasi Sarkodie-Mensah, PhD (No. 81, 2003). *An up-to-date guide on managing and maintaining a reference department in the twenty-first century.*

Digital Reference Services, edited by Bill Katz, PhD (No. 79/80, 2002/2003). *A clear and concise book explaining developments in electronic technology for reference services and their implications for reference librarians.*

The Image and Role of the Librarian, edited by Wendi Arant, MLS, and Candace R. Benefiel, MA, MLIS (No. 78, 2002). *A unique and insightful examination of how librarians are perceived–and how they perceive themselves.*

Distance Learning: Information Access and Services for Virtual Users, edited by Hemalata Iyer, PhD (No. 77, 2002). *Addresses the challenge of providing Web-based library instructional materials in a time of ever-changing technologies.*

Helping the Difficult Library Patron: New Approaches to Examining and Resolving a Long-Standing and Ongoing Problem, edited by Kwasi Sarkodie-Mensah, PhD (No. 75/76, 2002). *"Finally! A book that fills in the information cracks not covered in library school about the ubiquitous problem patron. Required reading for public service librarians." (Cheryl LaGuardia, MLS, Head of Instructional Services for the Harvard College Library, Cambridge, Massachusetts)*

Evolution in Reference and Information Services: The Impact of the Internet, edited by Di Su, MLS (No. 74, 2001). *Helps you make the most of the changes brought to the profession by the Internet.*

Doing the Work of Reference: Practical Tips for Excelling as a Reference Librarian, edited by Celia Hales Mabry, PhD (No. 72 and 73, 2001). *"An excellent handbook for reference librarians who wish to move from novice to expert. Topical coverage is extensive and is presented by the best guides possible: practicing reference librarians." (Rebecca Watson-Boone, PhD, President, Center for the Study of Information Professionals, Inc.)*

New Technologies and Reference Services, edited by Bill Katz, PhD (No. 71, 2000). *This important book explores developing trends in publishing, information literacy in the reference environment, reference provision in adult basic and community education, searching sessions, outreach programs, locating moving image materials for multimedia development, and much more.*

Reference Services for the Adult Learner: Challenging Issues for the Traditional and Technological Era, edited by Kwasi Sarkodie-Mensah, PhD (No. 69/70, 2000). *Containing research from librarians and adult learners from the United States, Canada, and Australia, this comprehensive guide offers you strategies for teaching adult patrons that will enable them to properly use and easily locate all of the materials in your library.*

Library Outreach, Partnerships, and Distance Education: Reference Librarians at the Gateway, edited by Wendi Arant and Pixey Anne Mosley (No. 67/68, 1999). *Focuses on community outreach in libraries toward a broader public by extending services based on recent developments in information technology.*

From Past-Present to Future-Perfect: A Tribute to Charles A. Bunge and the Challenges of Contemporary Reference Service, edited by Chris D. Ferguson, PhD (No. 66, 1999). *Explore reprints of selected articles by Charles Bunge, bibliographies of his published work, and original articles that draw on Bunge's values and ideas in assessing the present and shaping the future of reference service.*

Reference Services and Media, edited by Martha Merrill, PhD (No. 65, 1999). *Gives you valuable information about various aspects of reference services and media, including changes, planning issues, and the use and impact of new technologies.*

Coming of Age in Reference Services: A Case History of the Washington State University Libraries, edited by Christy Zlatos, MSLS (No. 64, 1999). *A celebration of the perseverance, ingenuity, and talent of the librarians who have served, past and present, at the Holland Library reference desk.*

Document Delivery Services: Contrasting Views, edited by Robin Kinder, MLS (No. 63, 1999). *Reviews the planning and process of implementing document delivery in four university libraries–Miami University, University of Colorado at Denver, University of Montana at Missoula, and Purdue University Libraries.*

The Holocaust: Memories, Research, Reference, edited by Robert Hauptman, PhD, and Susan Hubbs Motin (No. 61/62, 1998). *"A wonderful resource for reference librarians, students, and teachers . . . on how to present this painful, historical event." (Ephraim Kaye, PhD, The International School for Holocaust Studies, Yad Vashem, Jerusalem)*

Electronic Resources: Use and User Behavior, edited by Hemalata Iyer, PhD (No. 60, 1998). *Covers electronic resources and their use in libraries, with emphasis on the Internet and the Geographic Information Systems (GIS).*

Philosophies of Reference Service, edited by Celia Hales Mabry (No. 59, 1997). *"Recommended reading for any manager responsible for managing reference services and hiring reference librarians in any type of library." (Charles R. Anderson, MLS, Associate Director for Public Services, King County Library System, Bellevue, Washington)*

Business Reference Services and Sources: How End Users and Librarians Work Together, edited by Katherine M. Shelfer (No. 58, 1997). *"This is an important collection of papers suitable for all business librarians. . . . Highly recommended!" (Lucy Heckman, MLS, MBA, Business and Economics Reference Librarian, St. John's University, Jamaica, New York)*

Reference Sources on the Internet: Off the Shelf and onto the Web, edited by Karen R. Diaz (No. 57, 1997). *Surf off the library shelves and onto the Internet and cut your research time in half!*

Reference Services for Archives and Manuscripts, edited by Laura B. Cohen (No. 56, 1997). *"Features stimulating and interesting essays on security in archives, ethics in the archival profession, and electronic records." ("The Year's Best Professional Reading" (1998), Library Journal)*

Career Planning and Job Searching in the Information Age, edited by Elizabeth A. Lorenzen, MLS (No. 55, 1996). *"Offers stimulating background for dealing with the issues of technology and service. . . . A reference tool to be looked at often." (The One-Person Library)*

The Roles of Reference Librarians: Today and Tomorrow, edited by Kathleen Low, MLS (No. 54, 1996). *"A great asset to all reference collections. . . . Presents important, valuable information for reference librarians as well as other library users." (Library Times International)*

Reference Services for the Unserved, edited by Fay Zipkowitz, MSLS, DA (No. 53, 1996). *"A useful tool in developing strategies to provide services to all patrons." (Science Books & Films)*

Library Instruction Revisited: Bibliographic Instruction Comes of Age, edited by Lyn Elizabeth M. Martin, MLS (No. 51/52, 1995). *"A powerful collection authored by respected practitioners who have stormed the bibliographic instruction (BI) trenches and, luckily for us, have recounted their successes and shortcomings." (The Journal of Academic Librarianship)*

Library Users and Reference Services, edited by Jo Bell Whitlatch, PhD (No. 49/50, 1995). *"Well-planned, balanced, and informative. . . . Both new and seasoned professionals will find material for service attitude formation and practical advice for the front lines of service." (Anna M. Donnelly, MS, MA, Associate Professor and Reference Librarian, St. John's University Library)*

Social Science Reference Services, edited by Pam Baxter, MLS (No. 48, 1995). *"Offers practical guidance to the reference librarian. . . . A valuable source of information about specific literatures within the social sciences and the skills and techniques needed to provide access to those literatures." (Nancy P. O'Brien, MLS, Head, Education and Social Science Library, and Professor of Library Administration, University of Illinois at Urbana-Champaign)*

Reference Services in the Humanities, edited by Judy Reynolds, MLS (No. 47, 1994). *"A well-chosen collection of situations and challenges encountered by reference librarians in the humanities." (College Research Library News)*

Racial and Ethnic Diversity in Academic Libraries: Multicultural Issues, edited by Deborah A. Curry, MLS, MA, Susan Griswold Blandy, MEd, and Lyn Elizabeth M. Martin, MLS (No. 45/46, 1994). *"The useful techniques and attractive strategies presented here will provide the incentive for fellow professionals in academic libraries around the country to go and do likewise in their own institutions." (David Cohen, Adjunct Professor of Library Science, School of Library and Information Science, Queens College; Director, EMIE (Ethnic Materials Information Exchange); Editor, EMIE Bulletin)*

School Library Reference Services in the 90s: Where We Are, Where We're Heading, edited by Carol Truett, PhD (No. 44, 1994). *"Unique and valuable to the the teacher-librarian as well as students of librarianship. . . . The overall work successfully interweaves the concept of the continuously changing role of the teacher-librarian." (Emergency Librarian)*

Reference Services Planning in the 90s, edited by Gail Z. Eckwright, MLS, and Lori M. Keenan, MLS (No. 43, 1994). *"This monograph is well-researched and definitive, encompassing reference service as practices by library and information scientists. . . . It should be required reading for all professional librarian trainees." (Feliciter)*

Librarians on the Internet: Impact on Reference Services, edited by Robin Kinder, MLS (No. 41/42, 1994). *"Succeeds in demonstrating that the Internet is becoming increasingly a challenging but practical and manageable tool in the reference librarian's ever-expanding armory." (Reference Reviews)*

Reference Service Expertise, edited by Bill Katz (No. 40, 1993). *This important volume presents a wealth of practical ideas for improving the art of reference librarianship.*

Modern Library Technology and Reference Services, edited by Samuel T. Huang, MLS, MS (No. 39, 1993). *"This book packs a surprising amount of information into a relatively few number of pages. . . . This book will answer many questions." (Science Books and Films)*

Assessment and Accountability in Reference Work, edited by Susan Griswold Blandy, Lyn M. Martin, and Mary L. Strife (No. 38, 1992). *"An important collection of well-written, real-world chapters addressing the central questions that surround performance and services in all libraries." (Library Times International)*

The Reference Librarian and Implications of Mediation, edited by M. Keith Ewing, MLS, and Robert Hauptman, MLS (No. 37, 1992). *"An excellent and thorough analysis of reference mediation. . . . Well worth reading by anyone involved in the delivery of reference services." (Fred Batt, MLS, Associate University Librarian for Public Services, California State University, Sacramento)*

Library Services for Career Planning, Job Searching and Employment Opportunities, edited by Byron Anderson, MA, MLS (No. 36, 1992). *"An interesting book which tells professional libraries how to set up career information centers. . . . Clearly valuable reading for anyone establishing a career library." (Career Opportunities News)*

In the Spirit of 1992: Access to Western European Libraries and Literature, edited by Mary M. Huston, PhD, and Maureen Pastine, MLS (No. 35, 1992). *"A valuable and practical [collection] which every subject specialist in the field would do well to consult." (Western European Specialists Section Newsletter)*

Access Services: The Convergence of Reference and Technical Services, edited by Gillian M. McCombs, ALA (No. 34, 1992). *"Deserves a wide readership among both technical and public services librarians. . . . Highly recommended for any librarian interested in how reference and technical services roles may be combined." (Library Resources & Technical Services)*

Opportunities for Reference Services: The Bright Side of Reference Services in the 1990s, edited by Bill Katz (No. 33, 1991). *"A well-deserved look at the brighter side of reference services. . . . Should be read by reference librarians and their administrators in all types of libraries." (Library Times International)*

Government Documents and Reference Services, edited by Robin Kinder, MLS (No. 32, 1991). *Discusses access possibilities and policies with regard to government information, covering such important topics as new and impending legislation, information on most frequently used and requested sources, and grant writing.*

The Reference Library User: Problems and Solutions, edited by Bill Katz (No. 31, 1991). *"Valuable information and tangible suggestions that will help us as a profession look critically at our users and decide how they are best served." (Information Technology and Libraries)*

Continuing Education of Reference Librarians, edited by Bill Katz (No. 30/31, 1990). *"Has something for everyone interested in this field. . . . Library trainers and library school teachers may well find stimulus in some of the programs outlined here." (Library Association Record)*

Weeding and Maintenance of Reference Collections, edited by Sydney J. Pierce, PhD, MLS (No. 29, 1990). *"This volume may spur you on to planned activity before lack of space dictates 'ad hoc' solutions." (New Library World)*

Serials and Reference Services, edited by Robin Kinder, MLS, and Bill Katz (No. 27/28, 1990). *"The concerns and problems discussed are those of serials and reference librarians everywhere. . . . The writing is of a high standard and the book is useful and entertaining. . . . This book can be recommended." (Library Association Record)*

Rothstein on Reference: . . . with some help from friends, edited by Bill Katz and Charles Bunge, PhD, MLS (No. 25/26, 1990). *"An important and stimulating collection of essays on reference librarianship. . . . Highly recommended!" (Richard W. Grefrath, MA, MLS, Reference Librarian, University of Nevada Library)* Dedicated to the work of Sam Rothstein, one of the world's most respected teachers of reference librarians, this special volume features his writings as well as articles written about him and his teachings by other professionals in the field.

Integrating Library Use Skills Into the General Education Curriculum, edited by Maureen Pastine, MLS, and Bill Katz (No. 24, 1989). *"All contributions are written and presented to a high standard with excellent references at the end of each. . . . One of the best summaries I have seen on this topic." (Australian Library Review)*

Expert Systems in Reference Services, edited by Christine Roysdon, MLS, and Howard D. White, PhD, MLS (No. 23, 1989). *"The single most comprehensive work on the subject of expert systems in reference service." (Information Processing and Management)*

Information Brokers and Reference Services, edited by Bill Katz and Robin Kinder, MLS (No. 22, 1989). *"An excellent tool for reference librarians and indispensable for anyone seriously considering their own information-brokering service." (Booklist)*

Information and Referral in Reference Services, edited by Marcia Stucklen Middleton, MLS, and Bill Katz (No. 21, 1988). *Investigates a wide variety of situations and models which fall under the umbrella of information and referral.*

Reference Services and Public Policy, edited by Richard Irving, MLS, and Bill Katz (No. 20, 1988). *Looks at the relationship between public policy and information and reports ways in which libraries respond to the need for public policy information.*

Finance, Budget, and Management for Reference Services, edited by Ruth A. Fraley, MLS, MBA, and Bill Katz (No. 19, 1989). *"Interesting and relevant to the current state of financial needs in reference service. . . . A must for anyone new to or already working in the reference service area." (Riverina Library Review)*

Current Trends in Information: Research and Theory, edited by Bill Katz and Robin Kinder, MLS (No. 18, 1987). *"Practical direction to improve reference services and does so in a variety of ways ranging from humorous and clever metaphoric comparisons to systematic and practical methodological descriptions." (American Reference Books Annual)*

International Aspects of Reference and Information Services, edited by Bill Katz and Ruth A. Fraley, MLS, MBA (No. 17, 1987). *"An informative collection of essays written by eminent librarians, library school staff, and others concerned with the international aspects of information work." (Library Association Record)*

Reference Services Today: From Interview to Burnout, edited by Bill Katz and Ruth A. Fraley, MLS, MBA (No. 16, 1987). *Authorities present important advice to all reference librarians on the improvement of service and the enhancement of the public image of reference services.*

The Publishing and Review of Reference Sources, edited by Bill Katz and Robin Kinder, MLS (No. 15, 1987). *"A good review of current reference reviewing and publishing trends in the United States . . . will be of interest to intending reviewers, reference librarians, and students." (Australasian College Libraries)*

Personnel Issues in Reference Services, edited by Bill Katz and Ruth Fraley, MLS, MBA (No. 14, 1986). *"Chock-full of information that can be applied to most reference settings. Recommended for libraries with active reference departments." (RQ)*

Reference Services in Archives, edited by Lucille Whalen (No. 13, 1986). *"Valuable for the insights it provides on the reference process in archives and as a source of information on the different ways of carrying out that process." (Library and Information Science Annual)*

Conflicts in Reference Services, edited by Bill Katz and Ruth A. Fraley, MLS, MBA (No. 12, 1985). *This collection examines issues pertinent to the reference department.*

Evaluation of Reference Services, edited by Bill Katz and Ruth A. Fraley, MLS, MBA (No. 11, 1985). *"A much-needed overview of the present state of the art vis-à-vis reference service evaluation. . . . Excellent. . . . Will appeal to reference professionals and aspiring students." (RQ)*

Library Instruction and Reference Services, edited by Bill Katz and Ruth A. Fraley, MLS, MBA (No. 10, 1984). *"Well written, clear, and exciting to read. This is an important work recommended for all librarians, particularly those involved in, interested in, or considering bibliographic instruction. . . . A milestone in library literature." (RQ)*

Reference Services and Technical Services: Interactions in Library Practice, edited by Gordon Stevenson and Sally Stevenson (No. 9, 1984). *"New ideas and longstanding problems are handled with humor and sensitivity as practical suggestions and new perspectives are suggested by the authors." (Information Retrieval & Library Automation)*

Reference Services for Children and Young Adults, edited by Bill Katz and Ruth A. Fraley, MLS, MBA (No. 7/8, 1983). *"Offers a well-balanced approach to reference service for children and young adults." (RQ)*

Video to Online: Reference Services in the New Technology, edited by Bill Katz and Ruth A. Fraley, MLS, MBA (No. 5/6, 1983). *"A good reference manual to have on hand. . . . Well-written, concise, provide[s] a wealth of information." (Online)*

Ethics and Reference Services, edited by Bill Katz and Ruth A. Fraley, MLS, MBA (No. 4, 1982). *Library experts discuss the major ethical and legal implications that reference librarians must take into consideration when handling sensitive inquiries about confidential material.*

Reference Services Administration and Management, edited by Bill Katz and Ruth A. Fraley, MLS, MBA (No. 3, 1982). *Librarianship experts discuss the management of the reference function in libraries and information centers, outlining the responsibilities and qualifications of reference heads.*

Reference Services in the 1980s, edited by Bill Katz (No. 1/2, 1982). *Here is a thought-provoking volume on the future of reference services in libraries, with an emphasis on the challenges and needs that have come about as a result of automation.*

Outreach Services in Academic and Special Libraries

Paul Kelsey, MLIS
Sigrid Kelsey, MLIS
Editors

Outreach Services in Academic and Special Libraries has been co-published simultaneously as *The Reference Librarian*, Number 82 2003.

The Haworth Information Press®
An Imprint of The Haworth Press, Inc.

New York • London • Victoria (AU)
www.HaworthPress.com

COLORADO COLLEGE LIBRARY
COLORADO SPRINGS
COLORADO

Published by

The Haworth Information Press®, 10 Alice Street, Binghamton, NY 13904-1580 USA

The Haworth Information Press® is an imprint of The Haworth Press, Inc., 10 Alice Street, Binghamton, NY 13904-1580 USA.

Outreach Services in Academic and Special Libraries has been co-published simultaneously as *The Reference Librarian*™, Number 82 2003.

© 2003 by The Haworth Press, Inc. All rights reserved. No part of this work may be reproduced or utilized in any form or by any means, electronic or mechanical, including photocopying, microfilm and recording, or by any information storage and retrieval system, without permission in writing from the publisher. Printed in the United States of America.

The development, preparation, and publication of this work has been undertaken with great care. However, the publisher, employees, editors, and agents of The Haworth Press and all imprints of The Haworth Press, Inc., including The Haworth Medical Press® and Pharmaceutical Products Press®, are not responsible for any errors contained herein or for consequences that may ensue from use of materials or information contained in this work. Opinions expressed by the author(s) are not necessarily those of The Haworth Press, Inc. With regard to case studies, identities and circumstances of individuals discussed herein have been changed to protect confidentiality. Any resemblance to actual persons, living or dead, is entirely coincidental.

Cover design by Jennifer M. Gaska.

Library of Congress Cataloging-in-Publication Data

Outreach services in academic and special libraries / Paul Kelsey, Sigrid Kelsey, editors.
     p. cm.
    "Co-published simultaneously as The reference librarian, number 82."
    Includes bibliographical references and index.
    ISBN 0-7890-2431-4 (alk. paper) – ISBN 0-7890-2432-2 (pbk. : alk. paper)
    1. Library outreach programs–United States–Case studies. 2. Academic libraries–Public relations–United States–Case studies. 3. Special libraries–Public relations–United States–Case studies. 4. Libraries and community–United States–Case studies. 5. Libraries and minorities–United States–Case studies. I. Kelsey, Paul. II. Kelsey, Sigrid. III. Reference librarian.
  Z711.7.O88 2003
  021.2–dc22

2003021688

Z
711.7
.O88
2003

Indexing, Abstracting & Website/Internet Coverage

This section provides you with a list of major indexing & abstracting services. That is to say, each service began covering this periodical during the year noted in the right column. Most Websites which are listed below have indicated that they will either post, disseminate, compile, archive, cite or alert their own Website users with research-based content from this work. (This list is as current as the copyright date of this publication.)

(continued)

*Exact start date to come.

(continued)

Special bibliographic notes related to special journal issues
(separates) and indexing/abstracting:

- indexing/abstracting services in this list will also cover material in any "separate" that is co-published simultaneously with Haworth's special thematic journal issue or DocuSerial. Indexing/abstracting usually covers material at the article/chapter level.
- monographic co-editions are intended for either non-subscribers or libraries which intend to purchase a second copy for their circulating collections.
- monographic co-editions are reported to all jobbers/wholesalers/approval plans. The source journal is listed as the "series" to assist the prevention of duplicate purchasing in the same manner utilized for books-in-series.
- to facilitate user/access services all indexing/abstracting services are encouraged to utilize the co-indexing entry note indicated at the bottom of the first page of each article/chapter/contribution.
- this is intended to assist a library user of any reference tool (whether print, electronic, online, or CD-ROM) to locate the monographic version if the library has purchased this version but not a subscription to the source journal.
- individual articles/chapters in any Haworth publication are also available through the Haworth Document Delivery Service (HDDS).

ALL HAWORTH INFORMATION PRESS
BOOKS AND JOURNALS ARE PRINTED
ON CERTIFIED ACID-FREE PAPER

Outreach Services
in Academic and Special Libraries

CONTENTS

ABOUT THE EDITORS

Paul Kelsey, MLIS, is Agriculture Librarian at the Louisiana State University Libraries. Mr. Kelsey chaired the LSU Libraries Outreach Committee from 2001-2003. He is a member of USAIN (United States Agricultural Information Network) and serves on the Government and Legislative Relations Committee. He is the co-founder of the Louisiana Young Readers' Choice Award (LYRC). He has presented on the topic of outreach services at the 2002 Association of College and Research Libraries Louisiana Chapter Conference. Mr. Kelsey has contributed to several publications, including *Collection Building, Louisiana Libraries, T.H.E. Journal, College & Research Libraries,* and *The Best Books for Academic Libraries, Volume 1: Science, Technology, & Agriculture.*

Sigrid Kelsey, MLIS, is Electronic Reference Services and Web Development Coordinator at the Louisiana State University Libraries. She is the 2000 recipient of the American Library Association New Members Round Table Shirley Olofson Memorial Award. She has co-authored an "E-struction" (instruction by e-mail) program that has been adopted by libraries worldwide. Articles about her E-struction program are published in the *LLA Bulletin* and *The Reference Librarian.* Ms. Kelsey has written or co-written many articles which have appeared in *E-Libraries Proceedings: 2001, Colorado Libraries, Louisiana Libraries, Reference and User Services Quarterly,* and *Information Technology and Libraries.* She has also written a number of reference book entries, including one for the *Dictionary of Literary Biography.*

Introduction

Paul Kelsey
Sigrid Kelsey

Academic and special libraries offer a greater variety of exciting services and resources for their library constituents than in the past. For example, special libraries build or subscribe to databases designed to meet the information needs of their library patrons and create digital exhibits on the Web in tandem with thematic lecture series. Academic libraries subscribe to a rich array of electronic indexes and databases, full-text journals, and e-books, and offer virtual reference services, instruction by e-mail, and online classes. Library instruction is changing in new and highly creative ways by incorporating aspects of information literacy into the traditional library curriculum. Yet many students and faculty remain largely unaware of these relatively new library services and resources, or are simply content to access a limited sample of electronic resources remotely from their home, office, or dorm. Outreach services designed to promote awareness of the library and to meet the information needs of these constituents are of vital importance to academic and special libraries. This work presents a number of exceptional case studies and models devoted to the delivery of outreach services in academic and special libraries.

We begin the volume with several case studies describing the proactive efforts of librarians at academic libraries to build outreach programs and to form substantive partnerships with other university and college departments. Contributors from the Kresge Library at Oakland University discuss steps taken to build an outreach program designed to target underserved student populations; outreach efforts included participation in African American Celebration Month, Cultural Awareness Week, Disability Awareness Day, and

[Haworth co-indexing entry note]: "Introduction." Kelsey, Paul, and Sigrid Kelsey. Co-published simultaneously in *The Reference Librarian* (The Haworth Information Press, an imprint of The Haworth Press, Inc.) No. 82, 2003, pp. 1-3; and: *Outreach Services in Academic and Special Libraries* (ed: Paul Kelsey, and Sigrid Kelsey) The Haworth Information Press, an imprint of The Haworth Press, Inc., 2003, pp. 1-3. Single or multiple copies of this article are available for a fee from The Haworth Document Delivery Service [1-800-HAWORTH, 9:00 a.m. - 5:00 p.m. (EST). E-mail address: docdelivery@haworthpress.com].

http://www.haworthpress.com/store/product.asp?sku=J120
© 2003 by The Haworth Press, Inc. All rights reserved.
Digital Object Identifier: 10.1300/J120v39n82_01

1

reaching out to transfer students. Contributors from the Washington State University Libraries present a programmatic approach for initiating outreach partnerships at their university in the context of incorporating information literacy into library instruction. Next, librarians from the Arts & Sciences Libraries, University of Buffalo, SUNY, focus on multiple models of outreach, including library exhibits, book talks, interactive multi-media kiosks, and teaching assistant workshops, as an effective method for establishing collaborative partnerships and promoting library awareness to students. All of these case studies include examples of innovative outreach programs that take advantage of the resources and opportunities made available from collaborative partnerships.

The work also includes articles reporting on the outreach efforts of highly dedicated librarians working in special libraries to meet the very unique information needs of special groups of library constituents. Contributors from the Illinois Fire Service Institute Library, University of Illinois at Urbana-Champaign and Eastern Illinois University offer an in-depth analysis of a reference database containing requests made by Illinois firefighters and provide a model for delivering outreach services to groups of remote users. An outreach partnership between a special library, the Library and Information Center of the New York Center for Agricultural Medicine and Health, and the Mohawk Valley Library System of public libraries is the focus of an article submitted by librarians who participated at those institutions. The partnership, which also included several community organizations, resulted in a series of Library and Services Technology Act grants used to fund an outreach program targeting the farming and agricultural community in central New York State. These case studies serve as wonderful examples for special libraries considering outreach efforts to remote or underserved groups.

Multicultural outreach is also strongly represented in this work. Librarians from the Colorado State University Libraries created a bilingual research for teens web site in English and Spanish to reach the Hispanic community. The web site teaches teenagers strategies for conducting library research using a format with graphics especially designed to appeal to this age group. Contributors from Cornell University discuss and evaluate a unique recruitment program developed to attract people of color to the library profession. The summer program included a curriculum introducing high school students of color to library research and information literacy skills and provided students with the opportunity to job-shadow librarians at the Cornell University Libraries. Librarians from the health sciences library at the University of Rochester Medical Center formed an outreach partnership, funded by the National Library of Medicine, that reaches out to African American churches to expand access to important health care information. These exemplary outreach programs illustrate the continuing importance for the library profession to deliver outreach services in meaningful and innovative ways to multicultural groups.

We hope that you enjoy this publication. One of the great benefits of a work devoted entirely to outreach is the eclectic range of creative ideas and successful case studies presented by the contributors. We encourage readers to apply some of the models and ideas appearing in the following pages to the delivery of outreach services at their own academic and special libraries.

Beyond These Walls:
Building a Library Outreach Program
at Oakland University

Elizabeth W. Kraemer
Dana J. Keyse
Shawn V. Lombardo

SUMMARY. To enhance the learning experiences of all students, to-day's academic librarians must engage in outreach efforts that move beyond the walls of the library. In the past year, Oakland University's Kresge Library has made significant inroads in developing outreach initiatives that provide needed services to previously underserved student populations, such as transfer students, multicultural groups, and on-campus residents. These programs have increased the library's visibility, enhanced its image among the university's students, faculty, and staff alike, and positioned it at the heart of teaching and learning on campus. This article describes some of these outreach efforts. *[Article copies available for a fee from The Haworth Document Delivery Service: 1-800-HAWORTH. E-mail address: <docdelivery@haworthpress.com> Website: <http://www. HaworthPress.com> © 2003 by The Haworth Press, Inc. All rights reserved.]*

KEYWORDS. Transfer students, multicultural students, honors college, residence halls, disabled students, diversity, academic libraries

---

Elizabeth W. Kraemer, Dana J. Keyse, and Shawn V. Lombardo are all Assistant Professors and Reference Librarians, Kresge Library, Oakland University, Rochester, MI 48309.

[Haworth co-indexing entry note]: "Beyond These Walls: Building a Library Outreach Program at Oakland University." Kraemer, Elizabeth W., Dana J. Keyse, and Shawn V. Lombardo. Co-published simultaneously in *The Reference Librarian* (The Haworth Information Press, an imprint of The Haworth Press, Inc.) No. 82, 2003, pp. 5-17; and: *Outreach Services in Academic and Special Libraries* (ed: Paul Kelsey, and Sigrid Kelsey) The Haworth Information Press, an imprint of The Haworth Press, Inc., 2003, pp. 5-17. Single or multiple copies of this article are available for a fee from The Haworth Document Delivery Service [1-800-HAWORTH, 9:00 a.m. - 5:00 p.m. (EST). E-mail address: docdelivery@haworthpress.com].

http://www.haworthpress.com/store/product.asp?sku=J120
© 2003 by The Haworth Press, Inc. All rights reserved.
Digital Object Identifier: 10.1300/J120v39n82_02

INTRODUCTION

As college campuses grow increasingly diverse and academic libraries more complex, students are falling through the cracks of traditional approaches to information literacy education. Many students with special needs, including those with physical or learning disabilities, require individualized services and support that they cannot obtain in a one-shot library instruction session. Others, such as distance learning students, manage to avoid contact with library staff altogether. To enhance the learning experiences of all students, today's academic librarians must engage in outreach efforts that, as Lynn Westbrook and Robert Waldman assert, "reach patrons outside of the library—wherever they are accessing, evaluating, or manipulating information."[1] Effective outreach takes into account the information needs of the student as well as the potential barriers that may inhibit learning; for example, one goal of most library instruction programs is to create a more accessible learning environment for students, one that frees them to approach staff for assistance and to complete their work without feeling disconnected from the academic library setting. In the past year, Oakland University's Kresge Library has made significant inroads in developing outreach initiatives that provide needed services to previously underserved student populations. At the same time, these programs have increased the library's visibility, enhanced its image among the university's students, faculty, and staff alike, and positioned it at the heart of teaching and learning on campus. This article describes some of these outreach efforts.

BACKGROUND

Oakland University (OU) is a state-supported institution located in suburban Michigan, about thirty-five miles northwest of Detroit. The university has grown rapidly in recent years, with a fall 2002 semester enrollment of 16,059 students (12,634 undergraduate and 3,425 graduate students), marking the seventh consecutive year of rising enrollment. This growth has brought with it an increasingly diverse population. Approximately 16 percent of students identify themselves as members of a minority group, with the largest portions comprising African American students (7.2 percent), and international students (2.7 percent). In addition, about 330 students actively seek out the university's Office of Disability Services.[2] OU also has a large transfer student population, comprising approximately one half of new students each year.

One of the library's major service initiatives is its collaboration with the university's first-year writing program. In coordination with instructors of Rhetoric 160 (RHT 160), a required first-year writing course in which students must complete a major research paper, librarians have developed an instruction program to introduce students to the library, its services and the academic research process. This program uses both online instruction–in the form of a Web-based tutorial designed by librarian Beth Kraemer–and two hours of in-person instruction provided by librarians. Because RHT 160 is a required course, the library is able to reach a large number of students each year. During the 2001-2002 academic year, for example, OU librarians provided instruction for 102 sections of RHT 160, reaching 2,154 undergraduates.

A second library outreach initiative has focused on the library's liaison program with the university's academic departments. Each department is assigned a librarian liaison who coordinates collection development activities for that discipline. Liaisons also promote library instruction and other library services and resources to their respective departments. The purpose of the liaison program is to facilitate communication between the library and the university's academic units, and to expand the library's instructional efforts through the development of subject-based instruction sessions for individual courses.

It appears, however, that these efforts have fallen short of supporting the research and learning activities of every student at OU. For instance, students who delay taking RHT 160, sometimes until their senior year, are not introduced to library research methods until late in their academic careers. Moreover, a large number of transfer students opt out of RHT 160 by taking an equivalent course at their previous institutions, thereby bypassing an introduction to OU library services and resources altogether. Liaison relationships with academic departments also have failed to reach whole categories of students, though the liaison program with academic departments has been moderately successful. For example, the librarian liaison to the education department has developed an excellent relationship with that department, providing extensive instruction to both undergraduate and graduate students, and training sessions for faculty in new library resources and services. However, outreach to other departments, especially those in which faculty are not frequent library users, has proven more difficult. As a result, students in these disciplines are not exposed to the library's offerings as extensively as students in other disciplines. Other students may experience anxiety in a standard library instruction session because of their unfamiliarity with the library environment. International students, for example, may be unfamiliar with procedures in American libraries and thus have more difficulty with library protocols and jargon than the average undergraduate. Finally, many students, such as those with physical and learning disabilities, might benefit more from one-on-one instruction that takes their individual needs into consideration.

The library obviously needed to move beyond the academic departments to target underserved student populations. When planning a strategy for the marketing of library services and resources, Westbrook and Waldman recommend that institutions "determine the mechanisms on campus that provide students, staff, and faculty with information."[3] The library's first move, then–and the impetus for many of our accomplishments in the past year–was to reach out to the Student Affairs division. This university department oversees student activities and organizations, residence halls, new student programs, disability support services, advising, the academic skills center, and services to minority and international students. The Dean of the Library arranged for a group of librarians to attend a meeting of Student Affairs department leaders in the fall 2001 semester. The librarians' approach to this meeting was two-fold: to introduce themselves, and to market library services in terms of what Kresge librarians could do to help Student Affairs staff improve student retention and success. The participation of both the Dean of the Library and the Vice President for Student Affairs demonstrated a high level of administrative support for collaboration between the two units. Some ideas that were shared during this meeting included specialized library orientations and instruction, individualized research consultations for students, and ideas for creative programming such as a book discussion group for students living in the residence halls. A number of initiatives, described below, developed as a result of this meeting, while subsequent contacts presented additional outreach opportunities.

Since the librarians have become further acquainted with the directors and support staff in Student Affairs, they have been invited to do more than the outreach activities initially envisioned. Kresge Library is now heavily involved in campus-wide events such as Welcome Week, African American Celebration Month, Cultural Awareness Week, and Disability Awareness Day. This method of networking with students, faculty and staff has proved invaluable to the expansion of library outreach efforts across the campus.

CURRENT OUTREACH EFFORTS AT KRESGE LIBRARY

Outreach to New Students

One of the goals of Kresge Library is to introduce new students to library resources and services during their first year at the university. However, since most students take RHT 160 during the winter semester as the second of two required writing courses, they do not encounter a librarian until their second semester at OU. This can cause new first-semester students to feel overwhelmed and confused by an academic library, a situation that librarians wanted to alleviate through targeted outreach initiatives. Prior to the fall 2001 meeting with Student Affairs, the library had participated sparingly in new student orientation activities. In 2001, librarian Shawn Lombardo volunteered to serve as liaison to the Office of New Student Programs (ONSP), within the university's Student Affairs division, and worked to include the library in a variety of ONSP events to welcome and orient new students to the university. She designed handouts for students' orientation packets highlighting the library's timesaving and convenient services, including remote access to resources, full-text databases, electronic reserves, and e-mail reference services. And, because they felt that students would respond well to library tours led by their peers, Lombardo and fellow librarian Dana Keyse trained Orientation Group Leaders–upper-class students who plan and direct orientation activities for incoming students–to provide these tours to new students.

Lombardo, Keyse, and Kraemer also participated in a series of parent orientation sessions sponsored by ONSP in the summer of 2002. Paired with staff from the university's Office of Information Technology, they participated in interactive question and answer sessions for parents of incoming first-year students. Parents were interested in the university's information technology recommendations for student laptops and other technology needs, as well as the library resources and services that were available online, especially remotely. Since then, parents have accompanied their incoming students more frequently to the library to "check out" its services and resources. The three librarians believe that these visits, in part, demonstrate their success in publicizing library services to parents.

Throughout the fall 2002 semester, Kresge Library outreach specialists worked to continue building relationships with students new to the university. Lombardo and Keyse, for example, targeted students enrolled in the university's Peer Connections program, which supports student cohort groups taking many of the same courses during their first year at OU. Although most of these students will receive more comprehensive library instruction during their second semester at the university, Lombardo and Keyse wanted to introduce them to the library and its services early in their academic careers. They provided brief, casual presentations to these groups, with the goal of making the library less intimidating to students just out of high school. These sessions provided an opportunity for students to ask about library services and resources in a supportive, informal setting. The librarians received positive feedback for these efforts from Peer Connections group leaders, who indicated that students were both surprised and glad that a librarian was available to them. The librarians learned that a little effort goes a long way in improving the library's image and perceived accessibility.

Future projects for outreach to first-year students are being developed as well. To reach even more new students, Lombardo plans to target sections of Communications 101, a course introducing first-year students to university life. In coordination with other librarians, she will offer brief online tutorials and informal presentations to these groups before their more formal introduction to library research in RHT 160.

One important initiative still in its infancy is outreach to the university's transfer student population. It is crucial to target these students for library orientation and instruction to ensure student retention and success. According to

Staines, community college librarians report that a large number of transfer students return to their previous institutions to conduct research because they feel more comfortable in that setting.[4] In fact, Still posits that students who transfer to four-year institutions from community colleges and other two-year schools may be overwhelmed by a larger academic library.[5] Furthermore, according to a recent survey reported in the *Chronicle of Higher Education*, transfer students are less likely to feel connected to their institution than students who begin and end their academic careers at the same institution.[6] Unfortunately, many schools do not have instruction programs targeted specifically to transfer students. For example, Staines' 1996 study revealed that more than 35 percent of the four-year institutions and community colleges surveyed offered no special library instruction services to transfer students.[7] Moreover, transfer students are a difficult group to target. As a result, OU librarians planned outreach activities that were designed to make transfer students more comfortable at OU and at the library.

Using a multi-tiered approach, Lombardo collaborated with ONSP to reach out to OU transfer students. In doing so, she worked under the assumption that many transfer students are busy people, employed at least part-time and perhaps also caring for families. In fall 2001, Lombardo developed a handout specifically directed toward transfer students to include in their orientation packets. The handout emphasizes library resources and services, such as remote access, full-text databases, and electronic course reserves that can save students time and effort. More than half of OU's transfer students come from area community colleges. Because of this, Lombardo also stressed the availability of personalized research consultations and other reference assistance to address those students who may feel more overwhelmed at a larger institution than at their previous school. In addition, Lombardo held brief workshops at the beginning of the winter 2002 semester to orient students to basic library resources. Publicity for the workshops appeared on signs in the library, handouts distributed during transfer student orientation sessions, and the library's Web site. Although not initially well-attended, many transfer students expressed interest in the sessions, so they will be offered again each winter semester, when more transfer students enroll than at any other time of year. As Lombardo continues her work with transfer students, she plans to expand the library's marketing and outreach efforts, perhaps to include a designated Transfer Student Day at the library, where librarians offer tours, workshops, and free coffee to attendees. She also hopes to obtain a list of e-mail addresses of transfer students and check in with them over the course of the semester, offering research assistance during the midterm and final periods.

Along with these outreach efforts, OU librarians also began to think about programming that would increase the library's visibility and generally attract more students. Lombardo and Keyse served on the university-wide planning committee, responsible for organizing events to welcome new and returning students to OU during the first week of the semester. For the first time, the library participated extensively in Welcome Week activities at the beginning of the fall 2002 semester, and with much success. Library participation in Welcome Week included a daylong "library coffee house" with free mugs, coffee, and snacks, held in the library's student lounge. As part of this celebration, Lombardo and Keyse created a book display of faculty publications and invited faculty to view the display and chat with students. Library faculty and staff were encouraged to join the coffee house and conversation as well. Students voiced their appreciation of the event; in fact, one student suggested that the library host such an event every day! Other Welcome Week activities included library tours and a drawing in which students could enter to win a gift basket by registering their library cards at the circulation desk. These events proved to be very popular with students, as evidenced by the nearly 4 percent increase in the door count over the same period in the previous year. These numbers have encouraged Kresge Library to expand future Welcome Week participation, and perhaps bring back the very popular coffee house during midterms and finals.

Multicultural and Cultural Outreach

As Westbrook and Waldman state, "taking the time to accurately picture user information needs outside the library is crucial to effective, efficient outreach."[8] By attending, promoting and advising on various campus social activities as the diversity liaison to Student Affairs, librarian Dana Keyse serves not only as a representative of Kresge Library and a faculty advisor, but in some cases, as a mentor. Moving beyond the standard survey or focus group, perhaps the most effective way to assess students' information needs is to build relationships with them. While most students' tenure at a university will last fewer than five years, some of the relationships developed during those years will last into their professional careers. In terms of marketing, on and off campus, these alumni will gladly serve as library advocates. Word-of-mouth recommendations from respected peers to incoming students will always surpass any carefully planned marketing tool, though it is the carefully planned marketing tool–in this case, an outreach program such as the coffee house–that starts the cycle.

As a member of the African American Celebration Committee, Keyse currently advises students on a program about the history of African American music, which will be presented by Oakland University's Association of Black Students. She also is co-sponsoring campus showings of the speeches of Martin Luther King, Jr., to promote the campus unity march, and has participated in Disability Awareness Day with a kiosk of assistive technology equipment housed in the library. By attending campus events with related library resource handouts, and by creating displays and Web pages to support campus events such as Cultural Awareness Week and African American Celebration Month, Kresge librarians have not only made themselves visible, but invaluable as an information resource.

In a presentation at the American Library Association (ALA) 2002 Annual Conference, Isabel Espinal, of ALA's Office of Literacy and Outreach Services, defined multicultural outreach as "activities or organizational efforts to reach out to distinct cultural groups on your campus who are not part of U.S. mainstream or dominant culture."[9] With this in mind, Keyse created the *Kresge Library Diversity Resources* Web site,[10] http://www.kl.oakland.edu/ DiversityResources/DiversityResources.html, with input solicited from leaders of various minority-based student groups on campus and their faculty advisors. The site focuses on social and cultural studies of the following groups: African Americans, Arab Americans, Asian Americans, Hispanic Americans/ Latinos, Native Americans, Gay/Lesbian/Bisexual/Transgender, and Women. It aids students in their research for cultural studies and other diversity-related coursework with links providing access to primary documents through special archives, museum exhibits and research materials. The resource also links to bibliographies and online journals for cultural and diversity studies and provides scholarship and career information, lists of social organizations, and recreational sites. From the site, Keyse offers research consultations on cultural or other projects, providing yet another point of contact with students who may not be using library services otherwise. The Web site is meant to be a work in progress, promising something new and interesting with each visit, with continual development based on user feedback. While soliciting input from the leaders of student groups, Keyse has enlisted them to promote the site within their groups and elsewhere on campus. Additionally, librarians discuss the site in library instruction sessions with relevant courses. Keyse also promotes the site at various events on campus such as Hispanic Heritage Month, Cultural Awareness Week, and African American Celebration Month. By putting a face with the site at these gatherings, outreach becomes both high-tech and high-touch.

Residence Halls Outreach

There are more than 1,100 students living in the 6 residence halls on campus.[11] As outreach efforts at Kresge Library have expanded, so has the desire to connect with these students living on campus. Beth Kraemer volunteered to serve as the librarian liaison to the Residence Halls, and during the winter semester of 2001 she attended one of the monthly Residence Halls Council meetings to promote library services. Kraemer also began working with the library administration to develop a unique, educational and social program targeting on-campus residents, resulting in the OU Residence Halls Book Club. The plan for this program was for Kraemer to meet once or twice a semester with members of the book club to discuss a work of the group's choosing. By limiting membership to ten to twelve students, the book club would maintain a casual environment, avoiding the lecture hall feel. The University Housing Program Coordinator offered enthusiastic backing of the book club, and invited Kraemer to present the idea to students at a Halls Council meeting in the fall of 2002. Additional publicity was handled by mailing flyers to each Resident Advisor for posting on residence hall bulletin boards, and by setting up a display just outside of the cafeteria with book club flyers.

To get the group started, Kraemer chose Jean Hegland's *Into the Forest* as the book club's first selection. Because this new program was experimental, the purchase of the books was funded by the library administration so that the students would get to keep their copies, and the facilitator's copy would be added to the library's book collection. The book club held its inaugural meeting in November 2002, with a membership of six students. As a venue for the gathering, one of the members offered the student lounge located on her floor, where the book club gathered couches and comfortable chairs into a circle for the meeting. The library furnished light snacks and beverages, and the students were very pleased with their first meeting, indicating a desire to continue the program. The book club members voted unanimously to read the first two books in the Harry Potter series for the next meeting, held early in the winter 2003 semester. The library administration continued to fund the venture for the remainder of the 2002-2003 academic year. Beyond that, Kraemer planned to seek a grant over the summer of 2003 to cover expenses of the book club for several years, depending on the success of the next few meetings and continued interest from on-campus residents.

By offering programs such as the OU Residence Halls Book Club, Kraemer not only wants to raise the profile of the library on campus, but also to connect with students in a fun and casual way. The hope is that the next time those students need help with a class project or term paper, they will turn to a librarian before they turn to the Internet. And judging from the enthusiastic response to the book club from the students involved, it just might work.

Honors College Outreach

In the fall 2001 semester, the then-Interim Director of the Oakland University Honors College attended faculty meetings across campus to raise awareness of the program. As a result, the library administrators created the role of librarian liaison to the Honors College, asking Beth Kraemer to take the position because of her background as an honors college student in her undergraduate career. Kraemer accepted the responsibility and developed a flyer outlining library services to the Honors College, which she distributed among faculty members teaching in the honors program. Some of the services offered are customized library instruction sessions for honors classes, a display case for student work, presentation space for class projects, and individual research consultations with students working on a class project or their honors theses. The Honors College Director supported the outreach efforts fully, encouraging faculty members to contact the library for assistance.

During the summer of 2002, Kraemer sent a memo to the seven faculty members teaching honors courses in the upcoming fall semester. In her memo she once again outlined services available to the honors community, emphasizing that library instruction could be customized to suit each course. At the beginning of the fall 2002 term, Kraemer also attended the Honors College faculty orientation to publicize library services to the instructors. These marketing efforts resulted in two instruction sessions in the fall of 2002. Six honors courses were being offered in the winter 2003 semester, and Kraemer contacted those instructors in November of 2002. Several responses from interested faculty members were received within hours.

The Honors College faculty and staff have been eager to integrate the librarian liaison into the honors community on campus, and further outreach efforts with the Honors College are being discussed. For example, at least once each academic year, Kraemer will conduct a library instruction session for Honors College students to teach some advanced searching techniques and introduce specialized research databases. To ensure attendance, the sessions will be held at the Honors College facility, where there are several networked computers available to students. With the help of the new Digital Information Services Librarian at Kresge Library, Kraemer is also developing an online, searchable database of the honors theses collection that is housed at the honors facility. The two librarians met with the new Honors College Director in October 2002 to discuss the database design, which will be developed by the librarians and maintained by the Honors College staff. In addition, the honors students have begun publication of a newsletter, and Kraemer hopes to get involved with that project by submitting brief research tips for each issue. Future plans for the Honors College outreach also include more library instruction sessions, held at the honors facility, especially targeted at those students working on their theses. Finally, the Honors College Director has expressed interest in having the librarian liaison meet with faculty members serving as honors thesis advisors to promote research consultations and assistance that are available to their students.

PLANS FOR FUTURE OUTREACH EFFORTS

The outreach efforts described in this article are only the beginning for the librarians at Oakland University, as there are a number of additional groups on campus that the outreach specialists at Kresge Library hope to contact in order to establish partnerships. This section outlines some of those plans.

Due to Proposition 48, enacted in 1983 by the National Collegiate Athletic Association, student athletes have strict guidelines about securing acceptable grades in order to keep their scholarships, as well as their eligibilities to play.[12] Despite the rigors of both practice time and game schedules, these students are expected to be academic achievers in their institutions; because of this, library outreach to the Athletic Department would likely be very welcome. Services for student athletes could include specialized bibliographic instruction, fast turnaround e-mail reference assistance, and research consultations held at their practice facility.

OU has a growing number of undergraduate students who participate in high-level research projects of the type many other universities reserve for graduate students. The efforts of these student scholars are encouraged through the new Research Scholar Program, which annually awards twenty to forty $1,000 grants for approved projects.[13] Similarly high-performing students are found among other academic scholarship winners at Oakland; naturally, the criteria for these awards require students to maintain excellent grade point averages. Many possibilities for intensive library outreach programs exist among these academically motivated students. Librarians would develop information literacy workshops to help students better understand and navigate the information landscape by teaching them to use relevant research tools. Moreover, these workshops would address broader research issues such as the evaluation of information resources, intellectual property (especially in an online environment), academic freedom versus ownership, scholarly attribution and documentation, and plagiarism. Further efforts would include personal research consultations, promotion of a display case that could be used to spotlight student projects, and even quiet computer lab space in the library rooms normally reserved for bibliographic instruction. By offering such focused assistance, the OU librarians could help these students excel.

The Academic Skills Center at Oakland University offers services to encourage students seeking extra assistance, and supports their academic efforts. In the winter 2003 semester, Keyse participated for the first time in the Research Skills workshop offered by the Academic Skills Center to highlight services that the library can provide. By teaming up with this department, she hoped to build bridges with students needing supplemental instruction, tutoring, and study skills tips.

At many universities, graduate students are a difficult population to reach en masse, and Oakland University is no exception in this arena. Erroneously assuming that graduate students already are proficient in conducting research in their disciplines, many faculty do not perceive a great need for in-class library instruction. Contrary to this assumption, the provision of useful library services to this set of students is vital, and efforts to develop a strong relationship with the Department of Graduate Admissions and Student Services are already underway. Expanded efforts to graduate students could include dissertation/thesis writing workshops and research support groups. By catering to the research needs of graduate students with advanced services, the outreach librarians will help these scholars reach their academic and professional goals.

CONCLUSION

The number of librarians at Oakland University has not increased in proportion to the growth of the student population over the years, and Kresge Library and the university it serves are preparing for budget cuts in higher education at the state level. In spite of this, librarians are actively engaging in outreach. Student Affairs and Kresge Library have teamed up to integrate campus activities and services with students' classroom experiences in order to increase retention. As a result, the number of both in-person and electronic reference transactions has risen, after years of decline. Higher library door counts at the beginning of the fall 2002 semester indicate that outreach programs during new student orientations and Welcome Week are making a significant impact. Even as librarians are promoting the convenience of off-campus access to research services, more students are coming into the library.

External partnerships with the business community often increase a university's visibility; similarly, outreach projects enhance the library's position on campus. This heightened awareness can provide justification for increased library funding to meet student demands for improved library services, such as real-time online reference service and wireless networking. For example, even before Kresge Library initiated its outreach projects, the University administration heard the students' voice when OU's Student Congress successfully petitioned to increase the library's base budget. By reaching out to an even broader student population, the librarians hope to inspire student advocacy for all of the enhanced services that the library could offer.

Continued marketing of library services to all student populations will surely strengthen in time, and this will make outreach efforts more valuable and far-reaching. When university enrollment is rising and retention is key, the library plays a vital role. Kresge Library is already at the physical center of the Oakland University campus. Through progressive outreach programs, librarians will promote the library as the academic center as well.

REFERENCES

1. Lynn Westbrook and Robert Waldman, "Outreach in Academic Libraries: Principle into Practice," *Research Strategies* 11, no. 2: 62.

2. Oakland University Office of Institutional Research and Assessment, *OU Data Book: Student Information 2002*, (November 26, 2002). <http://aisnt.ais.oakland.edu/oira/Info_2002.htm>.

3. Westbrook and Waldman, 62.

4. Gail M. Staines, "Moving Beyond Institutional Boundaries: Perceptions toward BI for Transfer Students," *Research Strategies* 14 (spring 1996): 101.

5. Julie Still, "Library Services for Transfer Students," *Community & Junior College Libraries* 7 (1990): 52.

6. "Transfer Students Feel Disengaged from College Life, Survey Shows," *Chronicle of Higher Education* 49 (November 22, 2002): A55. Available online from http://chronicle.com/weekly/v49/i13/13a05502.htm.

7. Staines, 99.

8. Westbrook and Waldman, 62.

9. Isabel Espinal, "Multicultural Outreach in Academic Libraries." Paper presented at the American Library Association Annual Conference, Atlanta, Ga., June 2002.

10. Dana Keyse, *Kresge Library Diversity Resources*, (November 23, 2002). <http://www.kl.oakland.edu/DiversityResources/DiversityResources.html>.

11. *Oakland University Residence Halls: Try Us and See*, (November 23, 2002). <http://www2.oakland.edu/reshalls/try.cfm/>.

12. Melba Jesudason, "Outreach to Student-Athletes Through E-mail Reference Service," *Reference Services Review* 28, no. 3 (2000): 262-267.

13. *Spotlight on OU*, (October 19, 2002). <http://www3.oakland.edu/oakland/aboutou/spotlight.htm>.

Instructional Outreach Across the Curriculum: Enhancing the Liaison Role at a Research University

Corey M. Johnson
Sarah K. McCord
Scott Walter

SUMMARY. Over the past decade, there has been a steady rise in interest among academic librarians in the idea of outreach. Outreach from the academic library can take many forms, but it is often built around a commitment to instruction. At Washington State University, a commitment to information literacy instruction across the curriculum and an organizational structure that includes both an independent Library Instruction department and a network of subject specialists has facilitated the rise of a programmatic approach to instructional outreach that allows librarians and faculty to work together to develop creative approaches to the integration of information literacy instruction across the academic curriculum. This article identifies some of the characteristics of new models for

Corey M. Johnson (E-mail: coreyj@wsu.edu) is Instructional Design Librarian; Sarah K. McCord (E-mail: mccord@wsu.edu) is Electronic Resources Librarian for the Health Sciences Library; and Scott Walter (E-mail: swalter@wsu.edu) is Interim Assistant Director for Public Services and Outreach, and Subject Specialist for Higher Education, all at Washington State University Libraries, Pullman, WA 99164-5610.

[Haworth co-indexing entry note]: "Instructional Outreach Across the Curriculum: Enhancing the Liaison Role at a Research University." Johnson, Corey M., Sarah K. McCord, and Scott Walter. Co-published simultaneously in *The Reference Librarian* (The Haworth Information Press, an imprint of The Haworth Press, Inc.) No. 82, 2003, pp. 19-37; and: *Outreach Services in Academic and Special Libraries* (ed: Paul Kelsey, and Sigrid Kelsey) The Haworth Information Press, an imprint of The Haworth Press, Inc., 2003, pp. 19-37. Single or multiple copies of this article are available for a fee from The Haworth Document Delivery Service [1-800-HAWORTH, 9:00 a.m. - 5:00 p.m. (EST). E-mail address: docdelivery@haworthpress.com].

http://www.haworthpress.com/store/product.asp?sku=J120
© 2003 by The Haworth Press, Inc. All rights reserved.
Digital Object Identifier: 10.1300/J120v39n82_03

19

instructional outreach in the academic library and describes two instructional outreach programs at Washington State. *[Article copies available for a fee from The Haworth Document Delivery Service: 1-800-HAWORTH. E-mail address: <docdelivery@haworthpress.com> Website: <http://www.HaworthPress. com> © 2003 by The Haworth Press, Inc. All rights reserved.]*

KEYWORDS. Information literacy, library instruction, outreach, academic libraries, first-year experience, medical education

INTRODUCTION

Over the past decade, interest among academic librarians in outreach has risen steadily. Potential explanations for this new attention to a familiar subject include the increasing diversity of the student body (Westbrook and Waldman 1993), the rising importance of information technology and electronic information sources in higher education (Arant and Mosely 1999, Jacobson and Cohen 2000, Schillie et al. 2000), and the desire to provide specialized library services to target user groups, e.g., faculty, administrators, distance learners, international students, athletes, and transfer students (Cruickshank and Nowak 2001, Neely et al. 1999, Peyton 2000, Stebelman et al. 1999). Outreach from academic libraries takes many forms, often built around a commitment to instruction. At Washington State University, a commitment to information literacy instruction across the curriculum and an organizational structure, including both an independent Library Instruction department and a network of subject specialists, has facilitated the rise of a programmatic approach to instructional outreach. This approach allows librarians and faculty to work together, developing creative approaches to the integration of information literacy instruction across the academic curriculum.

OUTREACH IN THE ACADEMIC LIBRARY: LITERATURE REVIEW

The American Library Association defines "outreach" as any program of activities "initiated and designed to meet the information needs of an unserved or inadequately served target group" (Young 1983, 160). While "outreach" is a term most commonly associated with public libraries (Cruickshank and Nowak 2001), academic library outreach activities have expanded and evolved in recent years, responding to changes in the library profession and in the broader environment of higher education.

In the academic context, outreach has focused on unserved or underserved groups such as high school students and other community users, non-traditional students, international students, and distance learners. There is a rich history of this sort of outreach at the Washington State University Libraries (Gibson and Scales 2000, Nofsinger 1989, Washington State University Libraries 2002a, 2002b), and recent studies by Neely et al. (1999), and Cruickshank and Nowak (2001) demonstrate the ongoing importance of traditional outreach in academic libraries. Another traditional outreach activity is the liaison relationship between librarians and academic faculty, through which librarians work with faculty, using subject expertise to develop relevant library collections (Wu et al. 1994, Chu 1997). Recent studies by Frank et al. (2001), and Lougee (2002), explore how librarian expertise regarding concepts and skills associated with the location, use, and management of information, can reshape the meaning of outreach in the academic library, and redefine the academic librarian's place on campus.

Frank et al. (2001), for example, explore academic librarians' roles as "information consultants" on campus. The librarian-as-information-consultant provides specialized information services to library users and "cultivates active partnerships with students and scholars, collaborating on the design of learning experiences for students and providing value-added information [to students, faculty, and campus administrators]" (p. 90). While Frank et al. (2001), note the importance of traditional outreach models such as the liaison relationship, they argue that these models are too "passive" to be effective in the dynamic information environment of the 21st-century campus (p. 90).

Lougee (2002) also identifies new roles for academic librarians as a result of their expertise in information creation, dissemination, location, and management. She concludes that the rising interest in electronic information and the attendant transformation of scholarly communication provides an opportunity for academic librarians to take on new roles across the university. She argues that academic librarians should focus less on the value of their collections and the traditional role of collection development at the center of liaison relationships, and more on the value of their expertise in handling information. New roles for librarians include creating educational opportunities with active learning elements and incorporation of the information literacy concepts of information analysis, inquiry, and use (p. 18).

New models of outreach build on traditional models such as the liaison relationship, with several significant differences. Traditional outreach models focus on opening lines of communication with broad sets of underserved users, while new models emphasize enhancing existing relationships with users through programs with which they are associated. The primary aim of traditional models is to market the library's resources, enticing more people to visit these resources. New outreach models are characterized by the primary goals of marketing the librarians' expertise and using their information skills to augment a program's processes and products. Librarians are increasingly aiding university programs through the collaborative development of teaching curriculum and by facilitating instructional courses and class sessions.

INSTRUCTIONAL OUTREACH

Information literacy instruction is a vital area where librarian expertise has provided increased outreach opportunities over the past decade. The reasons for rising interest in instructional outreach include students' ability to think critically about information (Bodi 1988, Gibson 1995), and the rapid evolution of end-user information technology, such as the World Wide Web, and its incorporation into student and faculty research (Jayne and Vander Meer 1997, Walter 2000, Jacobson and Cohen 2000). Concerning traditional models, instructional outreach has encompassed both the provision of services to underserved user groups, and the continued delivery of "course-related" instructional services traditionally provided by instruction librarians and subject specialists. The new outreach models described by Frank et al. (2001) and Lougee (2002), bring to light new methods for instructional outreach, calling upon academic librarians to play proactive roles, collaborating with faculty members and instructional support programs on campus (Dewey 2001, Haynes 1996, Raspa and Ward 2000).

These emergent models of instructional outreach are rooted in the idea that the librarian brings to the collaborative enterprise an expertise in the location, evaluation, management, and use of information resources, that is significant to faculty and students teaching and learning in an increasingly complex information environment. Walter (2002) and Grafstein (2002) both describe how a campus-wide commitment to information literacy requires instruction librarians understand how to tailor instructional services to the needs and curricular content of specific disciplines. As classroom faculty commit to the integration of information literacy into the curriculum, they will depend on librarians for collaboration, expertise, and knowledge regarding the design of information literacy instruction, and for help developing assessment tools for information literacy.

As with the electronic collections issues identified by Lougee (2002), instructional issues require academic librarians to play increasingly "diffuse" roles on campus. Instructional outreach across the curriculum and across the campus requires an approach going beyond partnerships with individual librarians and members of the teaching faculty, and moving toward establishing ongoing collaboration between library-based instructional services and academic programs.

INFORMATION LITERACY INSTRUCTION
AT WASHINGTON STATE UNIVERSITY

Washington State University, one of two comprehensive research universities in Washington state, was established in 1890 as the state's land-grant institution. The university maintains a flagship campus in Pullman, a rural city in the southeastern corner of the state, and three "newer campuses" in Spokane, Richland, and Vancouver. The university also supports ten learning centers located around the state, and cooperative extension offices in each of Washington's thirty-nine counties. In 2002-2003, the Pullman campus enrolled approximately 19,000 students, while thousands more participated in undergraduate, graduate, and continuing education programs in the other locations, or delivered through teleconferencing and Web-based instruction.

The Washington State University Libraries provide a full range of collections, services, and electronic resources to the university community through a system of six libraries on the Pullman campus (Agricultural Sciences, Architecture, Education, Health Sciences, Humanities/Social Sciences, and Science & Engineering), and branch libraries on each newer campus. Each Pullman library is supported by at least one subject specialist responsible for reference, collection development, and instruction in relevant disciplines. Subject specialists provide instructional services to liaison departments and programs, and are supported by an independent Library Instruction department, which includes three full-time librarians and one instruction coordinator in each of the largest public service units (Humanities/Social Sciences, and Science & Engineering).

In addition to providing support for subject specialists, the Library Instruction department provides instructional services to a number of independent academic programs, such as World Civilizations, Freshman Seminar, English Composition, Distance Degree Programs, the Intensive American Language Center, and New Student Programs. The Library Instruction department also coordinates traditional instructional outreach services to groups such as K-12 students and members of Washington State University Athletic Programs. Each librarian in this department coordinates instruction for one or more of these programs while developing instructional materials for use throughout the Libraries, including resource guides, activity sheets, assessment tools, and Web-based instructional materials. Information about these programs can be found on the Library Instruction home page at <http://www.wsulibs.wsu.edu/usered/home.htm>.

The Instruction Department is moving to conform its instructional efforts to the ACRL Information Literacy Standards (Association of College and Research Libraries 2002). Drafted in 1989, these standards define a comprehensive set of skills people need to effectively find, retrieve, analyze, and use information. Librarians at the six public baccalaureate institutions in Washington state are working under legislative mandate RCW 28B.10.125 (Washington 2000) to assess student mastery of information literacy skills. This law is serving as a catalyst for programmatic collaboration between the libraries and academic programs across campus.

As a result, information literacy instruction at WSU is evolving to reflect new thinking about outreach from academic libraries. While continuing to support traditional outreach activities, the faculty are revising expectations for the program based on newer outreach models such as those articulated by Frank et al. (2001) and Lougee (2002). This new way of thinking about outreach activities is called a "programmatic" approach to instructional outreach throughout the remainder of this article. Like traditional outreach, the programmatic approach targets a defined user population. These users are not unserved or underserved in the traditional sense that they lack adequate access or orientation to library services and resources. Rather, they are underserved because they lack curricular needs, namely, fully developed information literacy skills. The innovative characteristics of the programmatic approach include librarians proactively collaborating with faculty members to impact the main processes and products of educational programs. The programmatic approach features librarian subject expertise used in the instructional setting as opposed to the collection development environment. Finally, the programmatic approach to instructional outreach includes significant librarian contributions to and involvement with course curriculum and student assessment. The following two case studies illustrate the programmatic approach to instructional outreach.

INSTRUCTIONAL OUTREACH
AT WASHINGTON STATE UNIVERSITY–
TWO CASE STUDIES

Freshman Seminar, a first-year-experience program, has been offered at Washington State University since 1996. First-year students joining the program enroll in a section of Freshman Seminar (General Education 104), linked either to a section of World Civilizations (Gen Ed 110/111), or a first-year course in disciplines such as Animal Sciences, Anthropology, Biology, Communications, and Sociology. Each student enrolled in Freshman Seminar becomes part of a learning community comprising the students in his or her section of Gen Ed 104 and the staff of the Student Academic Learning Center (SALC), who coordinate the program and the curriculum. In addition, students and staff trained in the Center for Teaching, Learning, & Technology (CTLT) provide information technology support for student projects, faculty, and librarians introducing the first-year students to library resources and to the research process.

The focal point of the Freshman Seminar experience is a research project that students design, conduct, and present under the guidance of the undergraduate Peer Facilitators (PFs). PFs are sophomores, juniors, and seniors drawn from Freshman Seminar alumni, who have prepared for their roles by completing an upper-division course in "peer leadership" (ED AD 497). PFs are assisted in their instructional work by Graduate Facilitators (GFs) drawn from programs across the curriculum and employed by SALC, and by "Hypernauts," a corps of undergraduates trained in technology support. The final results of this semester-long research process are presented at a "research symposium," where student groups present Web-based multimedia projects, and answer questions posed by members of the classroom and library faculty. More information on Freshman Seminar can be found at <http://salc.wsu.edu/ Freshman/>.

Librarians have been involved with Freshman Seminar since the program was launched six years ago. Each semester, librarians work with Freshman Seminar sections, introducing students to library resources and assisting with the design and development of the research projects. Instruction librarians and subject specialists work together, providing instruction on topics ranging from using the online catalog, to evaluating Web-based resources for use in academic research, to appropriate forms of citation for print and electronic sources. In each case, the librarian's overarching concern is to introduce students to resources and tools that will help them with their research projects. Like other faculty involved in the program, librarians have the opportunity to be involved in all phases of project development, from initial proposals to evaluation of the final product.

In the early years of the collaboration between Freshman Seminar and the Libraries, success was largely due to the efforts of individual librarians. The parameters of the relationship between the Library Instruction program and the Freshman Seminar program were loosely defined, with librarians and PFs determining the extent and nature of their instructional partnership on an individual basis. There was limited collaboration between the Freshman Seminar staff in SALC and the program liaison in the Library Instruction department, and little attempt to coordinate the work of the librarians involved. Over time, the lack of coordination and clear expectations led to disenchantment between librarians and PFs, and the quality of instruction provided in the library varied widely from section to section, and semester to semester. Librarians were uncertain about how to best provide instructional support to the Freshman Seminar program, or when during each semester to meet with their assigned sections.

This situation began to change in early 2002, when a more programmatic approach to the collaboration between the Library Instruction department and Freshman Seminar began to take form. The Head of the Instruction Department, the Director of the Freshman Seminar Program, along with representatives from both groups, devised a new collaborative model based on (1) the need to institutionalize an approach to information literacy instruction that could survive any change in program personnel, (2) the desire for librarians to have greater input into curriculum development, and (3) the interest in instruction librarians to provide a greater range of instructional support services to PFs. This new approach to instructional collaboration had three main components: PF enrollment in "Accessing Information for Research" (Gen Ed 300), an improved communication structure between librarians and the Freshman Seminar officials, and design of curriculum for new instructional sessions.

First, the group of Freshman Seminar and Library Instruction leaders agreed that each new cohort of PFs would enroll in a specially designed section of the Libraries' one-credit information literacy course (Gen Ed 300). This section of the course, meeting the same instructional objectives as other sections, would prepare students to be information literate themselves, as well as to be effective mentors for their future students in Freshman Seminar. Taught for the first time in Fall 2002, this new section of the course incorporates specific instructional elements with which future PFs must be familiar if they are to assist first-year students in the research process (e.g., critical evaluation of Web-based information resources). It also introduces them to professional concepts such as process models of information literacy instruction, and to resources they can use to develop their own instruction activities. Requiring participation in this course not only helps assure baseline information literacy among PFs, but provides PFs with a better understanding of information literacy instruction (something both parties agreed might translate into better working relationships between PFs and librarians).

Second, the Freshman Seminar and Library Instruction leaders created a structure to improve communication and feedback between the Freshman Seminar staff and students, and the Libraries. The commitment to improved communication began with meetings between the Freshman Seminar leaders and members of the Library Instruction department during Summer 2002. The goals were to outline a framework for instructional collaboration, and develop a shared understanding of how librarians would contribute to the Freshman Seminar program. The meetings allowed representatives of each program to brainstorm new ideas for information literacy instruction, and gain a better understanding of the instructional objectives guiding the others' work. Finally, long-standing miscommunications were addressed. For example, it was determined that the centerpiece of the instruction provided by librarians in previous semesters–evaluation of Web sites and Web-based information–was also part of the classroom curriculum, taught in the semi-weekly Freshman Seminar meetings outside the library.

Communication continued through the Fall 2002 semester as the Libraries' liaison to Freshman Seminar scheduled meetings for librarians involved in the program, and attended several PF and GF training sessions to prepare Freshman Seminar instructors and mentors for the planned instruction sessions in the library. These unprecedented meetings provided regular opportunities to solicit feedback from each other, identify problems, and provide enough guidance and support to librarians participating in the program to assure a more uniform instructional experience across the twenty-six sections of the course during Fall 2002. The semester ended with a number of librarians collaborating with Freshman Seminar officials in the formal assessment of student projects, many librarians attending the "appreciation lunch" sponsored by Freshman Seminar, and the Freshman Seminar coordinator attending a meeting in the library to discuss changes to the collaborative program for the upcoming semester.

Third, the new approach to collaboration focused on creating a new curriculum for the instructional sessions provided in the library. As noted above, librarian involvement in the program had usually been limited to a single instructional session introducing students to Web site evaluation for academic research, something also addressed by the PFs in the classroom. After discussion, the group of Freshman Seminar and Library Instruction leaders decided that PFs would continue providing instruction in Web site evaluation, with librarians providing instructional support in the form of resource sheets and classroom activities, to teach evaluation skills for the electronic environment. This freed librarians to focus on the provision of instructional content with which PFs felt less confident, including the identification of library resources germane to specific research topics and issues related to copyright, plagiarism, and the correct citation of sources.

In addition to changes to the instructional content provided during library visits, the pedagogical method changed. The Freshman Seminar and Library Instruction leaders determined that a key complaint students had regarding the information literacy instruction was that it often did not follow the model of discussion and active learning that the rest of the Freshman Seminar program provided. Likewise, librarians were eager to provide active learning opportunities, but reported that they felt pressed for time during the single instruction session scheduled each semester. During Fall 2002, each section of Freshman Seminar began to meet formally with its librarian twice, rather than once, with opportunities for active learning incorporated into each lesson.

This new approach to library involvement with Freshman Seminar demonstrates several elements of a programmatic approach to instructional outreach. First, it represents a team-oriented and proactive approach to outreach, with librarians identifying problems with an existing instructional collaboration and approaching their partners in the Freshman Seminar program to rethink how to more effectively involve librarians, both in curriculum design and delivering instruction. Second, it represents the development of a new version of a for-credit information literacy course aimed specifically at training the undergraduate Peer Facilitators, who are at the front lines of Freshman Seminar instructional efforts. Rather than individual outreach from a librarian to a faculty member, this approach demonstrates how two programs can work together, serving as a model for providing training and resources to help every individual involved address programmatic needs. Finally, it represents librarians taking the opportunity to use their expertise in information literacy instruction, thereby redefining ways in which first-year students enrolled in Freshman Seminar are introduced to library resources and the research process. Because of their recognized expertise, librarians contributed significantly to the program, training the Peer Facilitators, developing curricular resources and classroom activities, and collaborating in assessment of student projects. The newly defined program is young, but initial feedback from students and instructors has been positive, pointing toward a bright future for instructional outreach from the Washington State University Libraries to the Freshman Seminar program.

Just as instruction librarians serving as liaisons to the Freshman Seminar program are embracing new models for instructional outreach, the programmatic approach is demonstrated by subject specialists enhancing their traditional liaison relationships by engaging in new forms of collaborative instructional work. An exemplary model of the programmatic approach to instructional outreach by a subject specialist is found in the Washington State University Health Sciences Library and its faculty partners in the College of Pharmacy.

As noted above, the Health Sciences Library (HSL) is one of six library facilities on the Pullman campus. It is also one of only nine federally designated Resource Libraries in the National Network of Libraries of Medicine/Pacific Northwest Region. The two HSL librarians serve as subject specialists for fields including Nursing, Veterinary Medicine, and Pharmacology, and as liaisons to the College of Veterinary Medicine, the College of Pharmacy, and WWAMI, the cooperative medical education program serving the needs of medical students in eastern Washington, Wyoming, Alaska, Montana, and Idaho who complete their first year of medical school on their "home" campuses before moving to Seattle to continue their professional education at the University of Washington. HSL librarians provide information and instructional services to students and faculty involved in these programs, as well as practicing pharmacists, clinical pharmacologists, veterinarians, and physicians throughout the region. More information on the collections and services provided through the Health Sciences Library can be found online at <http:// www.wsulibs.wsu.edu/hsl/>.

The College of Pharmacy offers a variety of programs for graduate and professional students. Chief among these is the Doctor of Pharmacy degree (Pharm.D.), requiring two years of pre-pharmacy study at the undergraduate level, and four years of pharmacy study in the professional program. The first two years of the professional curriculum take place on the Pullman campus, while the final two years take place at the campus in Spokane. In addition to the Pharm.D., the College provides opportunities to earn Master's and Doctoral degrees in Pharmaceutical Sciences, as well as a Master's degree in Health Policy and Administration.

Traditional liaison relationships between HSL and the College of Pharmacy have always been strong, in part because information (specifically drug information) is a vital part of the Pharm.D. curriculum. The pharmacy subject specialist is introduced along with the College faculty at the formal matriculation ceremony beginning each academic year, and regularly attends departmental and College faculty meetings and other College activities. The librarian also plays an important role in the accreditation process for the College, which requires a detailed analysis of information resources available to students, faculty, and staff in the College. In addition, the librarian recruits representatives from the College faculty and students to serve on the HSL Advisory Committee, provides library resource seminars at faculty meetings, collaborates on research projects with College faculty, and serves as the primary liaison to instructional services, technical support, and administrative procedures. The librarian works with College information technology staff to provide information resources and services. Activities such as these fall within the traditional approaches to outreach from the academic library, and their presence provides the foundation for enhanced liaison activity through a program of instructional outreach.

Instructional outreach to the College of Pharmacy began with the regular meetings between the subject specialist and faculty to discuss collection support for teaching and research activities. As a result of these meetings, information literacy instruction has been successfully integrated into a variety of classroom experiences, and (as noted above), information literacy instruction is provided to Pharmacy faculty, staff, and students, in a number of ways and in a number of venues. Over the past year, this already successful approach to information literacy instruction developed into a programmatic program of instructional outreach focusing on the first two years of the professional education (Pharm.D.) program in the College of Pharmacy.

The first two years of the Pharm.D. curriculum are bracketed by library orientations–one during the second week of the first year, and one during the final month of the second year. Students also receive intensive instruction during the first semester of the second year, when the librarian provides two instructional sessions and two graded assignments as part of the hands-on Pharmaceutical Care Laboratory (PCL), a program comprising a one hour-long lecture section and four two-hour lab sections each week, allowing students to develop skills in areas such as patient counseling and practice guidelines for specific diseases and conditions. Information literacy instruction provided as part of the PCL curriculum focuses on building skills in database searching and developing the ability to critically analyze and review biomedical literature.

During their second week in the program, all first-year Pharm.D. students attend a mandatory two-hour orientation to both the physical and virtual library resources available to WSU students. The physical orientation consists of an HSL tour, explanations of library policies and procedures, and an introduction to the organization of the HSL stacks. The orientation to electronic library resources introduces them to the Washington State University Libraries Web site, online catalog, electronic journals, and basic database searching in PubMed, the biomedical database produced by the National Library of Medicine (NLM). Student response to this initial orientation has been positive, and faculty support has been strong enough that a longer time period has been allotted to the library orientation program beginning in Fall 2003, in order to accommodate instruction in the use of additional electronic databases.

The information literacy instruction provided during the PCL evolved through traditional liaison meetings and phone conversations with a number of College faculty. The meeting identified various areas where students needed instruction. For example, Pharm.D. students are required to take a Drug Information course during the first semester of their third year in the program, and the Spokane-based faculty member who teaches this course identified a number of gaps in his students' ability to locate and evaluate drug information. Several Pullman-based faculty members also noted occasions when students could not locate appropriate information effectively, nor evaluate information critically. Finally, a faculty commitment to introducing evidence-based practice earlier in the Pharm.D. curriculum provided an opportunity for the pharmacy librarian to contribute expertise based in her experience as an instructor in the WWAMI program (for which she team-teaches a class on the Critical Review and Analysis of Medical Literature). Evidence-based medicine, briefly defined, is "the process of systematically finding, appraising, and using contemporaneous research findings as the basis for clinical decisions" (Rosenberg & Donald 1995, 1122). In collaboration with the faculty member responsible for the PCL, and using the ACRL Information Literacy Standards (ACRL 2002) as a guide, the pharmacy librarian developed instructional sessions and graded assignments, addressing the perceived lack of information literacy skills among Pharm.D. students. As was the case in the Freshman Seminar experience, the College faculty were enthusiastic to incorporate an enhanced level of information literacy instruction into the Pharm.D. curriculum, because they saw such instruction as a service to help them meet instructional objectives already in place for the program.

The first PCL instructional session, "Database Search Skills," introduces students to coverage, applications, and search strategies of five biomedical and scientific databases: PubMed, Web of Science, Micromedex, Clinical Pharmacology, and the Natural Medicines Comprehensive Database. The instruction session and the related assignment use examples that are directly tied to work in other Pharm.D. classes. Examples used to illustrate search skills, for instance, relate to macrolide antibiotics, which are discussed simultaneously in a course on Selective Toxicity. Additionally, problems on the graded assignment relate to drugs that act on the cholinergic system, which is a topic of discussion in the Pharmaceutics course. This level of integration is possible because of the pharmacy librarian's comprehensive knowledge of the coursework offered and issues under discussion in the Pharm.D. program.

Students worked in small groups during one of their weekly laboratory sections to complete the graded assignment attached to the first instructional session. Because it was a skill-building assignment, the instructors used a grading scale based on correct completion of all questions assigned. Students would earn an "A" for an assignment completed in the lab without significant errors. Students could correct their answers and re-submit the assignment if there were significant errors. Assignments correctly completed after a single re-submission would earn a "B," while assignments requiring two re-submissions would earn a "C." Finally, students could negotiate with the PCL instructor and librarian for partial credit if additional submissions were required. This elaborate grading scheme used the first time proved unnecessary, as all students received top marks on the assignment. Student evaluation of this first instructional session was highly positive (drawing an average rating of 4.75 on a 5-point Likert Scale), with several students asking for "more homework," i.e., a more extensive set of information skills exercises to complete in the lab.

The second PCL instructional session, "Preparation for Evidence-Based Practice," takes place approximately one month after the first, allowing the librarian and the PCL instructor to introduce new concepts while determining what skills have been retained from the first session and assignment. This second session introduces students to the vocabulary of evidence-based practice, the distinctions between primary, secondary, and tertiary sources, the process of building a search strategy from the information needs presented in a clinical situation, and criteria for critically evaluating information sources. As before, examples used during the lesson relate to content in other courses, but this time the emphasis was on using "the software between the ears" to determine the scope of the information need and to evaluate the information located using library resources.

The graded assignment accompanying the second instructional session is based on a problem-based learning framework. Problem-based learning, which uses a case-based approach to engage students in the learning process, is not new to pharmacy education (Antepohl and Herzig 1999), and is increasingly being applied to information literacy instruction in higher education (Fosmire and Macklin 2002, Macklin 2001). For this assignment, students work in teams of three or four, and each team is given a sample case and an electronic copy of the Drug Information Request Response Form. During a two-hour PCL lab section, teams conduct a search in at least two different databases, cite at least one information source of each type (primary, secondary, tertiary), provide a summary of the data, and include a reference list with citations in correct NLM format. Even though two hours is considered very generous in most clinical situations, students are encouraged to review their Database Search exercises before coming to lab.

Again, the sample cases forming the foundation of the assignment are based on coursework in other Pharm.D. classes (focusing on antiviral and antifungal medications). Both the written assignment and the verbal instructions stress that the response should provide an overview of the evidence found in current literature, but not provide a clinical opinion. In other words, students are asked to locate and select high-quality information sources, and create a summary of the current literature, but not make a recommendation on what medication should be given to the patient. Grading for this assignment is done jointly, with 20% of the grade based on the quality of the cited sources, 20% based on correct use of NLM citation style, and 60% based on the content of the written response (with the two former elements evaluated by the librarian, and the latter element by the PCL instructor).

During this past year, the vast majority of students (96%) located high quality information sources relevant to their cases, and correctly identified them as either primary, secondary, or tertiary literature. Students had some difficulty citing journal articles and abstracts of journal articles located through an electronic database. A number of students, for example, cited the PubMed database (and used the correct citation style for an electronic database), rather than citing the source journal. This problem was especially evident when students used the PubMed "LinkOut" feature to access an electronic copy of the article from within the database. This indicates an opportunity for future instruction, teaching differences between an index and the document itself.

The aspect of the second assignment that students found most challenging was the preparation of the written response. At the beginning of the lab section, the instructors suggested that students spend 45-60 minutes researching the case, and 60-75 minutes preparing the written response. Students were also told that the assignment was designed to be challenging, and that they were not expected to locate every piece of literature relevant to their case. Even so, some students did not begin to prepare their written responses until the lab section was nearly over. This was true even of students who located a wide range of relevant information sources within the first forty-five minutes of the class. Student feedback on this assignment was positive, but many noted that their performance would have improved with additional time. Both the librarian and the PCL instructor are evaluating the results of this assignment to identify ways to facilitate student success in the writing portion of the assignment–for example, possible involvement with the campus Writing Program, and expansion of the Drug Information Request Response Form to include suggestions for content and format.

As students complete the second year of the Pharm.D. program, they must prepare to continue their professional education on the Spokane campus (located about seventy-five miles from Pullman), where the final two years of instruction take place. Information literacy instruction provided at this juncture must help students make the transition from the information sources and services they accessed during their first two years, to those they will access in their final two years. With the increase in electronic resources in the biomedical field, such as electronic books and journals, this transition is easier than it once was, because the majority of resources are available across campuses. However, a one-hour lesson on accessing these resources from remote locations (such as hospitals and retail sites), and an orientation to differences in library policies and procedures between the Pullman and Spokane campuses, remains a mandatory component of the second-year Pharm.D. curriculum. This session also introduces students to hospital-based library services that will be available to them during experiential rotations in the fourth year. This final instruction and orientation during the second year has traditionally been provided by the Pullman-based pharmacy librarian, but beginning in Spring 2003, will be delivered in collaboration with the director of the branch library on the Spokane campus.

As in the case of Freshman Seminar, the approach to instructional outreach embraced by the Health Sciences Library in its work with the College of Pharmacy builds upon and enhances the traditional outreach activities associated with the familiar liaison program. In this case, as with Freshman Seminar, instructional outreach is rooted in a proactive approach taken by the librarian. Again, the work with the College of Pharmacy demonstrates the significance of integrating information literacy instruction across a program, rather than attempting to piece together a successful approach from a series of individual relationships. Finally, and most significantly, as in the Freshman Seminar case, the success of the instructional outreach is based on the mutually compatible instructional objectives of two programs, and the combination of instructional and subject-specific expertise brought to the project by the participating librarian. In each case, librarians are involved in both the generation of curriculum and the assessment of student performance. This new approach to successful instructional outreach is rooted in the roles that academic librarians can play on a campus where their professional expertise is critical to meeting the instructional objectives of academic programs and departments across campus. Figure 1 provides a summative comparison of the College of Pharmacy and Freshman Seminar outreach programs, illustrating specific elements librarians can focus on in developing a programmatic approach to instructional outreach.

CONCLUSION

American higher education is changing in response to new trends in instruction, new calls for assessment of student learning, and new demands from local, state, and federal government, the business community, and others. Students educated in the 21st century must be well prepared for employment, citizen-

FIGURE 1. Programmatic Approach Analysis–Key Elements Across Examples

Concurrent Characteristics	College of Pharmacy	Freshman Seminar (FS)
Librarians recognize a program's need for help, enhancement	Spokane and Pullman faculty, along with the librarian, see a "skills gap"	FS officials notice students need training about plagiarism
Programmatic approach bolstered through key meetings and other organized contacts	Library Advisory Board, librarian attendance at ceremonies and faculty meetings, liaison work	Ongoing planning sessions between FS officials and librarians, feedback sessions
Collaborative environment increases librarian involvement in the program	Librarian and faculty members agree to increases in the time allotted for the lab sessions	Growth from one to two library sessions, librarians providing Web evaluation curriculum
Librarian-generated curriculum/sessions correspond to students' coursework, relevance increased	Drug types chosen for the library lab assignments tied to the drug family being studied and timing is critical to introduction to evidence based work	Library sessions and topics scheduled to correlate to course content and assignment due dates
Librarian involvement in the formal assessment process, help assign grades	Students receive letter grades for their written work from the library labs	FS librarians volunteer to be a part of the formal Web site evaluation process
Active learning in the instructional sessions	Problem-based learning in the library labs	Librarians given interactive lessons to use in their instructional sessions

ship, and lifelong learning in the increasingly dynamic world of the Information Age. Academic libraries are evolving to address these concerns. Library outreach has changed from a focus on bringing people into the library with the aim of resource discovery, to one of librarians bringing instructional and subject expertise to collaborative efforts with partners in academic departments and in other offices and programs across campus. Information literacy instruction is a key venue where this new paradigm is thriving.

The Washington State University Libraries are adopting the tenets of this new paradigm as instruction and subject-specialist librarians employ a programmatic approach to instructional outreach. The two representative examples described in this article illustrate librarians taking their collaborative work to new levels as they engage in the structural design and planning of courses, create active-learning curriculum, teach instructional sessions, and are strongly involved in coursework assessment. The two examples exemplify how a proactive and programmatic approach to instructional outreach helps librarians claim a new place in campus collaborations based on their expertise in the location, evaluation, management, and use of information.

Frank et al. (2001), and Lougee (2002) have articulated new roles that may become part of public services librarianship. Clearly these roles will be shaped by traditional elements of academic library outreach that remain at the heart of a programmatic approach to instructional outreach, but the opportunities are there to build upon these existing relationships and activities, providing enhanced instructional collaboration and outreach on the contemporary academic campus.

REFERENCES

Association of College and Research Libraries. 2002. Information Literacy Competency Standards for Higher Education [online]. Chicago: American Library Association [cited February 9, 2003]. Available from the World Wide Web: <http://www.ala.org/acrl/il/toolkit/standards.html>.

Antepohl, W. and S. Herzig. 1999. "Problem-Based Learning versus Lecture-Based Learning in a Course of Basic Pharmacology: A Controlled, Randomized Study." *Medical Education* 33 (2): 106-113.

Arant, W. and P. A. Mosley. 1999. Introduction. *The Reference Librarian* 67/68: 1-4.

Bodi, S. 1988. "Critical Thinking and Bibliographic Instruction: The Relationship." *Journal of Academic Librarianship* 14 (3): 150-153.

Chu, Felix T. 1997. Librarian-Faculty Relations in Collection Development. *Journal of Academic Librarianship* 23 (1): 15-20.

Cruickshank, J. and D. G. Nowak. 2001. "Marketing References Resources and Services through a University Outreach Program." *The Reference Librarian* 73: 265-280.

Dewey, B. I. (Ed.). 2001. *Library User Education: Powerful Learning, Powerful Partnerships.* Lanham, MD: Scarecrow Press.

Fosmire, M. and A. S. Macklin. 2002. "Riding the Active Learning Wave: Problem-Based Learning as a Catalyst for Creating Faculty-Librarian Instructional Partnerships." *Issues in Science & Technology Librarianship* 34. [cited November 17, 2002]. Available from the World Wide Web: <http://www.istl.org/02-spring/article2.html>.

Frank, D. G., G. K. Raschke, J. Wood, and J. A. Yang. 2001. "Information Consulting: The Key to Success in Academic Libraries." *Journal of Academic Librarianship* 27 (2): 90-96.

Gibson, Craig. 1995. "Critical Thinking: Implications for Instruction." *RQ* 35 (1): 27-35.

Gibson, Craig and Burley J. Scales. 2000. "Going the Distance (and Back Again): A Distance Education Course Comes Home." *The Reference Librarian* 69/70: 233-244.

Grafstein, Ann. 2002. "A Discipline-Based Approach to Information Literacy." *The Journal of Academic Librarianship* 28 (4): 197-204.

Haynes, E. B. 1996. "Librarian-Faculty Partnerships in Instruction." *Advances in Librarianship* 20: 191-222.

Jacobson, T. E. and L. B. Cohen. 2000. "Teaching about the Internet: An Opportunity for Faculty Outreach." *C&RL News* 61 (4): 302-304.

Jayne, E. and P. Vander Meer. 1997. "The Library's Role in Academic Instructional Use of the World Wide Web." *Research Strategies* 15 (3): 123-150.

Lipow, Anne G. 1992. "Outreach to faculty: Why and how." In L. Shirato (Ed.). *Working with faculty in the new electronic library: Papers and session materials presented at the nineteenth national LOEX library instruction conference held at Eastern Michigan University, 10-11 May, 1991, and related resource materials gathered by the LOEX Clearinghouse* (pp. 7-24). Ann Arbor, MI: Pierian Press.

Lougee, Wendy P. 2002. "Diffuse Libraries: Emergent Roles for the Research Library in the Digital Age." Washington, DC: Council on Library and Information Resources. [November 29, 2002]. Available on the World Wide Web: <http://www.clir.org/pubs/reports/pub108/pub108.pdf>.

Macklin, A. S. 2001. "Integrating Information Literacy Using Problem-Based Learning." *Reference Services Review* 29 (4): 306-314.

Neely, T. Y. et al. (1999). "Instruction and Outreach at the CSU Libraries. *The Reference Librarian* 67/68: 273-287.

Nofsinger, Mary M. 1989. "Library Use Skills for College-Bound High School Students: A Survey." *The Reference Librarian* 24: 35-56.

Peyton, G. 2000. "The Mississippi State University Libraries Outreach Program: Reaching Out." *Mississippi Libraries* 64 (4): 104-107.

Raspa, D. and D. M. Ward, eds. 2000. *The Collaborative Imperative: Librarians and Faculty Working Together in the Information Universe.* Chicago: Association of College & Research Libraries.

Rosenberg, W., & Donald, A. (1995) "Evidence based medicine: an approach to clinical problem-solving." *British Medical Journal* 310 (6987), 1122.

Schillie, J. E. et al. 2000. "Outreach Through the College Librarian Program at Virginia Tech." *The Reference Librarian* 71: 71-78.

Stebelman, S. et al. (1999). "Improving Library Relations with the Faculty and University Administrators: The Role of the Faculty Outreach Librarian." *College & Research Libraries* 60 (2): 121-136.

Walter, Scott. 2000. "Engelond: A Model for Faculty-Librarian Collaboration in the Information Age." *Information Technology and Libraries* 19 (1): 34-41.

Walter, Scott. 2002. "Information Literacy in the Disciplines: A New Phase in the Movement." *LOEX News* 29 (1): 6-9.

Washington. 2000. *Revised Code of Washington* 28B.10.125 (West Group).

Washington State University Libraries. 2002a. *Washington State University Library Instruction–K-12 Connections.* [cited November 29, 2002]. Available on the World Wide Web: <http://www.wsulibs.wsu.edu/usered/k12connect.html>.

Washington State University Libraries. 2002b. *WSU Distance Degree Library Services.* [cited November 29, 2002]. Available on the World Wide Web: <http://www.wsulibs.wsu.edu/electric/library/>.

Watson, P. G. and R. A. Boone. 1989. "Information Support for Academic Administrators: A New Role for the Library." *College & Research Libraries* 50 (1): 65-75.

Westbrook, L. and R. Waldman. 1993. "Outreach in Academic Libraries: Principle into Practice." *Research Strategies* 11 (2): 60-65.

Wu, Connie et al. 1994. "Effective Liaison Relationships in an Academic Library." *College and Research Libraries News.* 55 (5): 254-255.

Young, H., ed. 1983. *The ALA glossary of library and information science.* Chicago: American Library Association.

Multiple Models
for Library Outreach Initiatives

Carole Ann Fabian
Charles D'Aniello
Cynthia Tysick
Michael Morin

SUMMARY. Special programming and advanced technologies were used to attract diverse, underserved and expanded user populations to University Libraries resources and events. Arts and Humanities Team librarians collaborated with other University units and community organizations, adapted programming models from enterprise settings and non-academic libraries, and used multi-media technologies to deliver a variety of events over one calendar year. Library exhibits, book talks, teaching assistant workshops, and multi-media kiosks were planned, implemented and evaluated. *[Article copies available for a fee from The Haworth Document Delivery Service: 1-800-HAWORTH. E-mail address: <docdelivery@haworthpress. com> Website: <http://www.HaworthPress.com> © 2003 by The Haworth Press, Inc. All rights reserved.]*

Carole Ann Fabian (E-mail: cafabian@buffalo.edu) is Director and Michael Morin (E-mail: memorin@buffalo.edu) is Educational Technology Librarian, Educational Technology Center; and Charles D'Aniello (E-mail: lclcharl@buffalo.edu) and Cynthia Tysick (E-mail: cat2@buffalo.edu) are Humanities & Social Sciences Librarians, Arts & Sciences Libraries, all at University Libraries, University at Buffalo, Buffalo, NY 14260.

[Haworth co-indexing entry note]: "Multiple Models for Library Outreach Initiatives." Fabian, Carole Ann et al. Co-published simultaneously in *The Reference Librarian* (The Haworth Information Press, an imprint of The Haworth Press, Inc.) No. 82, 2003, pp. 39-55; and: *Outreach Services in Academic and Special Libraries* (ed: Paul Kelsey, and Sigrid Kelsey) The Haworth Information Press, an imprint of The Haworth Press, Inc., 2003, pp. 39-55. Single or multiple copies of this article are available for a fee from The Haworth Document Delivery Service [1-800-HAWORTH, 9:00 a.m. - 5:00 p.m. (EST). E-mail address: docdelivery@haworthpress.com].

http://www.haworthpress.com/store/product.asp?sku=J120
© 2003 by The Haworth Press, Inc. All rights reserved.
Digital Object Identifier: 10.1300/J120v39n82_04

KEYWORDS. Library outreach, collaborations and partnerships, faculty partnerships, book talks, library exhibits, teaching assistants, multimedia kiosks

INTRODUCTION

Academic libraries have relied on patron dependence on library print collections to attract users to their services. The introduction of greater electronic access to research materials, use of online reference utilities, and diverse user needs have caused many academic libraries to re-examine outreach efforts to their campus and community patrons. For some libraries, this initiates an exploration of new marketing and public relations activities. At the University at Buffalo (UB), special programming and advanced technologies were used to attract diverse, underserved and expanded user populations to the Libraries' resources and events. Arts and Humanities Team librarians collaborated with other UB units and community organizations, adapted programming models from enterprise settings and non-academic libraries, and used multi-media technologies to deliver a variety of events over one calendar year. Library exhibits, book talks, teaching assistant workshops, and multi-media kiosks were planned, implemented and evaluated.

LITERATURE REVIEW

Michele Russo and Nancy Colborn provide a useful definition and application of public relations in marketing library services and collections in the academic setting. Based on market research strategies, they describe a variety of activities targeted at specific user populations (students, faculty and community). In quoting Pamela Brown, they distinguish between marketing (used in long-range planning initiatives and documents) and public relations (PR), a marketing subset activity that stresses promotion of services to customers (Russo and Colborn, 2002). Wendi Arant and Charlene Clark build on this definition by adding an imperative to take the PR message outside the library to diverse constituencies. For them, libraries provide a value-added service seldom recognized by users: the ability of librarians to teach about information and technology as a distinguishing and valuable commodity in the information marketplace. A focus on "clientele" emphasizes two components of their PR model: fulfilling the service expectations of users and building strong relationships (Arant and Clark, 1999). The vernacular of marketing is aptly applied to the library setting in Maureen Brunsdale's analysis. She recommends a highly proactive marketing campaign as key to the success of academic libraries competing for consumer attention (Brunsdale, 2000). While these authors propose specific activities and strategies for increasing the visibility and centrality of libraries in the academic community, Nancy Marshall provides an interesting study of the views of academic library administrators on marketing and PR. Her introductory comments emphasize the importance of PR initiatives in securing the support of institutional leadership for library goals. However, in documenting library director attitudes towards PR initiatives, the study data demonstrate that outside of fundraising activities, public relations efforts are not always understood or valued by library leadership. Nonetheless, she continues, many academic libraries are launching creative programming activities as PR vehicles for their promotion of library collections and services. These activities are designed to increase the academic library's reach to its constituents, and to underscore the relevance of library services to the scholarly community. As part of these efforts, and to ensure their success, librarians are also strategically inviting the collaborative partnership of diverse individuals and organizations (Marshall, 2001). Jill McKinstry and Anne Garrison, reporting on the ACRL President's Discussion Forum, ALA Midwinter 2001, highlight the importance of identifying and nurturing critical campus partnerships as the basis for library outreach. Citing examples from three large public institutions, the report encourages academic librarians to plan library programs and services in response to community needs and wants (McKinstry and Garrison, 2001).

UB Arts & Humanities Team librarians developed outreach activities to encourage use and awareness of the Libraries' traditional collections, and to introduce users to the services offered and multi-format collections held. The Libraries serve approximately 25,000 users (undergraduate, graduate and faculty) across two campuses and hold over 3.25 million volumes. The UB Libraries are staffed by 162 full-time employees, including sixty-one librarians. The Arts & Humanities Team comprises eight subject specialist librarians that serve diverse academic disciplines including: Anthropology, Architecture, Art, Art History, Classics, History, and Romance Languages and Literatures, among others. They are charged by the Libraries' Directors to collaborate on projects of mutual interest, such as the development of programming and outreach initiatives. The Team explored, selected and tested emerging technologies and marketplace public relations strategies as outreach methods in a one-year series of events targeted at introducing library resources to hidden campus and community constituencies.

Librarians also identified and nurtured campus partnerships to engage a wider audience, and to instill a sense of community "ownership" of, and investment in, library collections and activities. Librarians identified partners within and beyond the University with shared goals and complementary resources. Program partners included individual faculty presenters, campus units with similar end goals and target audiences, and community cultural institutions, for example, the English Department, the UB Center for Teaching and Learning Resources, and the Albright-Knox Art Gallery. Motivating factors for collaborative activities included: intellectual engagement with the program theme, desire to co-promote complementary programs and events, economies of effort in terms of program implementation and associated costs, publicity, and maximizing the impact of related programs.

During the 2002 calendar year, the Team developed four program areas to promote library collections and services and to advance library outreach goals: collaboratively planned and implemented library exhibits, book talks, and multi-media exhibit kiosks, all tied to a central theme, and co-planned teaching assistant workshops that targeted outreach efforts to a special university population. Each programming effort tested the Libraries' ability to attract new University and community constituencies to the Libraries' resources and services. The following sections describe each of the four outreach programs, contextualized and described by lead librarians in the program.

LIBRARY EXHIBITS

When collaboratively developed and professionally executed, a library exhibit is a memorable, tangible, and easily documented outreach vehicle. Exhibits, whether physical or online, can be an important educational opportunity both for their developers and for those who view them. They can also be an enjoyable and effective focal point around which to build relationships with professorial faculty, librarians, and students, as well as with various University offices and community organizations and institutions. These outcomes are achieved through the development of an exhibit theme or story, the selection and interpretation of materials, collaborative relationships with colleagues and others, publicity, and associated programming. Moreover, a library exhibit reaches out to its viewers, demonstrating that libraries are sources of learning, even apart from the explicit advertising of their collections and services.

Collaborating with professorial faculty on interpretative issues, building programs featuring their participation, using an organization's public relations offices, or relying on colleagues with a diversity of topical knowledge or technical skills–from programming to graphic design–builds new relationships and enriches and strengthens established ones. In fact, building a web of relationships can set the stage for collaborations and interactions having little in common with the events that initiated them. The same is true for the skills one may develop to create an exhibit, from computer programming to carpentry. Exhibit design and execution can be a tremendously valuable exercise in self-education and interpersonal skills. In an academic setting, exhibit creation can demonstrate to professorial faculty that a librarian or group of librarians care about the substance of what interests them, beyond demonstrating how information may be found on the topic. Exhibits can also play an important and interesting role by explicitly demonstrating research strategies or publicizing locally available collections and resources. Each of these goals can be built into any exhibit. The mere existence of an exhibit can implicitly demonstrate how quickly information can be found and synthesized by a talented librarian. Further, the alliances and mutual positive perceptions nurtured during the design and execution of an exhibit–and the sense of ownership and teamwork between those even peripherally involved–can often be drawn upon in a variety of political situations. At the very least, successful collaborations on one exhibit may suggest other exhibits and make the execution of each successive collaborative exhibit easier. Mentioning that a particular individual assisted or is assisting with an effort sometimes is all that is needed to encourage another's participation. In short, the participation of certain individuals validates the effort for others. Further, while large attendance figures for an exhibit or event are important and gratifying, a well-executed effort can mitigate the need for large numbers–and have a powerful public relations impact–if the appropriate viewers and collaborators have found the effort enjoyable and intellectually stimulating.

The initial attractiveness of an exhibit to viewers–and the very reason for its existence–may well be its association with instruction, or community or institutional events. The latter may include lectures, concerts, conferences, or commemorations. Sometimes an exhibit may explicitly support instruction and students may be required to view it. And, of course, programming can be built around an exhibit. Programs can be powerful advertisements for exhibits and, likewise, exhibits can be powerful advertisements for programs. As the component of an outreach program, exhibits are most significant when they benefit from and contribute to these synergies. Several recent exhibits sponsored by the Arts & Humanities Team are fine examples.

"Fifties Flashback: Popular Culture and American Society" was designed to complement a large enrollment undergraduate course on the 1950s and a concurrent exhibit at Buffalo's Albright-Knox Art Gallery (AKAG). The library exhibit, installed in the entrance to UB's Lockwood Memorial Library, remained on display for a little over a semester and was advertised in the campus press. The exhibit featured a timeline; period photographs of Lockwood Memorial Library and the University, along with yearbooks and clippings from campus publications; a large and valuable collection of automobile memorabilia; selections from the Libraries' pulp fiction collection, with commentary focusing on period censorship efforts; four large hanging photographic collages of advertisements, events, and individuals from the '50s; and three cases of period comic books, with commentary. Hula hoops were hung from the ceiling above the exhibit and posters created from scanned comic book covers were mounted on columns and walls surrounding the comic book cases. One multi-media kiosk displayed a civil defense film and two kiosks offered music and television commercials and print advertisements from the period. Some of these exhibit components were assembled from responses to a request for exhibit-worthy materials that was sent across the Libraries' staff listserv by the exhibit coordinators. Individuals, not members of the Arts & Humanities Team, played important roles in creating the exhibit and many exhibit components had their own curators. One of the three coordinators was not a Team member, but a Libraries colleague. The exhibit was announced on the Libraries' exhibits web page <http://ublib.buffalo.edu/libraries/exhibits/>.

"J. M. Coetzee: Voicing the Heart of South Africa" was also installed in the entrance area of Lockwood Memorial Library and remained on display for about two months. It was initiated at the request of UB's English Department to advertise a reading at the University by this renowned South African novelist, literary critic, and former UB faculty member. We took this opportunity to create a multi-media exhibit kiosk consisting of text, timelines, video and audio files, and still photographs. Photographic portraits of Coetzee were displayed, along with a personal timeline and selections from his two "memoirs." To provide historical context, provocative photographs documenting apartheid-era social conditions and political events were shown, with descriptive labels, along with a detailed timeline of South African history, and a brief historical narrative. Some of these materials were displayed on walls surrounding the cases. Adapted or copied materials were appropriately attributed. In addition, the covers of his books were displayed, each accompanied by a brief summary. The exhibit was introduced in a short essay by a UB faculty member who was especially knowledgeable on Coetzee's writing, a South African himself, and a friend of the author. The text of an interview with the author and a review of his most recent work–both done by a member of our faculty–were displayed. Each of these faculty collaborators was involved in a panel discussion of the author's work that complemented the exhibit, and each offered advice on the exhibit and associated discussion. The former is chairman of our Department of Comparative Literature and served as a major advisor for the exhibit. The other faculty member, a regular reviewer for *The Buffalo News*, our local major newspaper, played a leading role in organizing the panel. In addition to the panel discussion, the Team sponsored a video screening introduced by an appropriate scholar. The exhibit, video screening, and panel discussion were advertised, along with the reading, using posters and in a sidebar to an interview with Coetzee published in *The Buffalo News*. The latter was conducted by the faculty reviewer mentioned above. In addition, the exhibit and programs were well-advertised in the campus press. A web-resident exhibit was also mounted <http://ublib.buffalo.edu/libraries/asl/exhibits/coetzee/> and, as previously noted, a PowerPoint kiosk exhibit with audio complemented the physical exhibit. The discussion was hosted by the Team in the Libraries' Special Collections Reading Room, was introduced by the Team's coordinator, and featured faculty members from the departments of English and Comparative Literature. Partnership with the Libraries was acknowledged by the Department of English throughout this effort and again at the author's reading. All programs were advertised on the English Department web site. A permanent J. M. Coetzee web site is under consideration, with the two faculty members mentioned above serving as advisors.

Years of sitting at the reference desk observing those who have visited our exhibits inform the following conclusions. Exhibits can play a uniquely important educational role. They can both complement and initiate formal and informal educational opportunities. An exhibit can also serve as decoration in an otherwise at best boring physical setting, and under cover of adornment, sometimes unconsciously encourage reflection. Exhibits are different from other learning opportunities, because they are "read" differently than traditional "texts" or "stories." Exhibits have always offered opportunities for "hyperlinked" discourse and the creation of virtual realities. This is because text and other elements such as images, sounds, and physical objects can readily be "linked" with one another through physical positioning within the exhibit or made readily accessible through explicit associations with other exhibit components–in our exhibits, for example, with multi-media kiosks. Further, ambiance and meaning can be created with words, sounds, images, physical surroundings, and even smell, taste, and feel. While an exhibit may be constructed with an overall story line, exhibits lend themselves more to a progression of vignettes or episodes and invite and support episodic and non-linear viewing and learning. A well-designed exhibit is constructed of discreet components that can stand alone, but when viewed together tell an even fuller story. This type of viewing seems to occur regardless of the content or technical sophistication of the exhibits we've mounted. Therefore, good exhibits have many teachable moments that are not necessarily dependent on one another, but, nonetheless, complement one another and often do have an explicit, although sometimes loose, linearity for those wishing to use it. They are most effective when they combine a variety of formats–object, text, video, image, and sound–any one of which may be operative in drawing a viewer into exploring other components or features of the exhibit. From a purely epistemological consideration, all of these formats have important roles in telling most stories. An exhibit can demonstrate to viewers the diversity of the "recorded" record–the "documents" out of which any description or history can be–and should be–constructed.

To have a significant educational and public relations impact, exhibits must demonstrate sensitivity to the interests of the local environment, a meaningful understanding of the topic, and a compelling technical execution. If one of these factors is absent, the effectiveness of the exercise is compromised, and outreach can result in demonstrating ignorance, carelessness, or technological wizardry without substantive content. A bad exhibit is like a bad piece of writing–it exposes one to a prolonged critical inspection. A good exhibit can make a library friends and earn it respect from the full range of its creators, collaborators, and visitors. It can draw people into the library who might never come otherwise, build positive perceptions of libraries and librarians, and build relationships across diverse groups and constituencies. A good exhibit is a demonstrable act of intellectual engagement and scholarship. It can be the very best kind of showing off and outreach.

BOOK TALKS

Because of its solitary nature, reading is a very personal activity. Alone with a book, we experience a wide range of emotions: joy, laughter, enlightenment, love, anger, fear, and confusion are just a few. Participating in book talks or book clubs encourages readers to candidly and openly discuss their reactions to a book, while gaining a deeper understanding through the exchange of ideas and perspectives with others. In some cases, when the author is leading the discussion, it allows the members to clarify aspects of the book or confirm their interpretation of specific passages or messages. Meeting and discussing books have been called many things: book clubs, reading clubs, book discussion groups, and book talks. The member demographics and size of the group may vary but they all have two common elements, a book and a discussion.

Book clubs and book talks are nothing new. They started in the United States in the late 1800s for immigrant women and men as a means to improve their use of the English language, to meet fellow immigrants, and to become "Americanized" (Larson, 2001). Meetings were held in the homes of middle-class patrons, community centers, or "radical" bookstores. Eventually, book clubs moved into subscription public libraries and were organized by librarians. Some of the original book clubs ran for over twenty years. Over time the popularity of book clubs and book talks waned. However, public libraries and bookstores continued the practice due in large part to small, committed groups of bibliophiles scattered in communities across the country. It wasn't until the early 1980s that book clubs and book talks began making their comeback. Many credit this resurgence to the hard work and determination of Virginia Valentine, Tattered Cover bookstore employee, Denver, Colorado (Abramson, 2002). Valentine has been organizing and continuously hosting book clubs for over twenty years; as a result she is considered one of the foremost experts. Following her lead, in the 1990s Oprah Winfrey and large bookstore chains like Borders and Barnes and Noble began organizing and marketing book talks with the authors. To support these efforts, book publishers began producing "Reading Discussion Guides" to facilitate the "fine art of conversation" (McGinley and Conley, 2001).

During the late 1990s, public libraries across the country partnered with city officials, literary guilds, and corporations in an effort to reach out to their communities. "One Book, One City" campaigns sprang up across the country. They encouraged the public in cities, both large and small, to share in the joy and fulfillment of reading. In most cases community arts programs, such as theater, fine art, and music also participated in the campaigns (Rogers, 2002).

While most academic libraries have been slow to realize the potential of book talks as a tool for outreach, marketing, and collaboration, an intrepid few have joined the book talk bandwagon. A recent Internet search shows that academic libraries like the University of Pennsylvania at Pittsburgh, UC Santa Cruz, Villanova University, Cornell University, Loyola Marymount University, and Boston College promote the pleasure of reading through library and/ or partner-sponsored book talks. Taking these initiatives into account, the UB Arts & Humanities Team soon realized that an individual or series of book talks promotes the university or college library as a vital component of the academic experience for both students and faculty. By co-sponsoring a talk or series of talks the academic library reaches out across the campus, enriching and diversifying its partnerships. In our experience, inviting English Department faculty to co-plan our initial book talk series set the groundwork for future collaborative programming with them and other academic departments. In addition to English, faculty from Comparative Literature, Asian Studies, Center for the Americas, and History subsequently recognized the Libraries as a locus for scholarly discourse and co-planned a wide range of collaborative activities including guest author visits, library exhibits, and multi-media presentations.

Deciding to host a book talk requires attention to detail. Early in the programming process, the Team considered a variety of presentation issues including: the number and frequency of talks, book length, target audience, format, program themes, potential partners, specific book titles and facilitators. The Team ultimately decided to pilot a book talk series, titled "Reading the '50s." The campus-wide reading program was conceived as part of a number of campus and community events focusing on the '50s which included: the Albright-Knox Art Gallery exhibition, film and lecture series, "The Tumultuous Fifties: A View from the New York Times Photo Archives"; a large-enrollment undergraduate course English 372: "The Fifties"; and the Lockwood Library exhibit "Fifties Flashback."

Librarians compiled a list of twenty "blockbuster" books from the 1950s. Books were chosen from best sellers lists, Pulitzer Prize winners, and Team member suggestions. Criteria for inclusion were intellectual accessibility to the widest range of University readers, length, availability, and significant representation of the decade. A group of ten faculty members from the departments of English, History, Political Science and Romance Languages and Literatures was consulted for critical input on the book list. They were asked to review the book list, to select a single title, and to lead an hour-long facilitated discussion. All responded enthusiastically to the book list programming. However, one of the English faculty challenged the librarians' scholarly authority in selecting the book list titles, commenting that the list should have been generated by literature specialists. Interestingly, this professor has become our most engaged faculty collaborator. In the end, three faculty (English, Political Science and Romance Languages and Literatures) and one librarian agreed to present four book talks in the spring semester, one every two weeks. The next step was marketing the series without a budget. The Team created a media campaign around their spring 2002 semester programs including a web page <http://ublib.buffalo.edu/libraries/units/lml/Collections/docs/reading_50s.html>, bookmarks, and high-quality program posters that were mounted across the campus. In addition, they worked with the Libraries' Office of University and External Relations to place ads at no cost in the student newspaper, and were given free public service announcements on the campus radio station, a National Public Radio affiliate serving western New York and southern Ontario.

Each talk in the series was scheduled for Thursday at 4 p.m. in the library; refreshments were provided. Discussion leaders provided a variety of supplemental materials, for example, one faculty member created a multi-media presentation that walked the audience through the literary narrative, while another used audio tapes of the author giving a dramatic reading of passages from his book. All provided background information on the author, critical and popular reception of the book during the 1950s, and its relevance to present day readers. While each discussion leader handled their groups differently, all were skilled in encouraging attendees to voice their insights and difficulties with the books. In most cases, the conversation was lively and flowed with minimal prodding.

At the end of the semester, the Team met to evaluate the effectiveness of the book talks and to determine what their next step should be. While book talk attendance was low, on average seven participants, it was a varied group of students, faculty, and members from the local community. Feedback from those who attended was extremely favorable and the Team received many requests to continue the series. However, the Team felt that the amount of time necessary to create a theme, choose the books, create promotional material, organize facilitators, and actually run the talks did not justify the benefits. They decided that one book per semester would be a better use of their time and if co-sponsored by another department on campus would increase the benefits of outreach and collaboration.

To that end, the Team collaborated with the English Department during the summer of 2002 in preparation for a visit by author J. M. Coetzee in fall 2002.

They organized one book talk titled "Reading J. M. Coetzee," that highlighted selected works by the author and featured a panel of three faculty members from the departments of Comparative Literature and English. The Team created a web site <http://ublib.buffalo.edu/libraries/asl/exhibits/coetzee/>, an in-house exhibit with a multi-media kiosk, and flyers. The collaborative effort resulted in enthusiastic support from both departments and a higher attendance rate than the four previous talks combined. As with the book talk series, attendance included students, faculty, and the local community. Given the success of the single book a semester project, the Team concluded that in order for book talks to be a successful outreach tool they should be based on quality and not quantity. By highlighting one book per semester, academic libraries can more easily focus marketing efforts across the campus and community, build collaborations with relevant departments, and create complementary multi-media kiosk exhibits.

MULTI-MEDIA KIOSKS

The Team also developed multi-media kiosks–free-standing digital audio/video presentations viewed via computer monitors–to accompany both the '50s and Coetzee exhibits. The kiosks provided an alternate mode for visitor interaction with the exhibit content, and a vehicle for presenting related non-textual materials. The Team's ability to envision and develop these kiosks added an enriched dimension to the exhibits, previously inaccessible to our collaborators due to their lack of technological skill and access to technology infrastructure. The Team's unique contributions in this technology area increased its value to partners, and enhanced the experience of exhibit visitors.

To supplement materials in Buffalo's Albright-Knox Art Gallery exhibit, "The Tumultuous Fifties: Photographs from The New York Times Archives," Team librarians amassed pop artifacts, print ephemera from the Libraries' collections, and media clips from the Web and realia from Libraries' staff personal collections. After the exhibit needs of the museum curators were met and materials used in displays at the Gallery, a second, large-scale complementary exhibit, "Fifties Flashback: Popular Culture and American Society," was planned, designed and curated by the Team and exhibited at Lockwood Memorial Library. The amount of visual material collected by the Team easily overwhelmed the exhibit spaces available in the AKAG and the Libraries. The Team introduced a plan for electronic kiosks as an additional display format for each exhibit space. Armed with more media elements than technical solutions to harness them, the Team worked together to develop methods to edit and convert all the media elements into a digital multi-media presentation for stand-alone computer viewing. Two self-running, stand-alone media kiosks were developed for the Libraries' exhibit and one of the workstations was replicated at the AKAG for the duration of "The Tumultuous Fifties" exhibit. All three kiosks contained consumer commercials, print ads, tobacco ads and government civil defense movie footage. The film clips were critical in bringing to the viewer the 3-dimensional look and feel of the '50s via sound, graphics and moving images. One of the Libraries' kiosks also included eighty musical selections–1950s pop hits whose copyright status prevented inclusion in a museum venue. The kiosks displayed five-minute continuously looping audio/video presentations. Viewers watched the media presentation via the computer monitors and simultaneously listened to the audio portion using provided headphones.

As with most multi-media projects, difficulties were encountered with the technology. For example, our early decision to rely on several web-based video archives as our primary source of period film artifacts presented two major problems: identifying workable video format, driver and player for files that weren't created in-house, and editing and separating each proprietary file into individual clips readable via one presentation software application.

A combination approach to opening, editing and converting the media files was developed using common features of Pinnacle Studio 7 and Windows Movie Maker home video editing software to clip to length and index the files by individual subjects as needed. Once the video files were successfully edited, a final version was saved to a new user-friendly Windows Media Player format. This was an important task and would also be a major factor in developing the kiosk application itself. Window Media Player file format also provided the kiosk designers total design control of the screen interface. The Windows Media Player can run a sound or video file within a presentation program without adding anything unnecessary to the visual display.

No special budget was in place to utilize museum-style touch screen technology or theater-style projection, so the kiosk team decided to use a continuously running, highly animated PowerPoint Kiosk presentation format. Keyboards were hidden or removed, speakers were used with the AKAG displays and headphones were supplied with the two library displays.

With the single biggest technical challenge solved, the librarians turned their attention to graphic design for the kiosk and related print materials. Team efforts to gather fascinating materials from the '50s also piqued interest in period design and provided a strong visual theme for our presentations. Photographs of local '50s architectural icons and period design elements were examined for possible use as backgrounds, directional menu buttons, and a "skin" for the media player. Boomerang countertop patterns, hot '50s colors and many graphic design elements found in diners, jukeboxes, hula hoops, hot rods and period appliances were combined with elements of '50s print design as found in popular ads, civil defense literature and the world of popular music.

The kiosk graphical interface was created by the librarian-designer, in a "Hot Rod Barbie" color scheme of black, chrome, pink, and turquoise. Videos were inserted in PowerPoint, superimposed over a screen image of a 1950s Emerson television. Multi-layered graphical screens were animated and repeated as many as twenty times each to simulate motion. The animated menu screen allowed viewers to navigate between '50s print advertising and film clips, with submenus linking to various textual, tobacco, government or civil defense content.

The codification of a standard graphic identity for all presentation elements helped pull together the diverse physical, electronic and virtual iterations of the '50s program. Title screens reminiscent of period neon, hot rods and comic book illustration were prominent in the animated kiosks, display designs, and related print graphics, tying each element to the overall project. PowerPoint allowed the consistent heavy use of a '50s style graphic design and typography. Print materials designed to reinforce the library kiosks and display cases included poster-sized color reproductions of comic book covers, and full-color broadsides that incorporated civil defense symbols from fallout shelter signage. Visitors to the Library were greeted by an entry poster depicting an altered American flag design of stripes of civil defense yellow/orange and black with a blue union field replacing the triangle/circle symbol for radioactive materials. Inscribed on the last stripe of the atomic flag poster was the library exhibition's title, "Fifties Flashback: Popular Culture & American Society" (see Figure 1).

Animated PowerPoint with embedded digital audio files were also used for the J. M. Coetzee exhibit kiosk. Three librarians and one English Department faculty member collaborated to select important works by Coetzee to highlight in a continuous-loop, narrated PowerPoint presentation. A slide for each work was created containing cover art, text of the back matter, narration of the back matter, and appropriate music. Five thirty-second musical excerpts were selected by the librarians and included the work of five African musicians. The last component, narration, was done using a script and Sound Forge software during two hilarious recording sessions by three librarians on the Team. When complete, the entire presentation ran for four minutes. The kiosk was placed adjacent to the physical exhibit in Lockwood Memorial Library.

The software packages used to develop our audio and video files have been updated since our exhibits and any librarians developing a multi-media kiosk today could take advantage of several "direct to DVD" authoring features. When used in a computer, DVD applications can be dynamically linked to standard HTML documents. Feature film DVD authors, combining a fixed video display linked with web-based content, are slowly advancing this technology.

FIGURE 1. Image of Flag Poster

The moment our first kiosk went live, two unexpected things happened. First, a student instantly walked up and started watching the self-running exhibit and secondly, librarians realized that multi-media kiosks present a new modality for library instruction. Using built-in DVD-ROM technology, a fresh approach to information literacy tutorials can be created. Video screen images of well-executed information searches can be captured, edited and formatted into visual exemplars, ready for use in library presentations or indexed as help screen videos linked from library web pages.

TEACHING ASSISTANT WORKSHOPS

Emerging technology platforms allow librarians to expand library instruction to a potentially new and wider audience. Similarly, library programs designed for select audiences provide new opportunities for collaboration, teaching and learning. Librarians often focus their services and efforts at two primary user groups: faculty and students. Overlooked is a uniquely important hybrid of university instructors and students, the ubiquitous teaching assistant (TA). The university teaching assistant is often the most immediate contact an undergraduate student has with a faculty, a department, or a discipline. Their scope for influence is enormous, and yet it is rarely the case that libraries engage these instructors as partners in advancing library instructional goals aimed at undergraduate students.

In an effort to reach this large and underserved university constituency, university librarians teamed with the University at Buffalo Center for Teaching and Learning Resources (CTLR) to deliver two Teaching Assistant Workshops. The workshops were designed to expose new teaching assistants to a variety of basic teaching methods, classroom techniques, support services, co-teaching opportunities and research resources provided by the Libraries. Two separate programs were planned and offered: a mid-winter one-day workshop, and a late summer three-day immersion program. CTLR handled marketing for both events. The Libraries and CTLR co-planned the programs, jointly selecting lecture and discussion topics and recruiting speakers, facilitators, and participants.

The Libraries' part of the program included a "welcome to the Libraries" virtual tour, introducing participants to the Libraries' web portal, a sampling of its research databases, and specific services in support of teaching. Packets of in-house brochures and supplemental literature were distributed to TAs, highlighting the Libraries' "Instant Librarian" real-time online reference service, library instruction information <http://ublib.buffalo.edu/libraries/faculty/instruction.html>, selected e-product information, course reserve information for instructors, and a variety of other library research informational handouts. The library introduction emphasized a multitude of library resources and services available to TAs in their roles as both graduate students and as instructors. The introduction also stressed that collaboration between the TAs and librarians would further support the research components of the courses, and offer individualized guidance for TAs and their students. This overview was typical of most library orientation sessions.

A unique aspect of the program was the Libraries-hosted luncheon. TAs were introduced to the subject specialist library liaison for their department, and were invited to share a facilitated lunch with the subject librarian and other TAs in their discipline. Approximately twelve librarians and eighty TAs participated in the luncheons during each session; representing approximately 10% of UB's total TA population. To accommodate the multi-disciplinary nature of the TA population, the Team invited librarians from all subject disciplines throughout the Libraries to participate. This casual social interchange gave both librarians and TAs an opportunity to make personal contact with potentially critical partners in teaching and learning. Librarians made use of the opportunity to market new products and services offered by the library, and to schedule follow-up research meetings with individual TAs. Participants were very enthusiastic. Most were surprised at the approachability of the librarians, the range of services and research supports offered by the Libraries, and the depth and breadth of library resources in support of their research interests. TAs reported that they were unaware of available library services, and since the majority were new graduate students to the University, they were largely unfamiliar with the Libraries' collections, including general and subject-specific databases and reference tools.

Library staff also facilitated a panel discussion focused on TA identity and balancing TA roles as teacher and scholar. Four experienced TAs were invited to discuss their experiences as instructors, each telling a story illustrating challenges posed by one of the discussion topics: relationships with students, relationships with faculty, teaching strategies, classroom conflict resolution, communication skills, establishing classroom authority, and balancing teaching and research. These personal narratives were highly valued by attendees, and established a sense of community among attendees, discussants and the facilitator. The facilitator, a librarian, interpreted the TA "stories" in terms of pedagogical methodologies, and encouraged attendee participation in the discussions. Many of the stories presented opportunities to introduce instructional services available to the TAs provided by the Libraries and other campus support units, and underscored the Libraries' enthusiasm for team-based instruction.

Benefits for the TAs were clearly articulated in workshop evaluation forms: typical comments stressed new knowledge of library services and resources, accessibility of library staff, and confidence in University-supplied support services. For the Libraries, the workshops provide a welcome opportunity to showcase our rich print and electronic collections, support services and dedicated research staff to a critical–yet often overlooked–University constituency. Reference librarians uniformly applauded the effort and reported an increase in requests for course-integrated library instruction in undergraduate course offerings as a direct result of their lunchtime interaction with the TAs. Although initiated by the Arts & Humanities Team, the TA Workshops proved to be a viable, sustainable effort for the entire library faculty. By including librarians from all units of the Libraries, the Team promoted and supported a library-wide initiative and contributed to the achievement of a stated Libraries' outreach goal. As a result, the Libraries plan to continue to co-host the semi-annual Teaching Assistant Workshops. The workshops answer an ongoing need and provide mutual benefits to all participants. They also underscore the value of well-selected and equal program planning partnerships. By identifying common teaching and learning goals, the Libraries and the CTLR envision additional ongoing collaborative programming efforts.

CONCLUSION

In each of the four outreach activities, the Team found that the efforts of partnership produced more effective and successful results. For the library exhibits, partnerships with area cultural institutions and academic departments helped to ensure not only stimulating content, but an expanded market for our offerings. Additionally, librarians found that embracing technology solutions for their exhibit space limitations not only engaged unexpected users, but also opened up new opportunities for applying emerging technologies to more traditional library services, for example, library instruction. The book talk programs successfully utilized a similar network of University scholars in a series of events modeled after public library and enterprise setting reading programs. The Teaching Assistant Workshops diverged from theme-based library programming, focusing attention instead on a special population. These programs were most successful because they targeted an underserved student group, and invested in building strong interdependent campus partnerships for their success.

The Arts & Humanities Team will continue to support exhibits, book talks, multi-media kiosks and TA Workshops as elements of our outreach to the University and our civic neighbors. By building strong partnerships and employing carefully planned PR strategies, we hope to increase our outreach efforts and to maintain the interest and support of our library community.

REFERENCES

Abramson, Maria. "Valentine's way: the woman who preceded Oprah as the country's book guru knows how to make a group a great one." *Book.* July-August (2002): 36-37.

Arant, Wendi and Charlene K. Clark. "Academic library public relations: an evangelical approach." *Library Administration and Management* 13, no. 2 (Spring 1999): 90-5.

Bowen, Laurel G. and Peter J. Roberts. "Exhibits: illegitimate children of academic libraries?" *College & Research Libraries* 54, no. 5 (September 1993): 407-415.

Brown, Pamela. "Marketing public library services." *Public Libraries* 29, no. 1 (Jan./Feb. 1990): 11.

Brunsdale, Maureen. "From mild to wild: strategies for promoting academic libraries to undergraduates." *Reference & User Services Quarterly* 39, no. 4 (2000): 331-5.

Forys, M. "Library buddies: librarians' partnerships with teaching assistants at University of Iowa." *Research Strategies* 16, no. 3 (1998): 231-3.

Larson, Kate Clifford. "The Saturday Evening Girls: a progressive era library club and the intellectual life of working class and immigrant girls in turn-of-the-century Boston." *Library Quarterly* 71, no. 2 (2001): 195-230.

Marshall, Nancy J. "Public relations in academic libraries: a descriptive analysis." *The Journal of Academic Librarianship* 27, no. 2 (2001): 116-21.

McKinstry, Jill and Anne Garrison. "Building communities @ your library." *College & Research Libraries News* 62, no. 2 (2001): 165-7, 186.

Rogers, Michael. "Libraries offer chapter and verse on citywide book clubs." *Library Journal* 127, no. 6 (2002): 16-18.

Russo, Michele C. and Nancy A. Wootton Colborn. "Something for (almost) nothing: public relations on a shoestring in an academic library." *Library Administration and Management* 16, no. 3 (Summer 2002): 138-45.

Faculty Outreach:
A Win-Win Proposition

Linda Reeves
Catherine Nishimuta
Judy McMillan
Christine Godin

SUMMARY. Librarians at Northwest Vista College, a new community college, speculated that keeping faculty members informed about the library and its various resources would result in more instructors sending students to the library for library instruction and, ultimately, it would result in more students who were familiar with and comfortable using the library. This paper describes the librarians' comprehensive faculty outreach effort, which involved putting on special workshops for faculty, creating online forms, and Web links on the library Web page, and taking every opportunity to increase contact and collaboration between librarians and other faculty and staff. *[Article copies available for a fee from The Haworth Document Delivery Service: 1-800-HAWORTH. E-mail address: <docdelivery@haworthpress.com> Website: <http://www.HaworthPress.com> © 2003 by The Haworth Press, Inc. All rights reserved.]*

Linda Reeves (E-mail: lreeves@accd.edu) and Catherine Nishimuta (E-mail: cnishimu@accd.edu) are Public Services Librarians, Judy McMillan (E-mail: jmcmilla@accd.edu) is Technical Services Librarian, and Christine Godin (E-mail: cgodin@accd.edu) is Director of Learning Resources, all at Northwest Vista College, 3535 North Ellison Drive, San Antonio, TX 78251.

[Haworth co-indexing entry note]: "Faculty Outreach: A Win-Win Proposition." Reeves, Linda et al. Co-published simultaneously in *The Reference Librarian* (The Haworth Information Press, an imprint of The Haworth Press, Inc.) No. 82, 2003, pp. 57-68; and: *Outreach Services in Academic and Special Libraries* (ed: Paul Kelsey, and Sigrid Kelsey) The Haworth Information Press, an imprint of The Haworth Press, Inc., 2003, pp. 57-68. Single or multiple copies of this article are available for a fee from The Haworth Document Delivery Service [1-800-HAWORTH, 9:00 a.m. - 5:00 p.m. (EST). E-mail address: docdelivery@haworthpress.com].

http://www.haworthpress.com/store/product.asp?sku=J120
© 2003 by The Haworth Press, Inc. All rights reserved.
Digital Object Identifier: 10.1300/J120v39n82_05

KEYWORDS. Faculty outreach, marketing, information literacy, library instruction

INTRODUCTION:
RECOGNIZING THE NEED FOR OUTREACH

Northwest Vista College is a young institution, the fourth college in the Alamo Community College District in San Antonio, Texas. The campus opened in the fall of 1998, but classes had been offered in other locations since 1996. Northwest Vista College has experienced phenomenal growth since it opened. When it moved into the new campus facilities, it had 800 students. It now serves over 7,000 students, of which 56.4% are female and 43.6% are male.

The library, with approximately 15,000 volumes, and eighty subscriptions to electronic databases, is located on the second floor of the Learning Center Building. The first floor is occupied by the President's suite and the Student Success Center (advising, financial aid, testing). The current plan is for the library to eventually occupy the entire Learning Center Building. The librarians offer library instruction classes tailored to each academic subject area. Presently, the library has five full-time professional librarians (including the director), one part-time librarian, one administrative secretary, and six student clerks.

A variety of factors contribute to our need to market the library. One clear indication of this need is that many instructors and students have told us they were not aware that the college had a library. Since the library occupies the second floor of a building housing other departments, it is not as prominent on campus as it might be. Furthermore, because our library is part of a new college currently consisting of just three permanent buildings, people may assume that the library has not been built yet. Some faculty members who knew of the library's existence were not familiar with what our library had to offer. For example, the low numbers of faculty who scheduled library orientation sessions for their students suggested that not all faculty knew the library offered orientations. In addition, students were continually given library assignments that could not be completed using the library resources, indicating that some faculty members were not familiar with the library resources.

Another explanation for faculty members' unfamiliarity with library resources is that the nature of libraries has changed dramatically in the past few years. New technologies have transformed the library, for some, into a bewildering place. For example, because information previously found in print now appears in Web format, the original source of information can be difficult to identify. An electronic encyclopedia article often looks like a journal article or an item from a newspaper. Students and faculty must learn to judge the validity and reliability of the resource using critical thinking skills not needed with print information. As we move away from the strict controlled vocabularies of print indexing to keywords and Boolean operators available in electronic formats, patrons must master further searching skills. Faculty and staff unfamiliar with the library's new electronic resources need instruction in how to use them for research. Librarians must be proactive and ready to teach the skills their patrons need to acquire.

As the 2000-01 academic year drew to a close, we concluded that our library needed an outreach program, something from which virtually every library can benefit. Educating the faculty about the library became a goal, and we realized that we would have to use a variety of means to market ourselves to faculty, especially adjunct instructors. Communicating with the large pool of adjunct faculty has always been a challenge at our college. Many adjuncts come on campus only to teach one or two courses, and most do not have an office on campus, nor are they on the college e-mail system. We wanted the faculty members to know that with the addition of the online subscription databases, the community college library is now a valuable resource for their own professional development.

REVIEW OF THE LITERATURE

Having recognized the need to undertake a faculty outreach effort, we sought to determine what forms that outreach effort should take. A review of the professional library literature produced many good practical ideas and several common themes, which helped shape and guide our outreach efforts.

The Information Explosion and the Need for Information Literacy

Prominent in the professional literature is the idea that the information explosion makes it imperative for everyone to keep up with current trends in technology and information resources. Colleges across the country are finding innovative ways to respond to the need for information literacy, with librarians responding to meet this need. Farber (1999) asserts that in the period from 1975 to 1999 librarians have taken on an increased instructional role due to the increase in online sources. In the 1970s it was rare for advertisements for reference librarians to mention instruction as a job responsibility, but twenty years later it was rare to find one that did not mention bibliographic instruction. Saunders (1999) reports that faculty requests for class training at Salem State College have doubled since the library began providing access to Web-based resources. She adds, "Every time that we link to a new Web site or subscribe to full-text electronic journals, we expand the need for training" (43).

Teaching Information Literacy to Students

Colleges around the country are looking at various ways to teach information literacy skills. Farber (1999) traces how the instructional role of academic librarians has increased from the 1970s to the present. Student orientation programs are one way librarians introduce students to the wide range of library sources, and give them instruction in search strategies to use with online databases (Farber, 1999).

Library instruction classes offer another way to teach students library research skills. Most colleges report marked increases in requests for library instruction classes in response to the online revolution. Saunders (1999) asserts that to access the information available through the World Wide Web and through electronic databases, books, and journals, today's students need to learn how to search electronic library resources, how to conduct an effective Web search, and how to evaluate information critically. Librarians are in a good position to provide training in these skills, because they study new information resources and work closely with teachers and information technologists.

Furthermore, colleges and universities are turning to credit courses in information literacy. Teaching a credit course in information literacy makes students more adept at finding information using the latest technologies, and allows librarians to be more directly involved with the educational mission of their institutions, benefiting the librarians as well as students. Donnelly (2000) states that teaching Information Literacy 101, a two-credit, core-curriculum information literacy course, has given librarians an additional impetus to keep up to date with, and to have a better understanding of the problems students have with research projects. The course has also brought about more professional equality between librarians and the rest of the college faculty. It has even "catapulted the library to the center of the college's teaching mission and made it an integral part of the students' college experiences" (Donnelly 49). Owusu-Ansah (2001) also argues for requiring a course in information literacy taught by librarians, asserting that today's college graduates need to navigate, find, and use information to answer questions and solve problems in an environment of constant change and an explosive amount of information. He insists that instruction in the retrieval, evaluation, and use of information must be provided to all those graduating from a college or university. Owusu-Ansah maintains that because academic librarians are the best equipped members of the academic body to provide information literacy, colleges and universities need to make the library a teaching department and make information literacy courses part of the basic requirements of undergraduate education.

Some institutions provide information literacy instruction through teaching collaborations between librarians and teaching faculty. Cudiner and Harmon

(2000) describe workshops on online search strategies taught by a librarian and a faculty member, concluding that use of electronic library resources should become an important part of the university curriculum and the teaching culture.

The Need for Faculty Support

In order for an information literacy effort to succeed, librarians must have the support and respect of the teaching faculty. Faculty who are knowledgeable about the information resources available through the library, and aware that the library provides instruction, are much more likely to send their classes for instruction. Librarians can therefore educate students by first educating faculty, a difficult goal to achieve because, as research shows, many faculty members do not have a high regard for librarians and what they do, and some faculty members are reluctant to receive instruction from librarians. Oberg, Schleiter, and Van Houten (1989) present the results of a survey soliciting faculty members' perceptions of the status, role, and contribution of librarians at Albion College, a small, liberal arts college in Michigan. The authors suggest that confusion about the librarian profession occurs because many of the visible library functions–circulation and interlibrary loan–are clerical in nature, and the actual work of professional librarians–teaching, research, and collection development–happens behind the scenes. The authors report that increasing the amount of contact between librarians and faculty members is associated with an increased respect for academic librarians and conclude that librarians must better define and communicate their role to achieve a status appropriate to their contributions to their institutions. Faculty perceptions of librarians, the authors insist, influence librarians' status, the degree to which the library is isolated within the institution, how well the library is funded, and how intensively and successfully library resources are used.

Ivey (1994) offers a similar explanation: that teaching faculty is not aware of the academic nature of the work of librarians. Faculty members who view the work of librarians as largely clerical, are less likely to send their students to classes offered through the library. Ivey (1994) reports on a study conducted at Memphis State University, corroborating many earlier findings: teaching faculty value the service academic librarians provide to the university but do not view them as peers. To achieve recognition within the university, Ivey recommends that academic librarians increase their visibility by publishing in professional journals, becoming involved in academic governance and committee assignments, and marketing their skills by offering presentations and workshops to the academic community. Major (1993) presents similar results from interviews with academic librarians at Old Dominion University, concluding that librarians may be accepted as the peers of teaching faculty by overcoming timidity, developing self-confidence, participating in campus governance and committees, becoming known on campus, and initiating contact with faculty and supportive library administrators.

Good relations between librarians and teaching faculty, then, are critical, and a variety of avenues should be explored to reach that goal. Kotter (1999), in a comprehensive overview of the literature focusing on librarian-faculty relations, reveals that this relationship must be improved in order to ensure the viability of academic librarians and their role in higher education. Programs and initiatives for improving faculty-librarian relations and increasing faculty awareness of library services have included receptions honoring the faculty, faculty brown bag seminars, office calls, faculty focus groups, bibliographic instruction, and library liaison programs. Isaacson (2001) describes a faculty liaison program in which librarians meet with new faculty members and give them a personalized orientation to library resources, including a tour of the relevant sections of the library and a demonstration of the databases pertaining to each professor's interests. Some colleges have hired faculty outreach librarians to ensure good communication between faculty and librarians (Stebelman, 1999).

Instructing Faculty in Use of Electronic Resources

Special informal workshops designed for faculty are another effective way to familiarize instructors with the library and the new information technologies available through the library. Day and Armstrong (1996) describe workshops held at Illinois State to teach faculty members about Internet resources in their disciplines. The authors urge librarians to keep up with technological advances, communicate with faculty about the rapidly changing resources on the Internet, and teach faculty effective search techniques. Hall (1999) describes a series of workshops at California State University, Sacramento, held in order to train faculty to use the electronic catalog and databases and to let them know about problems students encounter when doing research. The workshops were well-received and resulted in an increase in the number of requests for instructional classes for students.

OUR FACULTY OUTREACH INITIATIVE

Inspired by ideas from the professional literature, we planned how to make our college faculty more knowledgeable about our library. Our goals for the outreach program included responding better to college community needs, helping students by helping faculty, building relationships with faculty and staff, encouraging faculty and staff to help shape the library collection and services, and keeping faculty and staff updated about new information technologies. We planned to accomplish these goals through a three-part initiative:

1. Getting the librarians out of the library and mingling with the rest of the college community;
2. Facilitating communication between librarians and the rest of the academic community;
3. Getting the faculty into the library.

GETTING OUT OF THE LIBRARY

Participating in community college events held outside the library offered us opportunities to reach faculty members who were not regular library users. We began attending campus events, forming relationships with faculty members, learning about their courses, and informing them about our library services and resources. While waiting in line at a Thanksgiving potluck, for example, we talk with faculty members about courses they are teaching and preparing, their research interests, and books they would like the library to purchase. We attend campus Fiesta events, get out and plant native plants for Earth Day, attend Black History Month presentations, and participate in International Women's Week activities. We participate in graduation wearing academic regalia, so we are a recognizable part of the academic community. We frequently take part in campus training opportunities such as technology workshops, which offer valuable opportunities to see and chat with members of the faculty, as well as acquire new skills.

Professional development workshops offer librarians opportunities to discover academic trends like service learning or globalizing the curriculum. Although the topics may not appear to directly relate to the library, they provide us with knowledge needed to purchase materials. Faculty whose presentations we attend in turn attend our own presentations. We are creating a network of support within the faculty.

FACILITATING COMMUNICATION: WEB LINKS FOR FACULTY AND STAFF

As the second arm of our outreach effort, we created three links for faculty and staff on our library Web site under the Resources for Faculty & Staff menu: "Collection Development," "Request for Purchase," and "Request for Library Instruction." The Request for Library Instruction form helps keep us organized, and obtains as much information as possible about the type of instruction needed. Required fields include the date and time preference; type of instruction desired; type of assignment (research paper, speech, PowerPoint presentation, literary criticism or persuasive paper, etc.); and a detailed explanation of the assignment. Each instruction request is sent to a database, which enables us to search specific fields, making information gathering easy. For example, we can see which departments request the most classes, and we can tabulate the number of students receiving instruction each semester.

The Request for Purchase form was created to encourage faculty and staff to suggest materials for the library. On this form we require either the title of the book or the ISBN number and the requestor's name and phone number. This information is sent to a database similar to the database that receives the Request for Library Instruction forms. Furthermore, the Collection Development page lists the librarians and the subject areas that each librarian is responsible for developing. Each name is hyper-linked to e-mail, so instructors can easily e-mail the appropriate librarian with requests for purchase. We continue to solicit suggestions from faculty for collection development, and we make certain to add subscriptions to journals in subject areas in which the college is building new programs.

The number of faculty-initiated requests for library instruction has increased dramatically, but because most requests come by phone, we believe that the increase is related to our other marketing efforts and not to adding the forms. There has been an increase in the use of our forms over the past year, but clearly we will need to market them further to increase their use. For example, we will make announcements at faculty workshops and meetings. We also plan to advertise by sending e-mail announcements and putting up flyers.

GETTING THEM INTO THE LIBRARY

The third part of our initiative was inviting faculty to the library to help familiarize them with resources available in and through the library. We addressed this goal by offering a series of lunchtime library workshops focusing on multidisciplinary databases. The series started in January with a general overview of library services. We scheduled it before the students returned to classes for the spring semester, during the faculty's in-service week. This was our opportunity to meet new faculty members, re-establish contact with returning faculty, and put faces and names together in a relaxed and congenial atmosphere. We made sure the faculty knew the subject areas each librarian was responsible for developing, and encouraged their participation in the collection development process.

The second session, in early March, focused on multidisciplinary databases that would appeal to instructors in all disciplines, who may be working on advanced degrees in addition to teaching. This workshop covered two multidisciplinary databases, the *Academic Search Premiere* and the *Professional Development Collection*. For many, this was their first exposure to using online databases. Sensitive to the anxiety that some might feel using this new medium, we chose familiar examples and topics for our demonstrations, such as "service learning" and "distance education." Choosing these relevant topics not only held their interest but also demonstrated the benefits of using these research tools to fill an immediate need. We were delighted when the chairperson of one of our academic departments asked us to present a library instruction class especially for her faculty focusing on databases specific to their disciplines.

As the semester progressed, we observed many students with assignments to write informative and persuasive papers. Consequently, the third workshop, held in mid-April, highlighted two databases that would support this type of assignment. We showcased two databases with content covering a variety of topics and that work well together in a presentation on researching information for persuasive papers: *CQ Researcher* and *The Opposing Viewpoints Resource Center*. This presentation proved to be very successful. Since then, we have often been asked to provide instruction to classes on using these research tools.

Our organization benefited from the outreach efforts we undertook in this past year in a number of ways. The number of classes we taught skyrocketed, and we encountered an increasing number of faculty members telling us they intended to bring their classes in for library instruction. In September of 2001, we provided thirteen library classes. One year later, in September of 2002, we taught forty-nine–a 277% increase! There has also been an increase, though not as dramatic, in faculty and staff interlibrary loan requests. We have seen more requests submitted by those already using this service, as well as several new, first-time users. We are very pleased with the reception of our first series of lunchtime faculty workshops and look forward to providing additional sessions to departments on databases that are specific to their subject disciplines.

REFLECTIONS ON OUR FACULTY OUTREACH EXPERIENCE

A successful marketing program must be ongoing, and we have continued our existing outreach initiatives while adding new features in recent months, persisting in our determination to get out of the library and market library services around campus. This fall, we promoted library services at events such as the adjunct faculty convocation and the campus health fair. We created a faculty guide to library services, an instruction sheet for the online faculty Web forms, and designed library bookmarks for various occasions. A bookmark for students provides basic library information such as hours, phone number, and our Web address, and another for faculty features Web site directories of scholarly resources on the Internet. For a workshop on service learning, we designed a bookmark featuring the titles and call numbers of relevant books.

We have become acquainted with the editor of the campus newspaper and make sure that articles about campus events such as Black History month include mention of commemorative displays in the library. In addition, our librarians have joined campus committees such as the Distance Education Committee and committees charged with developing new programs of study.

We had the honor of presenting at the first faculty development seminar of the 2002-03 academic year, and the previous year we attended all of the faculty development seminars. We made our presentation at the beginning of the academic year so instructors could schedule library orientation sessions at the beginning of the semester if they wished. Our presentation, "Successful Library Research: How Faculty Can Help," began with an exercise in which faculty members reflected on their experiences with libraries and librarians, both as undergraduates and the most recent time they went to college. We wanted to make the point that both libraries and the kind of work librarians do have undergone tremendous changes in the past several years. To emphasize this transformation, we donned wigs of gray hair fixed in an old-lady bun, with pencils stuck over each ear. We brought the assembly of around fifty faculty members to order by going to the center of the room and shushing the crowd in the manner of stereotypical librarians. Our performance brought down the house and definitely got everyone's attention. We discussed the "Top 10 Things" faculty can do to help students succeed with library research. Our advice included becoming familiar with what is available in the library, trying out library assignments before giving them to students, and booking library orientation sessions for their classes. We also recommended letting the students and the instructional librarians know, before the orientation, the nature of the library research students will be undertaking. In addition to a handout on the "Top 10 Things," we made available all of the other brochures and bookmarks we had designed for faculty. Several instructors booked library orientations for the first time after learning about them at this seminar.

Similarly, at a college Halloween carnival, all of the librarians donned gray buns, marketing our library at a table decorated with posters such as the one reading, "Do Not Fear: This is Not Your Father's Library." We also won a prize in the Halloween costume contest! Judging from the positive comments we received about our performances in costume, the campus community admires us for having the courage to laugh at stereotypes about our profession.

As reported in the professional literature, librarians gain greater acceptance as peers in the academic community by engaging in professional activities. Therefore, as part of our effort to increase our visibility, we have made presentations at regional conferences and recently received a grant for instructional innovation.

Our faculty outreach project has been underway for less than a year, and we have already seen many positive results. Our prediction that faculty who are knowledgeable about the library are more likely to send their students for library instruction, seems correct. The requests we have received to host additional faculty workshops and to help develop new academic programs indicates that our faculty outreach effort has resulted in greater recognition of the academic qualifications of the college librarians.

WHAT'S NEXT?

From our literature review and our experiences with our faculty outreach initiative, we gleaned many ideas that we would like to try in the future:

1. *Office calls*–visiting faculty in their offices or making brief presentations at departmental meetings to find out how the library can provide better service to faculty;
2. *Taking our show on the road*–bringing library instruction classes to the academic classrooms. We tried this once during the fall semester, and the experience was very successful for all parties involved. We enjoyed being able to bring the library to the patrons, and the instructor and students were very grateful for the extra effort we had made.
3. *Team-teaching with classroom faculty*;
4. *Collaborating with faculty in creating pathfinder links* on the library Web page for recurring research assignments;
5. *Collaborating with faculty to develop online tutorials in research methods*–We are currently working on online tutorials.
6. *Teaching a credit course in information literacy*;
7. *Faculty workshops focusing on each academic discipline.* Since our faculty outreach effort began, faculty members have begun to request that we make presentations to their departments.

CONCLUSION

The information explosion makes it imperative for everyone to keep up with current trends in information technologies, and academic librarians are the best link between the new, evolving electronic technologies and the campus community. Librarians must be proactive in initiating contact with faculty and staff and making the invisible visible–letting everyone know the kinds of academic challenges at which librarians excel. Our experience with faculty outreach so far has borne out the experiences reported by Oberg, Schleiter, and

Van Houten and others, namely, that increasing the amount of contact between librarians and faculty members has a direct correlation on how highly academic librarians are regarded and how intensively and successfully library resources are used.

REFERENCES

Cudiner, Shelley and Oskar R. Harmon (2000), "An Active Learning Approach to Effective Online Search Strategies: A Librarian/Faculty Collaboration," *THE Journal* 28 (Dec.), 52-61.

Day, Pam., and Kimberly L. Armstrong (1996), "Librarians, Faculty, and the Internet: Developing a New Information Partnership," *Computers in Libraries* 16 (May), 56-8.

Donnelly, Kimberly (2000), "Reflections on What Happens When Librarians Become Teachers," *Computers in Libraries* 20 (Mar.), 46-49.

Farber, Evan (1999), "College Libraries and the Teaching/Learning Process: A 25-Year Reflection," *Journal of Academic Librarianship* 25, 171-77.

Hall, Leilani (1999), "A Home-Grown Program for Raising Faculty Information Competence," *Computers in Libraries* 19 (Sept.), 29-34.

Isaacson, David (2001), "Librarians Who Lunch: Liaisons with New Faculty," *College & Research Libraries News* 5, 532-33.

Ivey, Robert T. (1994), "Research Notes: Teaching Faculty Perceptions of Academic Librarians at Memphis State University," *College & Research Libraries* 55, 69-82.

Jacobson, Trudi E. (2001), "Partnerships between Library Instruction Units and Campus teaching Centers," *Journal of Academic Librarianship* 27, 311-16.

Kotter, Wade R. (1999), "Bridging the Great Divide: Improving Relations between Librarians and Classroom Faculty," *Journal of Academic Librarianship* 25, 294-394.

Major, Jean A. (1993), "Mature Librarians and the University Faculty: Factors Contributing to Librarians' Acceptance as Colleagues," *College & Research Libraries* 54, 463-69.

Oberg, Larry R., Schleiter, Mary Kay, and Van Houten, Michael (1989), "Faculty Perceptions of Librarians at Albion College: Status, Role, Contribution, and Contacts," *College & Research Libraries* 50, 215-30.

Owusu-Ansah, Edward K. (2001), "The Academic Library in the Enterprise of Colleges and Universities: Toward a New Paradigm," *Journal of Academic Librarianship* 27, 282-295.

Saunders, Laverna (1999), "Who Owns the Responsibility for Training? We do!" *Computers in Libraries* 19 (Feb.), 43.

Stebelman, Scott and Long, Caroline (1999), "Improving Library Relations with the Faculty and University Administrators: The Role of the Faculty Outreach Librarian," *College & Research Libraries* 60, 121-130.

Meeting Changing Information Needs of Illinois Firefighters: Analysis of Queries Received from Outreach Reference Service

Lian Ruan
Jan S. Sung

SUMMARY. The Illinois Fire Service Institute (IFSI) Library, established in 1990 to support instructional teaching and research, continued to support the academic programs in the Institute while initiating and developing its Outreach Program in 1998. This program provides library and information services to Illinois fire departments and firefighters throughout the state. Since establishing the Outreach Program, the IFSI Library has accumulated more than 7,000 entries in a "Reference Request Database."

This paper reports and analyzes the data, including request methods, delivery methods, types of requests, and types of resources. Trends indi-

---

Lian Ruan is Director/Head Librarian, Illinois Fire Service Institute, University of Illinois at Urbana-Champaign, 11 Getty Drive, IL 61820 (E-mail: lruan@uiuc.edu). Jan S. Sung is Assistant Professor, Booth Library, Eastern Illinois University, Charleston, IL 61920 (E-mail: jssung@eiu.edu).

The authors would like to thank Professor Pauline Cochrane and Professor Terry Weech for their generous guidance and stimulating suggestions, and students Nancy Huang, Lifan Zhang, and Nanette Wargo for their assistance. The authors would also like to thank the Illinois Fire Service Institute for its support of the study.

[Haworth co-indexing entry note]: "Meeting Changing Information Needs of Illinois Firefighters: Analysis of Queries Received from Outreach Reference Service." Ruan, Lian, and Jan S. Sung. Co-published simultaneously in *The Reference Librarian* (The Haworth Information Press, an imprint of The Haworth Press, Inc.) No. 82, 2003, pp. 69-105; and: *Outreach Services in Academic and Special Libraries* (ed: Paul Kelsey, and Sigrid Kelsey) The Haworth Information Press, an imprint of The Haworth Press, Inc., 2003, pp. 69-105. Single or multiple copies of this article are available for a fee from The Haworth Document Delivery Service [1-800-HAWORTH, 9:00 a.m. - 5:00 p.m. (EST). E-mail address: docdelivery@haworthpress.com].

http://www.haworthpress.com/store/product.asp?sku=J120
© 2003 by The Haworth Press, Inc. All rights reserved.
Digital Object Identifier: 10.1300/J120v39n82_06

cate a change over time in request and delivery methods. Different regions of the state and different user groups have begun to use the library. The research can serve as a model for designing, developing and evaluating outreach reference service in a special or small library dedicated to meeting the information needs of remote library users. *[Article copies available for a fee from The Haworth Document Delivery Service: 1-800-HAWORTH. E-mail address: <docdelivery@haworthpress.com> Website: <http://www. HaworthPress.com> © 2003 by The Haworth Press, Inc. All rights reserved.]*

KEYWORDS. Outreach programs, special libraries, reference service, firefighters, service models, electronic reference service, outreach service, Illinois Fire Service Institute

INTRODUCTION

Outreach has been traditionally associated with public library extension services to neglected user populations such as the rural and urban poor, non-readers, people with disabilities, and people generally discriminated against based on their race, ethnic background, social class, or age, who are in need of special attention. In contrast, academic outreach is a relatively new phenomenon and may have a variety of functions (Cruickshank and Nowak 2001). This view is applicable to outreach service in special libraries like the Illinois Fire Service Institute Library (IFSI Library) at the University of Illinois at Urbana-Champaign.

The IFSI Library was established in 1990 as an in-house library to support instructional teaching and research. The Illinois Fire Service Institute is the statutory state fire academy with the central objective to prepare and help Illinois firefighters and other emergency services providers develop the core skills required to effectively meet the emergency fire service needs of their communities. The Institute's major programs are managed by four full-time program directors and 350 part-time field instructors, who also work at local fire departments.

Under the Institute's new Vision for the Future, a goal is set each year to find the best ways to reach every Illinois firefighter with the training, education and information he/she requires. In order to integrate library goals and objectives into those of the Institute, to remain relevant within the Institute, and to add new values to the Institute's new mission and function (Lutz 2000), the IFSI Library initiated the Outreach Program in 1998. The program eventually grew into a statewide program with support from the Institute and the assistance of a series of grant awards from the Illinois State Library, a division of the Illinois Secretary of State's Office. While continuing to support the Institute's instructional and research programs, the IFSI Library's Outreach Program now provides no cost library and information services to Illinois fire departments (1,258) and firefighters (42,675) scattered throughout the state. The IFSI Library is the only fire-dedicated library in Illinois and one of the three state fire academy libraries in the nation (www.inFIRE.org).

This study reports how the IFSI Library has developed and practiced outreach reference service, and poses questions and generates new ideas for further examination and research. What emerges from this unique perspective can be used as a model for designing, developing, and evaluating outreach reference service in a special or small library devoted to meeting the information needs of library users who are never in the IFSI Library. The experiences of the IFSI Library in outreach reference service may be relevant to other types of libraries with an expanded user base.

Since the IFSI Library launched its Outreach Program, over 7,000 detailed queries were collected during the period of fiscal year 1999 to fiscal year 2002 (July 1, 1998 to June 30, 2002). These data were processed and subjected to an extensive statistical analysis. The paper presents the results of an exploratory study attempting to establish a methodology and model for the outreach service in small and special libraries. The study reports how the IFSI Library has responded to changes; the ways in which special librarians have been exploring new approaches; convictions regarding values that have defined the librarian's role as service provider; and the pervasive effect of information technology on outreach service in special libraries.

The wealth of data collected was analyzed based on the following categories: request method (how users submitted their questions), delivery method (how requests were handled and delivered), geographical distribution of users (where the requests came from), personnel type (who made the requests), type of request (factual/direct assistance or source), and type of resource (what users were looking for and where answers were found). The data show the importance of the IFSI Library's Outreach Program to reference service. Trends indicate a change over time in request and delivery methods. Different regions of the state and different user groups have begun to use the IFSI Library. Suggestions for enhancing outreach reference service are given in the later section of the paper.

A review of the professional and research literature produces few articles related to outreach service in special libraries in a largely digital age. The literature has primarily concentrated on outreach programs in academic and public libraries (Janes et al. 1999). Of the small amount of research that has been conducted in special library settings, the majority has focused on outreach service offered by medical libraries (Scherrer and Jacobson 2002). Consequently, there is a great deal to be learned about electronic reference service provided by special libraries. Users of special libraries do not necessarily share similar characteristics, patterns of use, and views about library service with users of electronic reference services provided by academic and public libraries.

Reference service has been one of the focal points of IFSI Library's Outreach Program and needs constant adjustment according to changes in users' information needs and behavior. Reference is a highly visible service point, staffed by one librarian at a time with two or three graduate assistants from the library school of the University of Illinois. As a small special library confined to a space of 700 square feet, with multiple tasks and functions, the reference desk takes all types of requests during regular business hours from 8:30 a.m. to 5:00 p.m., Monday through Friday. The requests range from simple and straightforward factual/direct assistance questions (such as the cost of a popular training manual) to source questions (such as information on high-rise building fire and rescue), which are complex questions requiring extended assistance in the fire service discipline. Due to the nature and characteristics of a single service desk, the IFSI Library takes all queries regarding not only reference, but also circulation and interlibrary loans. This practice is different from larger libraries, which usually have separate circulation and ILL departments.

The difference in practice makes it important to define reference service for the present study. There are many definitions of reference service in the literature and practice. For example, Riechel (1991) defined reference service as " . . . mediated searching, formal and informal instruction in information-seeking skills . . . and assistance in the use of reference sources." Reference and User Services Association (RUSA) of the American Library Association (2000) suggests a variety of forms for reference services in libraries, including direct personal assistance, directories, signs, exchange of information culled from a reference source, readers' advisory service, dissemination of information in anticipation of user needs or interests, and access to electronic information.

The definition of reference services should be chosen based on the users' needs and behaviors of a particular library (Bunge and Bopp 2001). The present study and analysis were conducted with the RUSA definition of reference service in mind, which covers a broad range of queries received from the IFSI outreach reference service.

CHARACTERISTICS OF USERS AND OUTREACH SERVICE

Unique User Population

Based on the current Illinois Office of State Fire Marshal (OSFM) statistics, 6% of all fire departments (1,258) in Illinois are paid/career fire departments, 70% are volunteer fire departments, and 24% are other types of fire departments. Due to a high number of volunteer firefighters, a 20% turnover rate, and the distance barrier between users and the IFSI Library, it has become extremely important and an ongoing challenge to develop and maintain a relationship with its users. These users are "invisible" people since the IFSI Library staff rarely meets them inperson. Because of the untiring outreach efforts of the IFSI Library, users have become willing to provide enough information to allow library staff to assist them with questions relating to access problems or requests for information about library systems and services.

The IFSI student education statistics (15,396) in fiscal year 2002 reflect Illinois firefighters' educational background in the 21st century: 35.90% of firefighters have only high school diplomas and 0.83% have less than a high school education. Twelve point thirty-nine percent have a bachelor's degree and 11.97% an associate's degree. Thirty-six point thirty percent have some college education. A very few held master's (1.71%) and doctorate degrees (0.31%). Few did graduate work (0.52%) and 0.07% have other education. The evaluations made at the statewide Internet outreach training workshops at fire stations and local libraries during the "Library Service and Technology Act" (LSTA) 2000 Full Year Grant project reveal that many firefighters have little library experience. Among 524 firefighter attendees, 15.6% indicate that they never used a local library and 38.9% seldom visited a library. Obviously, attracting and educating firefighters to use the IFSI Library is the top priority in the outreach reference service. Confidence is needed on both sides–users and library staff–in order to establish a valuable give-and-take relationship needed to succeed. The users have recognized that the value the IFSI Library has placed on personal service is a hallmark of IFSI outreach reference service.

In 1998, the library initiated the IFSI Library's Outreach Program Survey, conducted among all Illinois fire departments, with a 46% response rate (Ruan 1998). Among 310 survey respondents whose fire departments have a library, only 3% have over 500 titles and 49% have fewer than fifty. Similarly, among the twenty-eight County Firefighters' Association libraries, no library has over 500 titles and 39% have fewer than fifty. Among all twenty-eight libraries, no libraries have a librarian and 90% have no personnel at all. Apparently, local information resources are fragmented and unbalanced, lacking professional support for collection development, organization, and access to fire information resources.

The 1998 survey and the evaluations made during the LSTA 2000 Full Year Grant project show that not every fire station and firefighter has access to computers, e-mail, or the Internet (Figures 1-3). However, the trend of access is increasing rapidly from 1998 to 2000 and the numbers continue to grow each year. In 1998, among 586 survey respondents, 63% had access to a computer, 28% to e-mail, and 44% to the Internet. In 2000, among 583 workshop attendees, 84% (21% increase) had access to a computer, 72% (44% increase) to

FIGURE 1. Comparison of Computer Accessibility

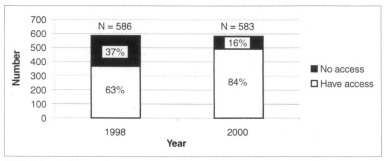

1998: Outreach Program Survey.
2000: Evaluations Made at the LSTA 2000 Internet Outreach Training Workshops.

FIGURE 2. Comparison of E-Mail Accessibility

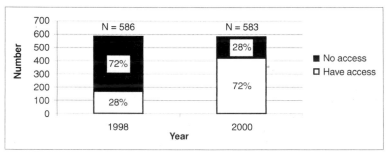

1998: Outreach Program Survey.
2000: Evaluations Made at the LSTA 2000 Internet Outreach Training Workshops.

FIGURE 3. Comparison of Internet Accessibility

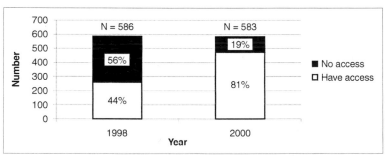

1998: Outreach Program Survey.
2000: Evaluations Made at the LSTA 2000 Internet Outreach Training Workshops.

e-mail, and 81% (37% increase) to the Internet. Internet use is growing exponentially in the fire service community in accordance with the national trend ("Internet Connectivity" 2000).

The inability of firefighters to access and use appropriate information resources may hinder their work and productivity. Overall, a high degree of reliance on outreach service is necessary to enable firefighters to meet their changing information needs. In the absence of a strong outreach initiative on the part of the IFSI Library, important information needs of firefighters often have gone unfulfilled. A total of 93% of survey respondents in 1998 supported the establishment of an IFSI Library Outreach Program. The survey respondents suggested that the Outreach Program should aim at those lacking funding and resources, particularly those working for small and/or volunteer fire departments in underserved urban and rural communities. Users from these small and rural fire departments are the type of unreachable users who often shy away from library services.

IFSI Library Outreach Program

Since the IFSI Library is the state fire academy library, it is in an ideal position and holds the responsibility to provide much needed library programming and information services to Illinois firefighters. At IFSI, the administration and the librarian realized the value of conceptualizing outreach service within the framework of a strategic plan. They understood the user culture and fundamentally transformed the IFSI Library's role accordingly. Without this process, any outreach service would miss the point and fail.

Respondents to the 1998 survey indicated that a majority of fire departments could not afford fee-based library services and 80.87% of 230 survey respondents had access to local public libraries. To broaden the capability of the IFSI Library serving the public interests in every community in Illinois and to provide no-cost services, the IFSI Library obtained full membership as a special library in the Lincoln Trail Libraries System (LTLS) in November 1998. LTLS is one of twelve library systems in Illinois (Figure 4). This membership connects the IFSI Library to over 3,000 libraries and allows the use of the no-cost statewide interlibrary loan system to physically deliver library materials to firefighters anywhere in the State.

Users can obtain articles not available in the IFSI Library's full-text databases through the interlibrary delivery system, which guarantees that copies of materials from the IFSI Library will be shipped to users' local libraries and then to firefighters within three to five days. Since fiscal year 2000, the outreach service through partnerships with local libraries and library systems has been so successful and cost-efficient that it has become an integral part of the IFSI Library operations (Figure 5). Materials the IFSI Library borrowed from

FIGURE 4. Library Systems in Illinois

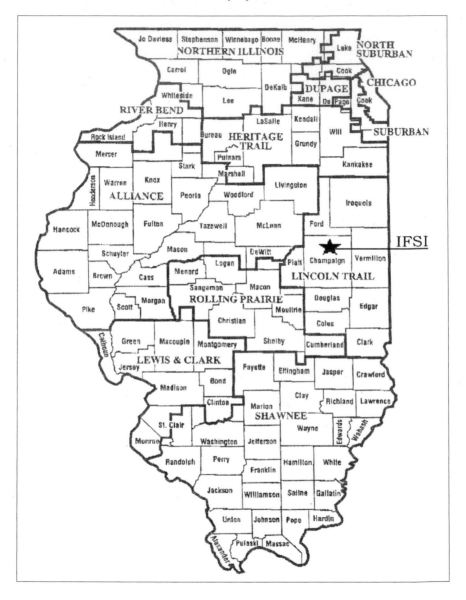

FIGURE 5. Items Delivered via Interlibrary Loan (N = 2,428)

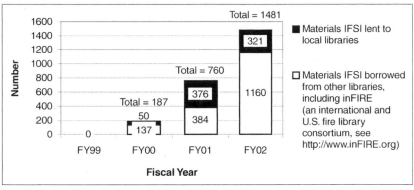

Note: FY1999: 7/1/1998-6/30/1999   FY2000: 7/1/1999-6/30/2000
FY2001: 7/1/2000-/6/30/2001   FY2002: 7/1/2001-6/30/2002

other libraries were the materials that firefighters requested directly through the IFSI interlibrary loan service and the sequential requests made by the IFSI library staff in response to user queries. These materials were then picked up at the IFSI Library or delivered (via ILL or mail) to patrons.

Distance alone may hamper an effective exchange of information, putting remote users at a disadvantage. Unlike their on-site counterparts, they do not have easy access to the IFSI library staff, who can help them with a variety of information needs from narrowing down a topic to choosing search terms and a database for an online search. They need to access the IFSI Library either through traditional means such as telephone, or through electronic means, such as e-mail.

Achieving equal access to information for all levels of users including remote users is a primary goal of outreach service at the IFSI Library. Advances in telecommunications technology make the IFSI Library resources increasingly available to remote users through the Internet. A fully electronic infrastructure for the purpose of broadening and enhancing access to the IFSI Library was developed with the support from the Institute and the LSTA grant projects (Ruan 2001). A wide range of web-based services (www.fsi.uiuc.edu) have been offered, including the IFSI Library Catalog; a web-based video tutorial which can be viewed using Quicktime; *FireTalk, IFSI Thesaurus;* integrated distance learning library services with IFSI online courses; digital archives; e-mail; and a listserv system (fsilib-1@listserv.uiuc.edu). Remote users can make direct requests via e-mail on the Web during an online search. Users are currently able to access a range of library databases, such as archives, articles, online courses, or Fire College supported by text or images, day or night, from their home, fire station, or local library.

Academic outreach activities have been often identified with the promotion of an established program of library resources and services (Cruickshank and Nowak 2001). Though it is a small special library, the IFSI Library's outreach activities have included aggressive and proactive approaches to market and promote the Outreach Program. The desire to transform the image of the IFSI Library from an in-house to an outreach library and the desire to enhance the perception of the librarian in the eyes of firefighters (by emphasizing her information expertise and skills which can help them do their job better) have resulted in open communication, statewide marketing, and the Internet outreach training workshops with firefighters and local librarians through grant projects. Some of the grant projects include the following: the FY 1999 "Library Service and Technology Act" (LSTA) mini-grant program–Bring in An Expert; the FY 2000 LSTA Full Year Grant–Internet Outreach to and Training of Illinois Fire Service Personnel, Public and Community College Librarians for Electronic Access to Fire Safety Information; the FY 2000 LSTA mini-grant program–Marketing; the FY 2001 LSTA: Libraries in the 21st Century–Developing the Distance Learning Library Services for Illinois Firefighters: An Integrated Information Service with Online Firefighter II Certification Program; and the FY 2002 LSTA mini-grant program–Grow with Pro. Seventy-nine workshops and ten demonstrations in sixty-four cities were conducted statewide during the LSTA 2000 Full Year Grant project. The workshops took place at 148 fire departments and thirty-six local libraries, reaching as far north as the Freeport Fire Department to the Carbondale Fire Department located in downstate Illinois.

During the LSTA 2000 grant project, IFSI reference requests doubled, and requests continued to increase after the grant project ended in September 2002 (Figure 7). Because of the increase in reference requests, in fall of 2002, a new graduate assistant position was added to the IFSI Library staff to conduct weekly training workshops and user instruction.

Increased knowledge about Illinois firefighters and their needs, and an ever-widening variety of service alternatives to serve them, have impelled the IFSI Library to build a "Reference Request Database" to analyze outreach reference service in order to get a more systematic view of the outreach operations and users' information-seeking behavior so that library services, activities, staffing, and resources can be modified and allocated to meet their changing needs over time.

REFERENCE REQUEST DATABASE

Reference questions can often be a good source of information to help librarians understand the needs of library users better (Bates and Allen 1994). In order to understand the reference usage, librarians need to quantify reference services (Dowling 2001). Some electronic reference services keep statistics automatically. A good example is Internet Public Library digital reference service (Carter and Janes 2000). A searchable Reference Request Database using inMagic software was initiated at the IFSI Library in 1999, and has been used to document interaction with firefighters, general users, and reference administration (Dennison 2000). Reassessment and modifications of outreach reference service in the IFSI Library are based on actual experience and analysis of this Reference Request Database rather than relying on educated guesses.

A trained hourly student worker enters all of the questions received by the IFSI Library from users via electronic reference service (e-mail, listserv, or web), or traditional reference service (phone, fax, ILL, mail or in-person) into the Database. Because the fire service discipline is a unique technical field and the IFSI library is a small special library, several attempts often have to be made in order to find a satisfactory answer either in the IFSI Library or at other libraries or organizations. The scope of the database is thus defined to cover and count queries made by users looking for any information from the IFSI Library (public interaction between the IFSI Library and its users), and sequential requests made by the IFSI library staff to other libraries and/or organizations while searching for the answer. This way of counting transactions reflects the true picture of IFSI Library reference practices and how much time was spent and allocated for the service, which also helps IFSI administrators understand the value of the services and provide much needed graduate assistants. Internal business and administration questions are excluded from the database. For example, questions from the IFSI Business Office regarding staff hiring, and from the IFSI Information Management Office regarding library computer maintenance would not be entered in the databases.

One of the pressing questions has been to determine the level of service to be offered through the outreach reference service. In spite of a single staff service desk and small size, the IFSI Library cannot restrict the service to brief, factual questions, but must take all types of questions ranging from factual/direct assistance to source questions–in-depth questions involving reference interviews and consultations. Based on the content of requests, all requests are categorized and indexed using the user's natural language, instead of using standard subject headings or *FireTalk, IFSI Thesaurus*. All e-mail messages are stored by cutting and pasting from the original message. Requests through the IFSI Library web site are stored in a Microsoft Access Database and transferred directly to the Reference Request Database. Guidelines for user confidentiality have been established. The content of all requests deserves special attention for content analysis and natural language studies, but that is beyond the scope of this paper. The main fields of the Database are shown in Figure 6, and fields indicating the requestors' personnel type, organizational type, and re-

FIGURE 6

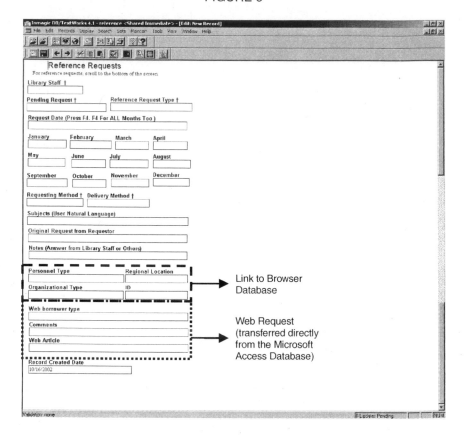

gional location are interconnected to the secondary Borrower (Profile) Database to avoid duplicate data entry.

The analysis of reference queries received from outreach service in this paper sheds some light on the remote users' usage and the information-seeking behavior of the IFSI Library.

DATA ANALYSIS AND DISCUSSION

For this study, data from both databases, the Reference Request and the Borrower Profile, was exported and processed with MS Excel and combined with FileMaker Pro. Once all necessary variables were exported, SPSS version 11.0.1 and Excel 2000 were used to analyze the data. The data analyzed in the present study are from July 1, 1998 to June 30, 2002 (i.e., FY 1999-FY 2002).

In order to analyze queries, it is necessary to group them into categories, covering all the queries, with each query ideally falling into only one category (White 1981). However, there is no consistent standard for categorizing reference questions (Sloan 2002). Dennison (2000) categorized reference questions into three basic groups–simple, medium, and harder–according to the level of difficulty of the questions. The questions were then further categorized by method of request: telephone or in-person. Carter and Janes (2000) categorized Internet Public Library reference questions into three groups: sources, factual, and rejected. Bushallow-Wilbur and others (1996) categorized their e-mail reference requests into four groups: basic reference, library policy, OPAC questions, and purchases requests. Warner (2001) addressed the importance of classification for reference statistics and categorized her data into four groups. Each categorization reflects its own environment or purpose of the study conducted. The present study groups the reference queries into three categories: source, factual/direct assistance questions, and other. Source questions need an in-depth reference interview and consultation whereas factual/direct assistance questions are those with straightforward answers. "Other" includes questions that do not fall into those two categories–for example a computer technical question. Classification types by different authors discussed here and for the present study appear in Table 1.

In the present study, besides type of request, an additional six variables were analyzed: request method, delivery method, type of resource, personnel type, organizational type, and region (Table 2). Key transaction data cap-

TABLE 1. Classification of Reference Questions by Different Authors

Dennison	Carter & Janes	Bushallow-Wilbur et al.	Warner	Present study (Ruan & Sung)
- Simple[1] - Medium - Harder[2]	- Sources - Factual - Rejected	- Basic reference - Library policy - OPAC questions - Purchases Request	- Level I[3] - Level II[4] - Level III[5] - Level IV[6]	- Source[7] - Factual/Direct Assistance[8] - Other[9]

Note: [1] Directional or ready-reference
     [2] Five minutes and more needed to answer
     [3] Nonresource-based
     [4] Skill-based
     [5] Strategy-based
     [6] Consultation
     [7] In-depth reference interview and consultation
     [8] Straightforward and simple answers
     [9] Answers or assistance which do not fall into source or factual/direct assistance categories

TABLE 2. Variables Used in the Study

Variable	Request Method	Delivery Method	Type of Request	Type of Resource	Personnel Type	Organiza-tional Type	Region
Category	√ E-mail √ Listserv √ Web √ Phone √ In-person √ Mail (U.S. Mail) √ Fax √ ILL[1]	√ E-mail √ Listserv √ In-person √ Mail[2] √ ILL[3] √ Phone √ Fax	√ Source √ Factual/direct assistance √ Other	√ Print √ Non-print √ E-resource	√ Fire Chief √ Firefighter √ Training officer √ Public √ IFSI	√ Paid/Career FD √ Volunteer FD √ Other FD √ IFSI √ Public √ Unknown	√ North √ South √ East √ West √ In-state √ Out of State & Int'l

Note: [1] Questions patrons asked IFSI through their local libraries
        [2] U.S. mail, campus-mail, FedEx, UPS
        [3] Answers IFSI obtained by asking other libraries

tured and analyzed in the study are from July 1, 1999 to June 30, 2002 (i.e., FY1999-FY2002).

Trends in Yearly and Monthly Usage

The total number of entries was 7,563. The dates of reference transaction were recorded to analyze and monitor the monthly and yearly usage. The number of total requests per fiscal year reached a peak of 2,751 in fiscal year 2001, and decreased slightly to 2,521 in fiscal year 2002 (Figure 7). The highest number of total requests per month was 368 in January 2001 and monthly requests have been stabilized around 200 requests per month since July 2002 (Figure 8). The number of reference requests increased after the LSTA 2000 Full Year Grant project, which ended in September 2000, proving the success of the Internet Outreach training program and the importance of marketing and promoting library services to users. After the events of September 11, 2001, reference requests climbed above 200 requests for three months (Figure 8).

The number of requests declined slightly in fiscal year 2002, but the number of items delivered via interlibrary loan more than doubled in fiscal year 2002 (Figure 5). The decline may indicate that users learned to obtain the information they needed without consulting the IFSI reference desk. As more users had Internet access in 2000 than 1998, they might have become more savvy information finders over time. The decline could also indicate that the IFSI Library's web site provided effective web-based training for using the OPAC, various online databases, and other fire emergency resources. It may also indicate that the IFSI Library's proactive training workshops have worked. While

FIGURE 7. Number of Requests per Fiscal Year (N = 7,563)

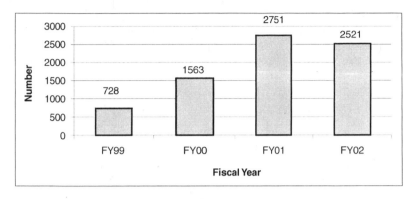

FIGURE 8. Number of Requests per Month (N = 7,563)

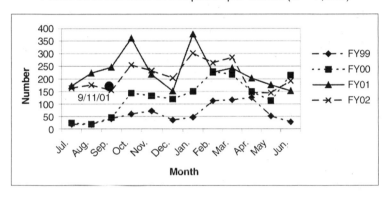

there has been no direct research on the effects of these programs, the decline in the number of reference requests may be a good indication of the success of these outreach efforts. It is also possible that users trained in the LSTA 2000 Full Year Grant project may have already left the fire service and new firefighters may not know how to access the IFSI Library. This study reminds the IFSI Library staff how important it is to promote and market library services through user education programs as an ongoing endeavor. The IFSI Library staff is planning a new user survey, which may answer some of these questions.

In addition, the study reveals that among over 7,000 requests, 59% of users made more than one reference query, and 41% of them used the service only once. Although online help text and video tutorials appeared in strategic points throughout the web-based system, users may still need or prefer personal assistance.

Request Methods

As discussed earlier, the library policy takes all types of requests that the IFSI Library receives both in-person at the reference desk and remotely through electronic requests. The request methods in Figure 9 demonstrate how users submitted their questions to the IFSI Library. Most often, users submitted their questions through electronic methods (overall 60.32%, including e-mail 51.32%, web 2%, and listserv 7%), followed by phone (24.91%), in-person (11.49%), fax (2.63%), mail (0.53%), and ILL (0.12%).

It has become an accepted fact that traditional reference statistics are declining in other library settings (Lipow 1999), similar to IFSI's experience (Figure 10). While there are no definitive answers to why this is the case, speculation is endless (Trump and Tuttle 2001), and there are many possible answers. The reason for decreasing traditional reference statistics at IFSI is partly attributed to the success of the IFSI Library web-based services and proactive outreach training workshops as discussed earlier. In addition, more users have regular Internet access, which may lead users to a vast array of electronic information. It is not surprising that instructional issues on how to use the Internet are considered an important area for the IFSI Library. The IFSI library staff is spending more time instructing users how to use technology, and less time trying to track down specific pieces of information. Some users want to learn about Internet fundamentals instead of finding a particular answer through the reference service. Teaching information literacy skills is

FIGURE 9. Request Method (N = 7,563, FY 99-02)

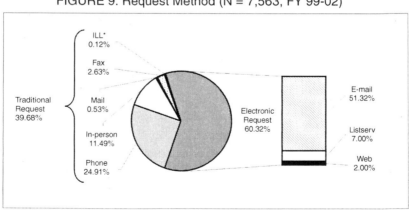

Note: *ILL: Questions patrons asked IFSI through their local libraries.

FIGURE 10. Request Method by Fiscal Year (N = 7,563)

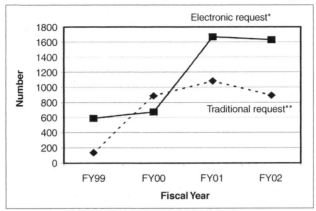

Note: *Electronic request methods include e-mail, listserv, and Web.
**Traditional request methods include phone, in-person, mail, fax, and ILL
(questions patrons asked IFSI through their local libraries).

becoming one of the definite roles of reference service in the Internet environment (Kautzman 1999). The IFSI librarian thought that phone and in-person requests were more numerous than electronic requests, because she and her students were swamped daily by phone calls and in-person visits. However, the findings show a different picture: phone and in-person requests comprised only 39.68% of total requests, compared to 60.32% of electronic requests. The data support offering additional electronic reference service.

There is no form for IFSI Library users to fill out (i.e., the initial form submitted by a user, a summary of the librarian's understanding of the request sent to the user, and confirmation of the summary message by the user) (Abels 1996), as the Internet Public Library reference service does (Carter and Janes 2000). Although providing more complete information up front by filling out comprehensive forms may make the reference transaction more efficient, the IFSI library staff agrees with Gray (2000) that for users who do not use traditional in-person or telephone services, complex forms may interfere with the perception that electronic reference services is a safe, relatively anonymous mode of communication with library staff. Filling out a complex form might not be considered worth the effort to some users, who may have considered their requests simple inquiries.

Telephone reference is the most long-standing and common remote reference service and will remain available in the IFSI library setting. Indeed, not every firefighter has e-mail, a computer or Internet access (Figures 1-3).

Visiting the IFSI Library for reference questions can generate time cost as well as the financial cost of traveling to the IFSI Library. From the findings, IFSI users still rely on the phone to make requests, since 24.91% of total requests were phone requests (Figure 9). It is very likely that all remote users have access to a telephone (and/or cell phone), and the IFSI Library offers a toll-free number. When requests are urgent and important to follow up, users prefer to use the telephone to contact the IFSI Library directly. There are some advantages of phone reference over electronic reference: questions can be negotiated in real-time, and there is generally no significant time lag in receiving an answer (Bushallow-Wilbur et al. 1996).

The number of questions received by fax is very low, only 2.63% (Figure 9). Some users in rural and small fire departments do not even have a fax machine, but more of them are getting a computer, e-mail and Internet access, either through home, local library, church, or fire station. The number of questions through ILL is extremely low (0.12%), mainly because the IFSI Library has suggested and trained users to contact IFSI directly when they have any questions to ask to avoid confusion and time delay.

Comparing the number of traditional requests to electronic requests broken down by user type, there are more electronic requests than traditional requests across all user types (Figure 11). Especially, e-mail makes it possible for more people to participate in potential reference interviews, since electronic interviewing is often less formal than traditional face-to-face encounters (Bristow and Buechley 1995). E-mail reference may have opened a way for people who cannot come to the IFSI Library due to distance to be a part of the in-person reference process.

FIGURE 11. Request Method by Specific Group of Users (N = 7,563, FY 99-02)

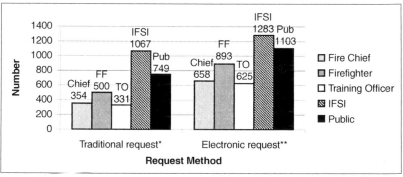

Note: * Traditional request methods include phone, in-person, mail, fax, and ILL (questions patrons asked
        IFSI through their local libraries).
      ** Electronic request methods include e-mail, listserv, and Web.

Delivery Methods

Reference interactions have changed as a result of information technology. Information delivery mechanisms help the IFSI Library place information onto the desktops of physical users throughout the state. The IFSI Library has physically reached out to its user population in many ways with more examples of electronic information delivery to them. It is not easy for remote users to come to the IFSI Library in person due to distance constraints. The Internet has irrevocably changed the pattern of delivery (as well as request) between the IFSI Library and remote users. Electronic delivery continues to grow while traditional delivery is declining (Figure 12), probably because the requests are more often electronic now (Figure 10).

However, no one delivery method is better than others, partly because there are differences in user needs, learning styles, and technological skill levels, and also because the impediment of distance limits the amount of in-person service the IFSI Library can deliver. Answers delivered through electronic methods totaled 54.39% (including e-mail 46.11%, and listserv 8.28%); followed by traditional methods at 45.61% (including phone 15.93%, ILL 10.13%, mail 9.12%, in-person 7.10%, and fax 3.33%) (Figure 13).

The IFSI Library listserv is one method preferred by some users: the IFSI Library receives 7.00% of requests through the listserv (Figure 9) and delivers 8.28% of answers through the listserv (Figure 13). Information available only through the listserv consists of invaluable expertise or internal documents such as standard operating procedures written and adopted by local fire depart-

FIGURE 12. Delivery Method by Fiscal Year (N = 7,563)

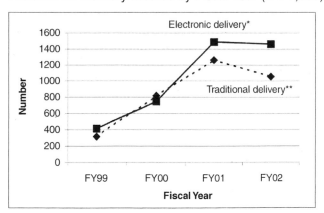

Note: *Electronic delivery methods include e-mail and listserv.
        **Traditional delivery methods include in-person, mail, phone, fax, and
        ILL (answers IFSI obtained by asking other libraries).

FIGURE 13. Delivery Method (N = 7,563, FY 99-02)

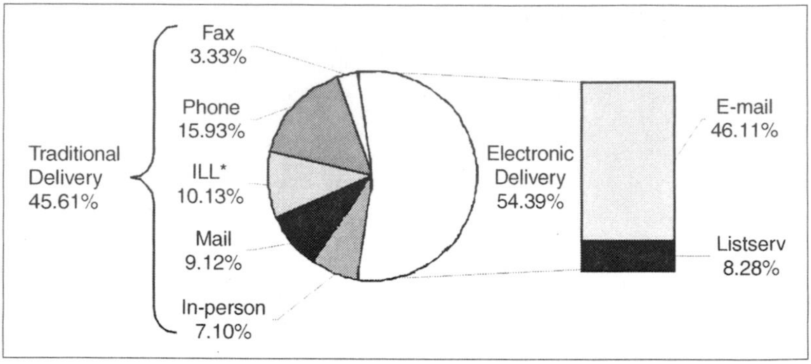

Fax
3.33%

Phone
15.93%

Traditional
Delivery
45.61%

ILL*
10.13%

Mail
9.12%

In-person
7.10%

Electronic
Delivery
54.39%

E-mail
46.11%

Listserv
8.28%

Note: *ILL: Answers IFSI obtained by asking other libraries.

ments. Often, these electronic responses from peers have no print equivalent. The listserv is an effective means of sharing and exchanging human expertise in the practical and technical fire service discipline. A growing trend, especially among young firefighters, is the tendency to consult electronic resources accessible through the Web to keep abreast of the latest research and developments in the field. The new IFSI Library survey will look into this trend.

Writing a response to a complex question can be much more difficult and time consuming than responding orally. It generally takes more time to respond to e-mail inquiries, which can often involve multiple exchanges and may require additional time to consult with colleagues if necessary. At a busy reference desk, there is often not enough time to provide a complete and thorough answer to every inquiry. This also means, even though the number of requests dropped in FY 2002 (Figure 7), the IFSI Library staff has very likely spent more time answering inquiries through electronic reference service, since the electronic response has increased since FY 2000 (Figure 12). A medium such as e-mail is ideal for handling short transactions that might require limited sources or limited follow-up. When short factual questions start to drift into detailed research questions, electronic reference negotiations can become a very involved process. Each transaction can mean a delay, and an extended question might take weeks to conclude (Roysdon and Elliott 1988). This is certainly an area that deserves further study and consideration.

Since serving IFSI users in a timely fashion is the IFSI Library's first priority, reference service is the central part of the IFSI Library operations. The goal of response time to requests is the same day, ranging from a few minutes to a few hours depending on the time when the user's request is received. The IFSI Library staff always notifies users regarding the status or progress of their request. For response times, staff usually notifies users if it will take more than a day to find the answer. Staff checks the electronic questions and follows up with users at least a few times a day, during regular business hours, 8:30 a.m. to 5:00 p.m., Monday through Friday.

By eliminating physical barriers and allowing reference transactions to take place outside the walls of the IFSI Library, e-mail makes it possible for more firefighters to take advantage of library services and brings users in rural areas into the information world. Comparing electronic delivery to traditional delivery methods, it is obvious that all types of users received the answers to their requests more through electronic delivery than traditional delivery methods (Figure 14). Firefighters can specify where, when and how they want to receive materials. Accordingly, the IFSI Library utilizes whatever methods, electronic or traditional, that users prefer and can reach them at their required timeframe.

Types of Requests

A reference query has been categorized either as a factual/direct assistance request, a source question (involving in-depth reference interview and consultation), or other question, indicating the most likely response given by library staff. The IFSI Library staff often asks users to specify whether they want their question answered with a brief factual answer, or with a list of sources to consult to help them with their request. Whether the question arrives via electronic or traditional reference service, a list of sources is usually provided. Users often seem optimistic that their questions can be answered simply and directly. No questions are routinely rejected for being outside the scope and purview of the IFSI library service.

FIGURE 14. Delivery Method by Specific Group of Users (N = 7,563, FY 99-02)

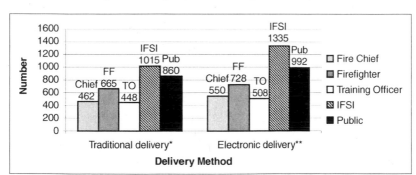

Note: * Traditional delivery methods include in-person, mail, fax, and ILL (answers IFSI obtained by asking other libraries).
      ** Electronic delivery methods include e-mail and listserv.

More source questions have been answered (77.77% of the total number of questions asked), than factual/direct assistance questions, comprising 21.05% of the total number of questions asked (Figure 15). Source questions indicate a measure of question difficulty, i.e., the harder a question, the longer it takes to answer, the more notes made to oneself, and the more assistance is offered. In addition, the study also found that the number of source questions received at IFSI has grown faster than the number of factual/direct assistance questions (Figure 16).

IFSI staff and public users asked more factual/direct assistance questions

FIGURE 15. Type of Request (N = 7,563, FY 99-02)

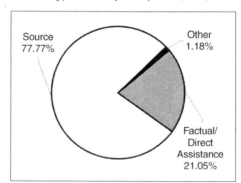

FIGURE 16. Type of Request by Fiscal Year (N = 7,563)

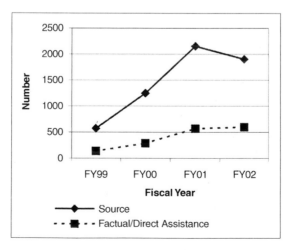

than fire chiefs, firefighters and training officers. Fire chiefs, firefighters and training officers asked more in-depth questions (comparing 2,874 to 1,630 from IFSI and 1,378 from the public) (Figure 17). This indicates that the IFSI Library staff spent more time serving remote users from fire departments.

Types of Resources

Print materials were used to answer 40.46% of the 7,563 queries; non-print materials (such as videotapes, CD-ROMs, transparencies, and slides), 24.61% of the queries; e-resources (web site 1.71% and listserv 11%), 12.71% of the queries (Figure 18).

Comparing all types of user groups in terms of materials delivered, more print materials were used across all user types (Figure 19). The findings may reflect that fire service publishers are relatively behind in developing electronic resources. There are not many electronic resources for the IFSI library to acquire and provide to users, and not many answers can be found in electronic resources.

Personnel Types

People who are involved with Illinois fire service use the IFSI Library the most. Of IFSI users, 45.09% are affiliated with Illinois fire departments, including fire chiefs (13.38%), training officers (12.64%), and firefighters (19.07%). Of users, 31.07% are affiliated with IFSI. Among them 25.61% are IFSI pro-

FIGURE 17. Type of Request Made by Specific Group of User (N = 7,563, FY 99-02)

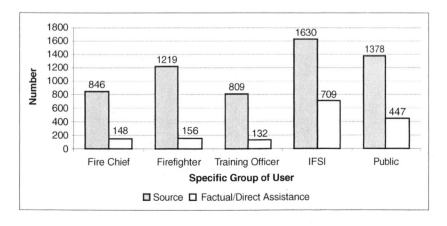

FIGURE 18. Type of Resource (N = 7,563, FY 99-02)

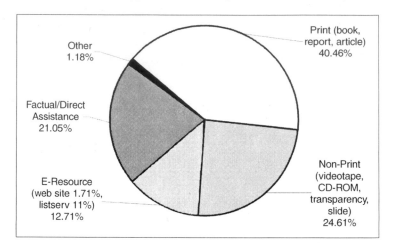

gram directors and 5.46% are part-time field instructors who are spread across different fire departments in Illinois. The general public comprises the remaining 23.84% of users (Figure 20). The data clearly shows that the outreach reference service has reached different types of users.

As Gray (2000) indicates, "Academic libraries as public institutions bear some responsibility to respond to reference requests from state residents and alumni, while public or special libraries might have a responsibility to serve an even wider population, depending on their individual missions." The findings indicate that both fire service-related personnel and the general public have used the IFSI Library (Figures 19 and 20). The loan policy of the IFSI Library states that it only provides interlibrary loan service to Illinois-based users. However, the IFSI Library answers a number of inquires from outside of Illinois and makes appropriate referrals, which is more in line with service philosophies related to in-person, telephone or e-mail services and generates good will toward the organization. There are no restrictions on the types of questions that IFSI e-mail reference will answer, including in-depth questions.

Organizational Types

Of the outreach reference services, 50.55% served the Illinois fire service community, including 17.12% for paid/career fire departments, 26.60% for volunteer fire departments, and 6.83% for other types of fire departments (Figure 21). This demonstrates that the outreach reference service is reaching all types

FIGURE 19. Type of Resource Delivered to Specific Group of User (N = 7,563, FY 99-02)

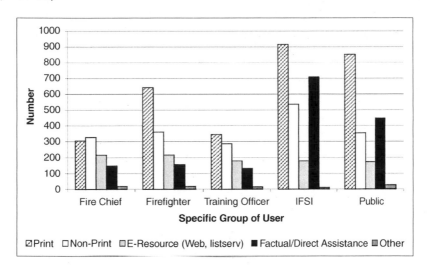

FIGURE 20. Number of Requests by Personnel Type (N = 7,563, FY 99-02)

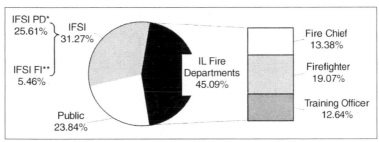

*IFSI Program Director   **IFSI Part-time Field Instructor

of fire departments. Meanwhile, the IFSI Library continues its service to IFSI program directors (25.61%) to support their statewide instructional and research activities. The IFSI Library also provides its service to the public (23.84%).

Geographical Distribution

The four regional boundaries for the state of Illinois are shown in Figure 22. Among all fire service related users, 75.51% have been scattered throughout

FIGURE 21. Number of Requests by Organizational Type (N = 7,563, FY 99-02)

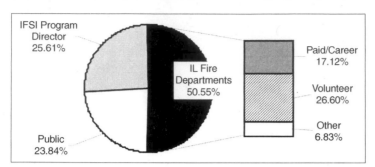

the state: 21.91% in the North region, 6.65% in South, 40.63% East, 6.31% West (Figure 23). Indeed, this distribution of requests resembles the distribution of population in Illinois (Figure 24).

The finding indicates that the outreach reference service has reached the whole state, but further study is needed to find out why the fewest requests are from the West and South regions. There are several possible explanations. It may be because most fire departments and firefighters situated in the south are volunteer-based with a high degree of personnel turnover. It may be also because of lower population and predominantly rural population in the area (Figure 24). North region (67.51% of population) includes Chicago, Chicago suburbs, and Rockford. East region (13.35% of population) includes Champaign-Urbana, Bloomington, Kankakee, Danville, Decatur, Ottawa, LaSalle, and Peru. All are large communities. South and West regions are overwhelmingly rural; since there are fewer people, there are fewer firefighters, which means fewer potential users. South region (9.96% of population) only includes Carbondale (not a very large community), and St. Louis metro whereas West region (9.18% of population) only includes Springfield and Peoria.

Of requests, 7.08% are from out of state, including out of the U.S. The IFSI Library received requests from many states, including California, Rhode Island, Florida, Nevada, Oregon, and New York, and from foreign countries, such as India, Korea, Mexico, and Peru (Figure 23).

The study shows that it is necessary for IFSI to maintain both electronic and traditional reference service to meet the unique needs of Illinois firefighters. However, the advance of information technology, particularly the Internet, has altered the values, attitudes, and beliefs of remote users (Wilson 2000). These changes have affected how users value the IFSI outreach service. Users prefer optimum library programs that meet the challenge of providing timely and interactive reference service. Clearly, electronic reference service can provide a

FIGURE 22. Map of the State of Illinois in Four Regions

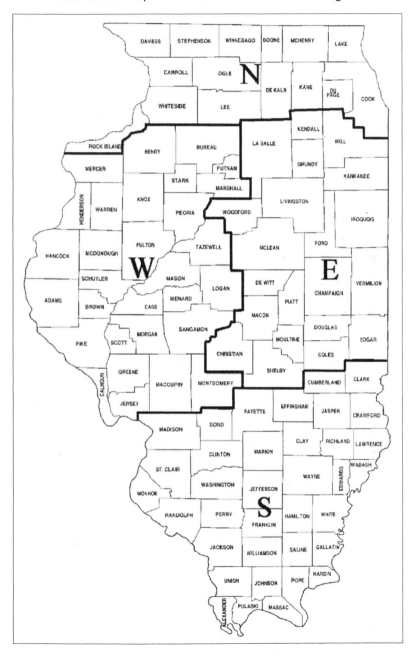

FIGURE 23. Requests in Four Regions and Out of State (N = 7,563, FY 99-02)

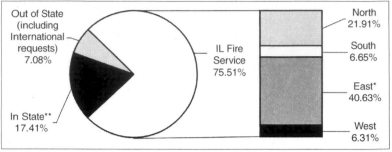

Note: *East region includes IFSI program directors and field instructors.
         **Public users from Illinois, but unknown regions.

FIGURE 24. Illinois Population in Four Regions

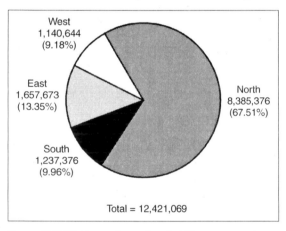

Source: 2000 U.S. Census Bureau (http://quickfacts.census.gov)

focal point for development and delivery of high quality reference and instructional support to all users of the IFSI Library at all times and from all locations, "commensurate with the expansion of the information and resources available for unmediated access from remote locations" (Ferguson and Bunge 1997). Indeed, as more and more library services are being delivered remotely, electronic reference service has become an important offering to remote users (Bushallow-Wilbur et al. 1996). Wilson (2000) argues that "something has decisively altered in the user culture and that librarians must comprehend this changed culture and fundamentally transform their role to accord with it."

While trends analyzed earlier indicate a change over time in request and delivery methods towards the electronic reference service, this trend is discussed below and some suggestions are offered to enhance the IFSI outreach reference service.

ELECTRONIC REFERENCE SERVICE: SOME SUGGESTIONS

During the study period, the IFSI Library's reference interactions have expanded from traditional face-to-face encounters at a reference desk to include 24-hour electronic options such as e-mail, listserv, web request, and web-based instruction. Some of the services are prominently featured on the IFSI library's gateway web site. Users' Internet knowledge has changed the IFSI reference desk from a static place to a fluid platform, connecting users to information anywhere and any time. However, the findings also reveal that the IFSI Library's electronic reference service is still very much in its infancy. It appears that the IFSI Library has made a solid beginning using simple but effective technologies (e-mail, listserv, web forms), guided by policies to provide focus, and to some extent, driven by the broad institutional mission. The FAQ lists posted on the web site are far from functional in terms of a "reference" perspective, though they are useful regarding procedural matters. No experiments have been undertaken yet to test videoconferencing or virtual reference in an effort to create interactions more closely approximating those that take place in a face-to-face reference transaction. Even though the technology involving these services has existed for many years, a number of factors, such as staffing, funding, or lack of interest of users or staff have prevented the IFSI Library from using it. The IFSI Library is planning to conduct experiments in its new virtual reference service.

This study has provided insight into who was asking what types of questions via which methods of reference service. It is useful to compare patterns of electronic and traditional reference service to help understand what types of users are using electronic library services, what types of users prefer in-person and traditional services, and why. This will assist the IFSI Library in better planning for the appropriate mix of remote and in-house services and in deciding how to market these services. A study of the cost-effectiveness of electronic versus in-person reference service would be of great use and interest, especially in these times of budget constraints.

While it is clear that users are becoming more aware of information resources and services available to them at IFSI, the extent to which many of their information needs are being met may not be clear. More interaction with users on an ongoing basis will be necessary to identify many of their information needs and to determine how well they are being addressed. Based on the study, electronic reference traffic will continue to increase. Thus, improvements in the management of these services will be critical.

Since more users can obtain information outside of the physical library building, the need for user support, such as technological support, should be re-examined. Users' demand and need for services over the network will continue to increase as more digital resources become available via the IFSI Library, other fire libraries, and fire service publishers. Therefore, the IFSI Library has to expand and improve its electronic outreach reference service to meet these demands in a way that is as obvious and convenient to the remote user as is access to the information itself. Such a service needs to be built into the infrastructure of the Internet (Lipow 1999). Rather than thinking of IFSI users as remote, the IFSI Library should, instead, recognize that it is the IFSI Library that is remote from users. Thus, the IFSI Library needs to change how it conducts business in order to make the IFSI Library more available to users.

The IFSI Library also needs to seek ways to provide a fuller range of services over the network, either digitally or through real-time interactions. The IFSI Library should aggressively experiment with such projects–offer quick turnaround or immediate information services so that the IFSI Library is ready when the technology advances. Options for providing real-time reference service can be as diverse as the needs of the users. These products offer a variety of features, such as chat, slide shows or video with users, co-browsing, form sharing, and more. Virtual reference has become commonplace and the interfaces are more user-friendly than in the past. Some IFSI users have already used virtual reference successfully in completion of the Online Firefighter II Certification Program. Chat software may provide a new mode of point-of-need service, recognizing that those who need assistance may not want to come into the IFSI Library to find the information they need, freeing users from the restrictions of place of traditional reference services.

Winstart Telebase, a commercial information service, has developed an interactive reference service based on widely used and distributed Windows or Internet chat technology. Changing to a new virtual reference service such as the Telebase system or real-time reference may make real-time transaction log analysis possible to support a better outreach reference service. Electronic reference service will enable the IFSI Library to accumulate data more easily because data can be obtained automatically without need for manual entry. Since transaction of questions and responses in e-reference allows the storage of the full record, analysis of these data will be a great source for understanding the dynamics of e-referencing (Roysdon and Elliott 1988). Reference request data have been used at IFSI to customize collection development policies to reflect the sources that are being consulted by users (Still and Campbell 1993). This data also can be used to diagnose and correct problems with systems and services for training and planning purposes. Online help tools, such as guides or tutorials, can be improved, and FAQ web pages linked to the electronic reference service can be further enhanced. Additionally, IFSI can use data gathered from these services to drive the design of integrated, user-friendly search interfaces for electronic resources.

The improved management of electronic reference traffic and the development of knowledge bases from accumulation of answers to questions–using software which allows searching–will lead to shorter response time for IFSI staff and users, because staff will be able to reuse responses to common reference questions. New developments in software, and adaptation of existing software packages to special libraries like the IFSI Library, will require continual reassessment, as will the needs of the user community. The IFSI Library frequently struggles with a lack of funding and staffing to support its reference service, as do other libraries (Ferguson and Bunge 1997). The large amount of e-mail transactions, both incoming and outgoing, is also a major technical problem to solve. If electronic traffic is increasing, the IFSI Library may need to use cutting-edge software solutions.

Use of real-time reference software will expedite service, which may require somewhat different communication skills from e-mail or traditional reference service. Expanding hours of service and shortening response time for users are necessary improvements to IFSI electronic reference services. IFSI needs to further analyze response and turnaround time in order to change the methods of handling questions delivered during weekends and evenings. A user having difficulty using online resources on a Friday evening should not have to wait until Monday morning to obtain one-on-one assistance. Response time should be cut down to hours or minutes rather than days. However, virtual reference desks have to be staffed like a traditional reference desk, which means that the IFSI Library has to stay open during weekends and evenings.

Although promoting electronic reference services remains critical to success, responding to the rapidly growing volume of electronic reference questions appears to be a concern in a library the size of the IFSI Library with limited staff. Asynchronous reference service is not inherently less time consuming than in-person service since typing answers usually takes longer than speaking, although it gives the librarian a chance to try research strategies using a variety of sources without the questioner needing to wait at a desk or on the telephone. Most of the time, this would cause conflicts with the reality of IFSI's single staffed reference desk. Should the IFSI Library give a level of priority to real-time reference service over in-person or phone service? Sloan's (1998) model of electronic reference service is not practical in the IFSI Library because it requires additional reference personnel.

The IFSI should continue to emphasize marketing and promoting the IFSI outreach reference service to reach a dispersed user population with a high turnover rate. Instructions should also be specialized for different user groups (e.g., field instructor, fire chief, training officer, paid/career or volunteer firefighter).

COLORADO COLLEGE LIBRARY
COLORADO SPRINGS
COLORADO

Development of computer-assisted instruction and the integration of information literacy into the training curriculum should also be considered. These will help outreach reference service integrate into fire service education and system design at the Illinois Fire Service Institute and throughout the fire service community. User instruction service will play a prominent role in the IFSI Library of the future and will be responsible for assisting users and the general public in understanding technologies and procedures to access information.

Roysdon and Elliott (1988) were first to address the inherent difficulties in conducting reference negotiations electronically, especially when questioners lead their questions into research questions rather than short factual questions. According to Roysdon and Elliott "[F]or both librarians and patrons, there are limitations to electronic communication for the reference function." Although reference negotiation is possible electronically, it is a slow and often frustrating process (Roysdon and Elliott 1988). Tomer (1994) remarked, "no matter how powerful the technologies become, there will be many circumstances under which face-to-face interaction with a reference librarian is preferred." In a comprehensive and analytical review of present and future issues in remote reference services, Sloan (1998) stressed the importance of librarian/user collaboration in an age of digital libraries. He challenged libraries to provide reference service with the human touch to widely dispersed users whenever and wherever they want it or need it. The issue of approachability is just as important in the electronic environment as it is at the traditional reference desk. The perception of accessibility sets the tone of the user's entire encounter with the IFSI Library (Straw 2000). In moving toward more electronic reference service and toward a digital library, it is crucially important for the IFSI Library to maintain its personal touch, tailored individual service and user-centered approach.

CONCLUSION AND FURTHER STUDY

Collecting and managing the reference transaction log database is time-consuming but worthwhile, because the findings allow the IFSI Library to improve and enhance its services effectively. Monitoring usage of reference transactions reveals needed improvements in the IFSI Library, modifications in staffing levels, and reconsideration of service hours. As seen in the analysis, there is a potential wealth of information that can be culled from the data collected from outreach reference service. It is obvious (but often forgotten) that when designing a reference request database, librarians should consider not only what they will need to answer the question, but also what sort of data analysis they wish to do in the future. The preceding analysis aims to broaden reference librarians' understanding of some quantitative operations and the thinking behind them at the IFSI Library. There is no "one-size-fits-all" answer to providing outreach reference service.

With 70% of Illinois firefighters serving as volunteers and a 20% turnover rate among all firefighters, developing and maintaining a high quality and dynamic outreach reference service has proven to be an exciting journey with many challenges. The 1998 Outreach Program Survey and a series of grant projects, in particular the LSTA 2000 Full Year Grant, have enriched our understanding about remote users. The Outreach Program has given the IFSI Library an invaluable opportunity to initiate innovative reference service as the central focal point of outreach service, and to personalize and customize these services based on direct knowledge of user needs and expectations. Technology has had a revolutionary impact on the IFSI Library as it did on librarianship as a whole, from the ways the IFSI Library staff views its services and users. The technology compels the IFSI Library to seek new alliances, to radically change our perspectives on user needs, and even to transform the ways in which the IFSI Library organizes itself to serve these needs. The IFSI Library has recognized the need and worked aggressively to bring the IFSI Library to users via the Internet instead of users to the IFSI Library.

Analyses of user needs and library use patterns have played an important role in the evolution of the new service models discussed in this article. Respecting users in all of their diversity and complexity will continue to be at the center of the IFSI Library's value system. The constant pursuit of knowledge of users' needs and their information-seeking behavior, based on actual data, will increase the effectiveness of information services better than wishful thinking and untested assumptions (Ferguson and Bunge 1997). Experimental digital methods of referencing will be further combined with classical reference archetypes to form a constantly evolving model of providing information services in a continually changing information environment. Evaluating important issues such as staffing, resources needed (financial, human, and information), training, users and situations best suited to the limitations and possibilities of outreach reference services, and potential cooperative models with commercial services will be very important as well. With this knowledge, the IFSI Library will be able to continue to keep momentum and provide high-quality outreach service to remote users.

Reaching a wider audience of remote users has provided good opportunities for IFSI to showcase library professional's skills and "sell" the services of the IFSI Library. Marketing through reference service and user training is the key to success in building these services and continuing to attract users to the IFSI Library. An indisputable result of the outreach reference service is a renewed commitment to a user-based philosophy of user services that now forms the essence of the mission statement of the IFSI Library. Working with the IFSI Director for Marketing, the IFSI library staff has marketed and advertised the library through flyers, conference presentations and posters, training workshops, the *IFSI Newsletter*, the IFSI web site, and word of mouth, to let firefighters around the state know about the library services.

Reviewing the outreach reference service allows IFSI to understand how far the IFSI Library has come and, more importantly, to prepare for the future. By understanding the continually evolving roles and expectations, organizational structures, and user culture that impelled the IFSI Library to successfully move from an in-house library to an outreach library, IFSI can thus understand the skills and qualities necessary for future success of outreach reference services.

Special libraries often share challenges and interests with their parent organization. The study suggests that the outreach reference service is mature when its activities are woven into the fabric of its parent organizations. Because of the success of outreach service, the management has recognized the IFSI Library as a "central, essential element of the Institute's Vision 2000 for the Future." The solo librarian was promoted to Director/Head Librarian in 1999 and the IFSI Library budget has been increased substantially. A feasibility study of a new IFSI Library building has been completed and the IFSI Library is being expanded from 700 square feet to 10,000 square feet by 2007.

Still, the challenges of providing access to information in print and electronic formats, along with meeting the information needs of firefighters continue to test the resources and creative problem-solving abilities of the IFSI Library staff. Information technologies will continue to change rapidly as will the understanding of how they can be used to support outreach reference services and library services in general. With no foreseeable increase in staffing, the IFSI Library is seeking the most cost-efficient plan to retain and improve the outreach reference services, such as hiring graduate assistants and supervising practicum and Independent Study students from the University of Illinois Graduate School of Library and Information Science (GSLIS). The IFSI Library will continue to add new elements selectively as the need for them arises.

The IFSI Library is shifting from a classical collection development model of material ownership to a model of providing timely access to materials. Every day, the need becomes more apparent to deliver high-quality reference and instructional support through the IFSI Library to all users at all times and from all locations, commensurate with the expansion of the information and resources available for unmediated access from remote locations. This points to an exciting future for the IFSI Library to continue to forge closer connections with Illinois firefighters and meet their changing needs.

Despite increasing outreach service in public and academic libraries, outreach service in special libraries has not been studied much, and a systematic study is needed in this area. Further studies could include the kinds of services that are needed, how information needs can be met, and the methodologies of providing answers to reference questions or information needed. It is especially interesting to map the use of reference in an environment of a special library as the general public becomes increasingly electronically savvy (Bushallow-Wilbur et al. 1996).

The present study raises as many, if not more, questions than it answers. While the data analysis is, in many aspects, interesting in its own right, it can also serve as a powerful tool for further exploration. Equipped with such knowledge, the IFSI Library staff can now examine other avenues of exploration–such as content analysis of the questions, a patron satisfaction survey, and librarian attitudes–with a much better background than can be accomplished in evaluating "traditional" reference services. Furthermore, comparisons of data across other libraries, as well as other services such as commercial question and answer services, or other outreach reference services would also be constructive.

Outreach service will continue to evolve, as a critical service point to meet the information needs of library users of the future. Nofsinger (1999) has noted that the essential core competency for reference professionals in the 21st century will be a personal commitment to users, especially by "serving as essential conduits for information . . . between library managers and customers." Thus, the advocacy role of outreach service will enhance the IFSI Library's ability to adjust its products to accommodate changes in user expectations. It is only through this activity that the special library can justify its existence and flourish in the years to come.

REFERENCES

Abels, Eileen G. "The E-Mail Reference Interview." *RQ* 35, no. 3 (Spring 1996): 345-358.

Bates, Mary Ellen, and Kimberly Allen. "Lotus Notes in Action: Meeting Corporate Information Needs." *Database* 17, no. 4 (August 1994): 27-38.

Bristow, Ann, and Mary Buechley. "Academic Reference Service over E-Mail: An Update." *College & Research Libraries News* 56, no. 7 (July/August 1995): 459-462.

Bunge, Charles A., and Richard E. Bopp. "History and Varieties of Reference Services." In *Reference and Information Services : An Introduction*. Edited by Richard E. Bopp, and Linda C. Smith. Englewood, CO: Libraries Unlimited, 2001.

Bushallow-Wilbur, Lara, Gemma DeVinney, and Fritz Whitcomb. "Electronic Mail Reference Service: A Study." *RQ* 35, no. 3 (Spring 1996): 359-371.

Carter, David D., and Joseph Janes. "Unobtrusive Data Analysis of Digital Reference Questions and Service at the Internet Public Library: An Exploratory Study." *Library Trends* 49, no. 2 (Fall 2000): 251-265.

Cruickshank, John, and David G. Nowak. "Marketing Reference Resources and Services through a University Outreach Program." *The Reference Librarian* 73 (2001): 265-280.

Dennison, Russell F. "Usage-Based Staffing of the Reference Desk: A Statistical Approach." *Reference and User Services Quarterly* 39, no. 2 (Winter 2000): 158-165.

Dowling, Thomas. "Lies, Damned Lies, and Web Logs." *Library Journal: Net Connect Supplement* (Spring 2001): 34-35.

Ferguson, Chris D., and Charles A. Bunge. "The Shape of Services to Come: Values-Based Reference Service for the Largely Digital Library." *College & Research Libraries* 58, no. 3 (May 1997): 252-265.

Gray, Suzanne M. "Virtual Reference Services: Directions and Agendas." *Reference & User Services Quarterly* 39, no. 4 (Summer 2000): 365-375.

"Internet Connectivity: The Promise Fulfilled." (December 2000) (Retrieved November 18, 2002 from http://www.nclis.gov/statsurv/bookmark.html).

Janes, Joseph, David Carter, and Patricia Memmott. "Digital Reference Services in Academic Libraries." *Reference & User Services Quarterly* 39, no. 2 (Winter 1999): 145-150.

Kautzman, Amy. "Digital Impact: Reality, the Web, and the Changed Business of Reference." *Searcher* 7, no. 3 (March 1999): 18-24.

Lipow, Anne G. "Serving the Remote User: Reference Service in the Digital Environment." (Keynote Address). *Ninth Australian Conference and Exhibition: Information Online & On Disc 99. (19-21 January 1999)* (Retrieved October 12, 2002 from http://www.csu.edu.au/special/online99/proceedings99/200.htm).

Lutz, Judie. "Keeping a Competitive Edge in Special Libraries." *Texas Library Journal* 76, no. 3 (Fall 2000): 104, 106-7.

Nofsinger, Mary M. "Training and Retraining: Reference Professionals: Core Competencies for the 21st Century." In *Coming of Age in Reference Services: A Case History of Washington State University Libraries.* Edited by Christy Zlatos. New York: The Haworth Press, Inc., 1999.

Riechel, Rosemarie. *Reference Services for Children and Young Adults.* Hamden, CT: Library Professional Publications, 1991.

Roysdon, Christine M., and Laura Lee Elliott. "Electronic Integration of Library Services Through a Campuswide Network." *RQ* 28, no. 1 (Fall 1988): 82-93.

Ruan, Lian. "Illinois Fire Service Institute Library (IFSI Library) Outreach Program Survey Report." Unpublished, December 1998.

Ruan, Lian. "Libraries in the 21st Century: Developing the Distance Learning Library Services for Illinois Firefighters: An Integrated Information Service with Online Firefighter 2 Certification Program, Final Narrative Report." *Illinois Libraries* 83, no. 4 (Fall 2001): 19-63.

Ruan, Lian. "Final Narrative Report, Internet Outreach to and Training of Illinois Fire Service Personnel, Public and Community College Librarians for Electronic Access to Fire Safety Information, Final Narrative Report." *Illinois Libraries* 83, no. 1 (Winter 2001): 18-33.

RUSA. *Guidelines for Information Services.* (July 2000) (Retrieved November 18, 2002 from http://www.ala.org/rusa/stnd_consumer.html).

Scherrer, Carol S., and Susan Jacobson. "New Measures for New Roles: Defining and Measuring the Current Practices of Health Sciences Librarians." *Journal of Medical Library Association* 90, no. 2 (2002): 164-172. (Retrieved October 30, 2002 from http://www.pubmedcentral.gov/tocrender.fcgi?iid=2747).

Sloan, Bernie. "Service Perspectives for the Digital Library." *Library Tends* 47, no. 1 (Summer 1998): 117-143.

Sloan, Bernie. E-mail to Lian Ruan, November 18, 2002.

Still, Julie, and Frank Campbell. "Librarian in a Box: the Use of Electronic Mail for Reference." *Reference Services Review* 21, no. 1 (Spring 1993): 15-18.

Straw, Joseph E. "A Virtual Understanding, the Reference Interview and Question Negotiation in the Digital Age." *Reference & User Service Quarterly* 39, no. 4 (2000): 376-379.

Tomer, Christopher. "MIME and Electronic Reference Service." *Reference Librarian* 41/42 (1994): 347-373.

Trump, Judith F., and Ian P. Tuttle. "Here, There, and Everywhere, Reference at the Point-of-Need." *The Journal of Academic Librarianship* 27, no. 6 (November 2001): 464-466.

Warner, Debra G. "A New Classification for Reference Statistics." *Reference & User Services Quarterly* 41, no.1 (Fall 2001): 51-55.

White, H. D. "Measurement at the Reference Desk." *Drexel Library Quarterly* 17, no. 4 (1981): 3-35.

Wilson, Myoung C. "Evolution or Entropy? Changing Reference/User Culture and the Future of Reference Librarians." *Reference & User Services Quarterly* 39, no. 4 (2000): 387-90.

Grassroots to Grassfed:
Libraries Partner with Local Organizations to Address the Information Needs of Farming Communities in Upstate New York

Bernadette Hodge
Rebekah Tanner

SUMMARY. A partnership formed between a special library and a public library system to address the information needs of local farmers is the subject of this paper. The special library partner is an information center for agricultural medicine and health. The public library system is one which serves its fourteen member libraries in central New York. These libraries, together with several community-based organizations, com-

Bernadette Hodge is Health Science Librarian, New York Center for Agricultural Medicine & Health Library & Information Center, One Atwell Road, Cooperstown, NY 13326 (E-mail: info@nycamh.com). Ms. Hodge is also part time Reference Librarian and nursing division liaison, Fulton Montgomery Community College in Johnstown, NY. Rebekah Tanner is Polaris Site Manager, GIS Information Systems, Inc., 7272 Morgan Road, Liverpool, NY 13090 (E-mail: Rebekah.tanner@gisinformationsystems.com).

[Haworth co-indexing entry note]: "Grassroots to Grassfed: Libraries Partner with Local Organizations to Address the Information Needs of Farming Communities in Upstate New York." Hodge, Bernadette, and Rebekah Tanner. Co-published simultaneously in *The Reference Librarian* (The Haworth Information Press, an imprint of The Haworth Press, Inc.) No. 82, 2003, pp. 107-124; and: *Outreach Services in Academic and Special Libraries* (ed: Paul Kelsey, and Sigrid Kelsey) The Haworth Information Press, an imprint of The Haworth Press, Inc., 2003, pp. 107-124. Single or multiple copies of this article are available for a fee from The Haworth Document Delivery Service [1-800-HAWORTH, 9:00 a.m. - 5:00 p.m. (EST). E-mail address: docdelivery@haworthpress.com].

http://www.haworthpress.com/store/product.asp?sku=J120
© 2003 by The Haworth Press, Inc. All rights reserved.
Digital Object Identifier: 10.1300/J120v39n82_07

bined their leadership, resources, and expertise in a successful outreach effort that saved a village library, improved community relations, enhanced awareness of the role of libraries, and disseminated information necessary for sustaining a viable and healthy farming community. *[Article copies available for a fee from The Haworth Document Delivery Service: 1-800-HAWORTH. E-mail address: <docdelivery@haworthpress.com> Website: <http://www.HaworthPress.com>* © *2003 by The Haworth Press, Inc. All rights reserved.]*

KEYWORDS. Agriculture, special, farming, rural, outreach

BACKGROUND

Libraries working in partnership are well-documented in the literature. Public libraries, in particular, have collaborated with school libraries to the mutual benefit of both the libraries and the students.[1] Public library partnerships with a variety of groups, including public agencies, foundations, non-profit, business, and the media, are described in a document by G. Francisco et al., in which the library's role is both participant and leader in the design of solutions to meet the needs of several communities.[2] An article by Tomasulo-Mariano describes the Connecting Schools and Libraries Program (CLASP) which began as a pilot in a few branches of the New York Public Library and eventually expanded to provide opportunities for collaboration between public, private and religious schools and local public library branches in all five boroughs of New York City through the New York Public, Queens Borough Public and Brooklyn Public Libraries.[3]

This paper describes how the collaboration between a special library and a public library system resulted in greater accomplishments than could have been possible by the efforts of either alone. These library partners, together with several community organizations, combined their leadership, resources, and expertise and challenged themselves to address the needs of the farming population in their community. Their grassroots efforts resulted in saving a village library, improving community relations by facilitating communication among residents, increasing and facilitating access to agricultural information, and providing educational programs and information dissemination necessary for sustaining a viable and healthy farming community. The special library partner is the Library and Information Center of the New York Center for Agricultural Medicine and Health (NYCAMH), located near Cooperstown, NY. NYCAMH, which provides health and safety services for the farm communities in New York State, is a program of Bassett Healthcare, and is funded by the National Institute for Occupational Safety and Health (NIOSH) and the New York State Department of Health. NYCAMH has also been designated by NIOSH as one of nine national agricultural centers, the Northeast Center for Agricultural and Occupational Health (NEC), to promote farm health and safety research, education, and prevention in a thirteen-state region from Maine through Virginia.

The public library partner in this collaboration is the Mohawk Valley Library System (MVLS), one of New York State's twenty-three public library systems, consisting of fourteen member libraries in the four counties of Fulton, Montgomery, Schoharie, and Schenectady, and the nine branches of the Schenectady County Public Library. The fourteen member libraries that MVLS serves from administrative offices in Schenectady, NY, include ten free-association libraries, three public libraries, and one county library, all located along the Mohawk River.

In New York State, the source for both federal and state funding is the Division of Library Development (DLD) at the New York State Library. Funding is then filtered through the public library systems to the member libraries. It was through the leadership of MVLS that three proposals were submitted for Federal Library Services and Technology Act (LSTA) grants to DLD, which made funding possible in the 1998-1999, 1999-2000 and 2001-2002 federal fiscal years.

In the spring of 1998, when MVLS determined to pilot this project, a search of general and professional periodical literature revealed no clear model upon which to base it. A similar search in April 2003, unfortunately, finds the situation little changed. One must go back to Curry's 1988 reporting on the project of the Jefferson County Public Library: "Cows to Computers"[4] for anything similar. More recently, one brief article by Wiese, offers some agriculturally related collection development suggestions and states: "At the local level, universities, agricultural extension offices, and state departments of agriculture should not be overlooked. They can be valuable sources for publications, services, and recommendations and may even have programs designed specifically for beginning or small farmers in their state."[5] Note that Wiese lacks any mention of special or public libraries or library collaborations.

INTRODUCTION

"It's the squeaking wheel that gets the grease," is a familiar adage and one applicable to the beginning of a unique partnership between a public library system, its member libraries, a special library, a number of community-based organizations, and the agricultural community of the Mohawk Valley region in central New York State. The squeaking wheel in this case was a group of farmers in the rural village of St. Johnsville, NY, who declared, by a ballot referendum, that they were unwilling to continue paying taxes for library services in 1998. Feeling overburdened with property taxes, these farmers publicly questioned the benefits of library services that they felt did not address their needs. The concerned but empathetic library director of the Margaret Reaney Memorial Library in St. Johnsville, NY, took the farmers' concerns to the director of MVLS. From there, those concerns became the responsibility of one member of the system staff who astutely identified this valuable opportunity for member libraries to reach out in their communities and address the information needs of an underserved population. As a result, an outreach partnership plan developed, aimed at improving the resources available to the farmers in MVLS' four-county service area.

Two tasks had to be undertaken to keep the Margaret Reaney Memorial Library viable: first, an intensive campaign to "get out the vote" at the local elections in May 1998 was required, because rescinding the tax levy would have resulted in the library's immediate closure. Then, with the help of an LSTA grant awarded by the New York State Library, which MVLS applied for in June 1998 and which was awarded in the late summer of 1998, groups composed of library staff, community members and farmers were given opportunities to communicate. The information needs of the agricultural community and ways in which library services might assist in meeting them were explored. The economics of farming emerged as the predominate concern in these earliest conversations, the first and largest of which was held in St. Johnsville in January 1999, facilitated by Duane Dale of Dale Associates, a consulting firm located in Amherst, MA. The Regional Farm & Food Project (RF&FP), a not-for-profit membership organization of farmers and citizens concerned with the local food supply, located in Albany, NY, and its director, Tracy Frisch, assisted MVLS in its outreach to farmers. After this initial assessment, a series of study circles[6] met five times over a ten-week period with an average attendance of thirteen farmers. By building rapport with a consistent small group it became evident that their concerns centered around questions such as: can small farms survive in today's corporate economy, and what knowledge is needed to secure success in farming today? The feedback from the study circles also corresponded to a study by Bundy, which found farmers tended to read selectively from a variety of media about agricultural practices that increase efficiency rather than entire books.[7] This finding served as a useful directive in the selection of grant-funded resource materials to be purchased by the participating libraries.

One of the stated goals of the proposal was to "make the community aware of the role of public libraries in their communities." The means by which MVLS set out to accomplish this objective was to launch a publicity campaign consisting of press releases, public service announcements, and flyers distributed in all of the MVLS member libraries, at the sites of partnering organizations, and through the mail to the membership list of the RF&FP. Over the course of the project, this mailing list grew ten-fold in response to publicity and by collecting additional names at each public event.

An article in the local newspaper, *Amsterdam Recorder*, following the community meeting in St. Johnsville was read with interest by yet another librarian who is employed at a nearby agricultural research/education center, the New York Center for Agricultural Medicine and Health (NYCAMH). This librarian noticed that agricultural health and safety concerns were not among the issues identified for inclusion in the MVLS project, a point for concern, since the National Safety Council places agriculture among the most dangerous industries.[8] In 1988, it was the recognition of these unacceptably high rates of occupational injury and illness in New York State's agricultural industry that led to the establishment of NYCAMH by the New York State Legislature to provide: research and education into the causes and prevention of agricultural injury and illness; education and prevention activities within the farm community; education of professionals serving the farm community; and clinical help for farm-related health problems. A health science librarian collects and maintains resources that support these research and educational activities. This specialized collection of monographs, serials, slides, videotapes, and electronic databases are organized around farm health and safety research conducted by NYCAMH, including occupational arthritis, hearing loss, tractor safety, skin cancer, emotional stress, pesticide exposure, and zoonoses. Hence, to the agricultural center's librarian, the MVLS project looked like a valuable outreach opportunity, particularly since the target audience was the farming population in nearby counties not regularly served by NYCAMH. A letter to this effect was sent to the MVLS project's director, initiating a discussion of outreach collaboration between the two libraries.

RESOURCES FOR ECONOMIC VIABILITY IN SUSTAINABLE AGRICULTURE

Farmland is a primary part of the scenic central Mohawk Valley region of New York State that lies between the Adirondack and Catskill Mountains, where small family farms characterize agriculture in much of this region. Situated along the Mohawk River in a four-county region are communities served by MVLS, ranging from the city of Schenectady and its suburbs to the smaller cities of Amsterdam, Gloversville, and Johnstown, and the small towns and villages in Fulton, Montgomery and Schoharie counties. In all, fourteen member libraries and nine branch libraries serve a population of 238,003 with

45,020 living outside the four cities in communities that are largely rural and where farming has been a way of life since before the American Revolution.[9] Through their membership in the MVLS consortium, each library can avail itself of funding and services it could not provide alone. In order to address the information needs of the agricultural community, MVLS used LSTA funds and formed partnerships with area organizations, groups, and individuals interested in the economic survival of farms and communities to form the *Resources for Economic Viability in Sustainable Agriculture (REVSA)* project. The proposal requested funding for collection development and outreach activities intended to serve the agricultural community in light of the recent situation in St. Johnsville. MVLS proposed that by offering resources and services that would contribute to the economic viability of farming in the region, libraries could begin building mutually beneficial relationships with farmers. MVLS submitted a proposal to the New York State Library in June 1998 and that autumn was awarded a grant for $25,195. This funding was used to build collections focusing on sustainable farming methods and sound business practices, develop linked annotations to web-based information, fund the initial community meeting, study circles, two farmer-to-farmer workshops and an in-service training workshop for system and library staff on the "Bibliography of Agriculture" presented by Eric Toensmeier of the New England Small Farms Institute in Belchertown, MA. Two libraries in western Montgomery county were the focal point for this project, the Margaret Reaney Memorial Library in St. Johnsville, NY and the Fort Plain Free Library in Fort Plain, NY.

RESOURCES FOR ECONOMIC VIABILITY IN SUSTAINABLE AGRICULTURE: YEAR TWO: BEYOND THE PILOT PROJECT

The need for, and responsiveness to, quality information by farmers was so overwhelming in this pilot project, as demonstrated by program attendance, press coverage and the high rate of completed attendee evaluation forms, that the New York State Library suggested its expansion in a second year, with eight libraries in all four counties participating in the *Resources for Economic Viability in Sustainable Agriculture: Year Two: Beyond the Pilot Project (REVSA Year Two)*, funded through a second successful proposal written by MVLS requesting LSTA monies.

Having opened up communications with MVLS during the first year of the project, NYCAMH joined in the proposal-drafting phase for the second year as an interested partner, along with the continued efforts of the Regional Farm & Food Project (RF&FP). A number of other community organizations, including the Hudson-Mohawk Resource Conservation and Development Council, Inc. (H-RC&DC), the Montgomery County Chamber of Commerce, and the

Schoharie County Cornell Cooperative Extension had also learned of the efforts MVLS was making to provide information to farmers, and came onboard at this time.

In addition to its librarian, the NYCAMH staff of twenty-five includes medical doctors, nurses, social workers, educators, and researchers, among other support personnel. The usual customers for NYCAMH safety and health resources include occupational health professionals, educators, schools, students, community organizations, and farmers. By collaborating with local public libraries in some of the counties NYCAMH is chartered to serve, but in which they had not had much previous visibility, NYCAMH could expand their ability to disseminate their message and at the same time provide MVLS with subject expertise that the organization had previously lacked.

MVLS wrote their second proposal in the spring of 1999 and that autumn was awarded a grant in the amount of $51,900. The target audience for the grant totaled 966 individuals, including 846 small family farmers in the largely rural, four-county area, forty Amish farmers, and eighty next-generation farmers.[10] In this second year, project goals were: to continue providing useful information to farmers about agricultural systems that are ecologically, economically and socially viable, including information on health and safety, economic development, financial planning, business management and sound farming practices; to mobilize the "creativity and courage of"[11] local youth by forging partnerships with the library, the community and the current generation of farmers, "in order to achieve sustainable development and ensure a better future for all";[12] and to open lines of communication further to and from the Amish community and provide information resources to support their "vital role in environmental management and development because of their knowledge and traditional practices."[13]

Staff in the MVLS member libraries were assisted in increasing their own knowledge about agriculture and provided with further training that they might enhance their collections with appropriately selected books, periodicals, videos, and CD-ROMs on topics covering health and safety, economic development, financial planning, business management and sound farming practices. Eric Toensmeier of the New England Small Farms Institute returned to provide a second in-service workshop, this time focusing on the business aspects of agriculture. Through the *REVSA* (1998-1999) and *REVSA: Year Two* (1999-2000) projects a total of 605 items were purchased, including: 446 books, seventy-six audiovisuals, seventy-two CD-ROM products and eleven periodical publications. Having learned in the first year of the project that farmers' willingness to read lengthy texts was limited, a concerted effort to provide as much information as possible in alternative formats, especially video, was employed in the second year.

Library staff and individuals representing each of MVLS' community partners were invited to attend a two-day training opportunity. Facilitated by Duane Dale (the same individual who had facilitated the project's initial community meeting), a modified study circle format was used to clarify the project's goals and objectives, define what is meant by "Sustainable Agriculture," and enable staff at the participating libraries to be more effective when recruiting individuals in the agricultural community to participate in a second study circle series scheduled for five consecutive weeks at the Frothingham Free Library, Fonda, NY. As in the previous year, Shannon Hayes of Sap Bush Hollow Farm in Warnerville, NY served as facilitator for the study circle. Using Joel Salatin's book *You Can Farm: The Entrepreneur's Guide To Start and Succeed in a Farming Enterprise*[14] as a background text, this group, which ranged from eight to twelve participants, met to explore the economics of sustainable agriculture versus scale dependent technologies.

The winter months, when farmers have some time available for off-farm activities, were an ideal time to schedule fifteen workshops of a very practical nature, demonstrating sustainable production methodologies. These included six farmer-to-farmer seminars and five presentations donated by professionals at cooperating agencies. Workshop titles such as, "Genetically Engineered Foods," "Selling What You Grow," "Animal Health and Nutrition from the Ground Up" and "Farm Safety, Health and Managing Stress" reflect the diversity of topics covered.

As an enhancement to the linked Web site resources developed during the first year of the project (http://www.mvla.org/revsa/index.html), an online resource directory for agricultural related services was created (http://www.mvlafarm.org). Electronic resources on a wide variety of topics were made available via CD-ROM products. These materials extended the focus of the grant with resources on landscape architecture, business planning, encyclopedias of world mammals, and topics in local government. To inform farmers of both the Internet-based and CD-ROM resources that were now available to them through their local public libraries, librarians worked at information booths at the *Central New York Farm Progress Show*, the *Montgomery County Fair*, the *Cobleskill Dairy Days*, and at a grant-sponsored event called "Food for Thought" held at Sap Bush Hollow Farm. At each of these venues, library staff demonstrated electronic resources using laptop computers. Individual librarians also made use of the laptops by visiting the agriculture students in local high schools, at the farmers market and other venues closer to home.

Another project goal was to make appropriate information available to the Amish community of western Montgomery County. Since the late 1980s, Amish farmers have been moving into the area and while some families visited the library's children's section, few adults used the library. With assistance from some long-term local residents who had contact with these Amish farmers, programs and resources appropriate to them were publicized in the Amish community. Efforts were made to purchase print materials regarding draft-animal techniques of farming, non-mechanized production methodologies, and one library even decided to subscribe to a weekly newspaper of Amish interest. Success in reaching this target population was limited during the grant period, but in the two years since, the number of adult Amish library users has slowly increased. More outreach to the Amish community is needed.

During the summer months, as part of summer reading programs at four participating libraries, programs for young people were offered using materials supplied by local 4-H and the Montgomery County Cornell Cooperative Extension around the theme of the many uses for corn.

SAFE FARMS, SAFE FOOD, AND SAFE FUTURES

At the conclusion of the 1998-1999 and 1999-2000 *REVSA* projects, the evaluative direction given to MVLS and its partnering agencies by the farming community was to enhance learning and information-sharing activities through dialog with other members of their communities, especially government officials and consumers. Following a one-year hiatus, MVLS applied to the New York State Library for another LSTA grant in 2001, and in the early autumn was awarded $29,760 for the *Safe Farms, Safe Food, Safe Futures (SFSFSF)* project, which continued through September 2002. In this project MVLS worked with NYCAMH, HMRC&DC, Dr. Shannon Hayes and her parents, Dr. James and Mrs. Adele Hayes of Sap Bush Hollow Farm, to plan and present a three-day conference, a series of community dialogs, a mobile farm hazard display, three safety day camps for children, Internet training on agriculturally related consumer health and safety resources for both staff and the public, additional Web-based resources, and collection enhancement.

Three of the libraries that had participated in *REVSA: Year Two* decided not to participate, while two additional MVLS member libraries joined, determining this newly formulated focus was better suited to their users. They were particularly excited about the fact that state and local legislatures were to be targeted to participate in dialogs open to the general public and agricultural community in the comfortable setting of local libraries. During the winter of 2002, a series of five of these dialogs took place. Attendees at these meetings included residents, community and church leaders, government officials, farmers, educators, agricultural administrators, and library staff. As with the earlier study circles, these discussions were facilitated by Shannon Hayes and tended to focus on such issues as concerns about food safety, security of the food supply, and the safety, financial security and well-being of the local farmers who will grow it. Meetings typically included the identification of significant local concerns, appropriate community resources, and opportunities for public action.

The Farm Hazards Display, an educational tabletop exhibit, was circulated for a one-month stay at each of six libraries. Provided by NYCAMH, the exhibit, through the depiction of farm-related hazardous situations and accompanying literature, increased awareness of farm injuries and fatalities common to New York State. Other activities related to farm safety included the presentation of one-day Farm Safety Day Camps for children six to twelve years of age, at three member library sites. NYCAMH staff presented safety topics relevant to living on or visiting farms through demonstrations, games, and interactive educational techniques.

In March of 2002 the three-day *Safe Farms, Safe Food, Safe Futures Conference (SFSFSF)* provided further study of safety issues in the production and consumption of food. Jo Robinson, bestselling author, presented the keynote address, "Why Grassfed is Best!" which challenged the healthfulness of modern food processing methods, and advocated livestock raised for consumption, dairying or egg production are more healthful when raised on a grassfed diet. Eight other conference workshops covered various aspects of food safety, farm economics, and sustainable cuisine. Also available at this conference, to both librarians and the public, was hands-on Internet training for accessing consumer information related to agricultural health and safety, provided by Peggy Falls of the Mid-Atlantic Region of the National Network of Libraries of Medicine. Ms. Falls returned several weeks later for additional Internet training of a more specialized nature for member library staff.

Collection development for *Safe Farms, Safe Food, Safe Futures* continued to include print and audio-visual materials, but with a much clearer focus on the issues related to safe farming and safe food production. Because this project also included direct services to young people, added emphasis on juvenile materials about agriculture, farming, gardening, etc., were given consideration when developing buying lists for the participant member libraries.

The *SFSFSF* Web site: (http://www.mvla.org/SFSFSF/index.html) serves both as a publicity tool and as a vehicle for the post-conference publication of presentations and therefore includes much more original content material developed by MVLS and its partners than the earlier linked resources of the original *REVSA* project.

Thus, the squeak made by the farmers and heard by the librarian in a rural village in upstate New York resulted in outreach activities spilling benefits beyond village, county, and even state limits. During three non-consecutive years of a four-year period, the outreach activities used over $106,000 in federal funds, and staff from MVLS and its member libraries, NYCAMH, the H-MRC&DC, RF&FP, the Schoharie County Cornell Cooperative Extension, and countless individuals dedicated thousands of hours to make the efforts a success. Community meetings organized by librarians became the first important step in helping the farmers and their communities to share concerns, identify needs, and organize plans to improve the situation. Dedicated staff from a growing number of libraries and organizations, working together with interested community members, achieved the numerous and successful outreach efforts herein described.

DISCUSSION AND EVALUATION:
FROM THE SPECIAL LIBRARIAN PERSPECTIVE . . .

Rural community residents objecting to paying taxes for their library is not a unique occurrence. A recently reported situation describes a campaign by local residents in Stevens County, Washington to dissolve an entire county library system by referendum.[15] Whereas these community dissenters are not farmers, the objection to paying taxes for something viewed as unnecessary holds the potential for the elimination of valuable information resources and services. Working to overcome this same dilemma, library partners in the MVLS grant projects capitalized on the opportunity to prove that libraries have value through the responsive actions they took to identify and address unmet information needs.

A library responding to farm crisis is not unique. Responding to the farm economic stresses of the 1980s, the Jefferson County Public Library in Florida partnered with a county Extension Service and received support from other farm-related community groups such as FFA (Future Farmers of America) and Farm Bureau to "develop a wide range of information services responsive to the changing needs of contemporary farmers." The county library visualized "acting as an agent of change" through the development of a farm information center of books and periodicals, reference services with remote access to databases in agribusiness, and a computer literacy in farm management program.[16] For the NYCAMH Library and Information Center, the attraction of the MVLS grant projects was not only the vision and effort of the public libraries but also the expanded outreach made possible by the partnering opportunity. While NYCAMH is a state-mandated organization, many residents in counties served by the MVLS libraries were unfamiliar with this agricultural organization. The idea of using local libraries as a vehicle for disseminating farm health and safety information was new to NYCAMH. Usual outreach avenues are places where farmers gather in large numbers such as at farm organization meetings or at regional farm shows. Presenting programs in the small rural library setting facilitated the dissemination of farm health and safety information to residents and also offered the very valuable opportunity for personalized contact with local farmers and their families.

There were valuable lessons to be gained by presenting programs in unfamiliar localities. NYCAMH staff, during the winter and early spring of 2000 presented a program titled, "Farm Safety, Farmer Health and Managing the Stresses of Farm Life" in three MVLS libraries. The attendance numbers for these programs were markedly disappointing when compared to other *REVSA* workshops with titles such as, "Making the Most of Your Pasture and Improving Your Land: Pasture Management for Healthy Livestock" or "Marketing Your Own Farm-Raised Meats and Poultry." Not an entirely surprising outcome, since farmers tend to be most interested in farm economic topics. However, our experience was similar to county Health Departments in Wisconsin, who, in collaboration with cooperative extension agents, offered agricultural safety programs but had difficulty getting farmers to attend. In the evaluation of their efforts, staff saw this low attendance as a barrier to safety.[17] Agricultural educators generally acknowledge that safety is a hard sell and unfortunately tends to become important only after an injury or fatality has occurred.[18] Farmers have a tendency to rely on knowledge that is intergenerational; believing that what was good for my grandfather is good enough for me. A very unfortunate practice given that today's farming environment poses more serious hazards to health and safety with the use of dangerously large equipment and the exposures to highly toxic chemicals. While the feedback was positive from those few people who did attend the in-library safety programs, NYCAMH staff learned an important lesson—a more popular topic increases the size of an otherwise reluctant audience.

On a national level, enlightenment resulted from the MVLS and NYCAMH presence as co-poster presenters at the NIOSH conference, *Agricultural Safety and Health in a New Century*, held April 28-30, 2000 in Cooperstown, NY, when the MVLS project director recommended attendees at a plenary session to consider statewide public library systems as a means to assist in the dissemination of the *National Agricultural Guidelines for Children* to farm families. Safety educators and farm families, in an effort to assist parents in determining their child's readiness and needs in the assignment of farm chores, developed the guidelines in Marshfield, Wisconsin. At the time of the conference, these guidelines were newly ready for public distribution.[19]

The roving Farm Hazard Display and the Farm Safety Day Camps presented by NYCAMH staff during the *SFSFSF* project were very successful means to promote injury prevention and safety awareness information to community library patrons. The Farm Hazard Display depicted unsafe situations using toy tractors, implements, animals, and people along with explanatory literature, and was placed in busy areas in six participating libraries. The exhibit tended to attract children who would then discuss the purpose with adults. Evaluations from the library staff reported that the display was a popular exhibit and tended to generate discussion among the patrons. Staff from several libraries hosting the display expressed the wish "to be able to keep it" and it remains on permanent exhibit at the Margaret Reaney Memorial Library in St. Johnsville (see Photo 1).

Three Farm Safety Day Camps for children were one-day sessions at local libraries. In addition to learning about farm family safety, the host librarian introduced the children to the related resources available in the library. All of these child-focused outreach and education activities support the important goal to make farming a safer and healthier occupation for those who will be the "next generation farmers." Teaching these future farmers to associate farm health and safety information with library resources could be an important means to achieve this goal (see Photo 2).

FROM THE PUBLIC LIBRARIAN PERSPECTIVE . . .

Throughout the grant period, MVLS and its member libraries had many opportunities to speak in forums not generally open to them, including a number of radio presentations, attendance at the Montgomery County Chamber of Commerce, the Montgomery County Supervisors meeting on the issue of establishing an Agriculture Sub-committee within the Economic Development Committee, a number of meetings of H-MRC&DC, the NIOSH conference, and others. In addition, a truly massive publicity machine was put in place, which grew to include over 2,000 individuals who regularly received flyers announcing events

PHOTO 1. Hazard Display

Used with permission.

PHOTO 2. Farm Safety Day Camp in Library

Used with permission.

and over seventy press, television and radio media outlets. In preparation for the *SFSFSF* conference, arrangements were made with Northeast Public Radio for the project director to be live in-studio while Jo Robinson was contacted via telephone for a ten-minute interview on "The Roundtable"–a feature that explores a wide variety of issues. This broadcast brought MVLS into the homes of many individuals who might otherwise never have known that "public libraries" and "agriculture" could go together in the same sentence.

Three years of federal funding did much to benefit the member libraries of MVLS, and by extension, the patrons of those libraries. These include the books, videos, CD-ROMs and other materials which will not quickly date and which are available without restriction throughout New York State via Interlibrary Loan; the development of relationships with individual farmers to provide informative and educational programs; the network of partnerships formed with community agencies, the numerous individuals who made presentations, and the project consultant, Dr. Shannon Hayes; the presentation of the idea to young people that farming can be a safe and viable occupation, and more–but it was this new-found visibility that was the most advantageous aspect of the projects for MVLS itself.

What lessons can be learned? How much more can be done is the most obvious! If public libraries which are dependent upon their local constituents for on-going funding are to survive, then public libraries will have to continue to listen to the "squeak of the wheel" and become proactive to meet the information needs of the communities they serve. In this case, it was the agricultural community, and the public library system was fortunate to find and ally with community agencies that could help the libraries learn new subject matter, even as they began providing that content to their users.

Having noted the scarcity of information on similar projects in professional journals, MVLS made a deliberate effort to include *Library Journal, American Libraries,* and other professional publications in project-related mailings that might have been of interest to the editors of professional journals. A search of the literature will find that none of these journals chose to include any information regarding the *REVSA/SFSFSF* successes (nor on any similar efforts to meet the information needs of farmers, if they have recently been taking place elsewhere). Perhaps, as is the vision of the Federal Library Services and Technology Act, these three MVLS projects, now completed and documented herein, will become a demonstration of what can be done in the public library setting to outreach to the non-traditional user who is the local farmer.

CONCLUSION

Identification of the community's needs is an important first step, but the process cannot stop there. How much does the local library reflect the current interests and needs of its patrons? The experiences described herein are focused on how the farmers in a rural village made known that their local library was not addressing their needs. This situation could be repeated in any locality where frustrated residents protest a perceived inequality. Certainly public libraries can respond, but so can other information disseminating organizations such as special libraries. In this scenario the noise made by the farmers to their local library resulted in the formation of networks and partnerships among community libraries, individuals, and organizations that otherwise may never have happened.

The expertise and resources of a special library in agricultural medicine and health became an integral part of a public library system's response to the "squeaking wheel," which was the outcry of overburdened farmers in one community. In so doing, the public library system serving that region became better known in the several communities it serves, and the information needs of farmers in central New York are now better known and receiving well-deserved attention because listening librarians and information providers in their communities became unlikely, but successful partners.

NOTES

1. R. T. Malito, "Intergovernmental Partnerships: A Town/School Library," *The Clearing House* 68 no. 1 (1994): 30 and M.C. Saccardi, "Can We Read You Our Story? The Tale of a School-Public Library Partnership," *The Reading Teacher* 51 no. 5 (1998): 445.

2. Grace Francisco et al., "Joint Ventures: The Promise, Power and Performance of Partnering." Accessed 31 March 2003, available from http://www.library.ca.gov/assests/acrobatr/JointVentures.pdf.

3. M. Tomasulo-Mariano, "Libraries and the Many Faces of Reading: Reading Around the Block," *Library Talk* 13 no. 2 (2002): 10.

4. Elizabeth Curry, "Cows to Computers: The Impact of Adult Library Services on a rural Community," *RQ* 28 no. 1 (1998): 17.

5. William H. Wiese, "Green Acres: Small-Farm Resources" *Library Journal Online* (May 2001); accessed 7 November 2002, available from: http://libraryjournal.reviewsnews.com/index.asp?layout=articleArchive&articleid=CA154504.

6. The Study Circles Resource Center was established in 1990 to promote the use of study circles on critical social and political issues. It is a project of the Topsfield Foundation, a private, nonprofit, nonpartisan foundation whose mission is to advance deliberative democracy and improve the quality of public life in the United States. The study circle is a democratic process for small-group deliberation. There are just a few defining characteristics: a study circle is comprised of ten to fifteen people who meet regularly over a period of weeks or months to address a critical public issue. One or two people facilitate, not acting as an expert on the issue, but by keeping the discussion focused and helping the group consider a variety of views with the sessions progressing from a session on personal experience ("how does the issue affect me?") to sessions providing a broader perspective ("what are others saying about the issue?") to a session on action ("what can we do about the issue here?"). For additional information contact the Study Circles Resource Center, 697 Pomfret Street, P.O. Box 203, Pomfret, Connecticut 06258. Telephone: 860-928-2616, Fax: 860-928-3713, E-mail: scrc@neca.com.

7. M. L. Bundy, "Attitudes and Opinions of Farm Families in Illinois Toward Matters Related to Rural Library Development" (Doctoral Dissertation, University of Illinois at Urbana-Champaign, 1960), 1-50.

8. In 2000, the injury rate for the agricultural industry was 20.1 deaths per 100,000 workers compared with the injury rate of 3.7 percent for every 100,000 workers in all other industries combined. From National Safety Council, *Injury Facts 2002 Edition* (Itasca, IL: National Safety Council, 2002), 50.

9. Dawn Capece, Director of the Margaret Reaney Memorial Library, as well as a number of the local farmers, all reported at various times during the project that the Mohawk Valley region was considered the "bread basket of the Revolution." However, Dave Rickard, Interpretive Specialist at the Farmers Museum in Cooperstown, NY, has researched this bit of local folklore and feels that while the region was fertile enough, it is probably closer to the truth that crops were often burned by Tories and Native Americans and General George Washington got food for his troops when and

wherever possible. Mr. Rickard feels that these ideas are more reflective of long-lasting patriotic ideals than actual facts.

10. The next generation farmers concept came from conversations with Shannon Hayes, a twenty-four year old, third generation family farmer, who in 1998, while doing research toward her Master's Degree at Cornell University, Ithaca, NY, conducted focus groups in Schoharie county to examine ways in which families and communities could contribute to profitable family farming for the generation of young farmers coming of age in the early twenty-first century.

11. United Nations, "Rio Declaration on Environment and Development," Principle 21, 12 August 1992, accessed 11 November 2002, available from: http://www.un.org/document/ga/conf151/aconf15126-1annex1.htm.

12. United Nations, Principle 21.

13. United Nations, Principle 22.

14. Joel Salatin, *You Can Farm: The Entrepreneur's Guide To Start and Succeed in a Farming Enterprise* (Swoope, VA: Polyface, 1998).

15. Timothy Egan, "Tax Revolt Takes Aim at a County's Libraries," *The New York Times*, 20 Aug 2002, late edition.

16. Elizabeth Curry, "Cows to Computers," 16.

17. L. Chapman et al., "Agricultural Safety Efforts by County Health Departments in Wisconsin." *Public Health Reports* (1966): 37.

18. D. J. Murphy et al., "An Occupational Health and Safety Intervention Research Agenda for Production Agriculture: Does Safety Education Work?" *American Journal of Industrial Medicine* (1996): 393.

19. B. Lee and B. Marlenga, eds. *Professional Research Manual: North American Guidelines for Children's Agricultural Tasks* (Marshfield, WI: Marshfield Clinic, 1999).

REFERENCES

Bundy, M. L. "The Attitudes and Opinions of Farm Families in Illinois Toward Matters Related to Rural Library Development." Ph.D diss., University of Illinois at Urbana-Champaign, 1960.

Boyce, J. I. and B. R. Boyce, "Library Outreach Programs in Rural Areas." *Library Trends.* Summer (1995): 112-128.

Campbell, Sarah, Catherine Flavin-McDonald and Molly Holme Barrett. *A Guide for Training Study Circle Facilitators.* Pomfret, CT: Topsfield Foundation, Inc., 1998.

Chapman, L. J., R. T. Schuler, T. L. Wilkinson, and C. A. Skjolaas, "Agricultural Safety Efforts by County Health Departments in Wisconsin," *Public Health Reports* 111 (1996): 437-443.

Curry, Elizabeth, "Cows to Computers: The Impact of Adult Library Services on a Rural Community," *RQ* 28, no.1 (1988): 16-20.

Francisco, G. et al. *Joint Ventures: The Promise, Power and Performance of Partnering.* Sacramento: California State Library, 2001.

Dale, Duane and Deborah Cavanaugh-Grant, eds. *Advancing Sustainable Agriculture Through Small Group Discussions: A Guide for Group Leaders and Members.* Urbana, IL: University of Illinois and Illinois Department of Agriculture Conservation, 2000.

Egan, Timothy, "Tax Revolt Takes Aim at a County's Libraries." *The New York Times*, 20 August 2002, late edition.

Lee, B. and B. Marlenga, eds. *Professional Research Manual: North American Guidelines for Children's Agricultural Tasks*. Marshfield, WI: Marshfield Clinic, 1999.

Malito, R. T. "Intergovernmental Partnership: A Town/School Library," *The Clearing House* 68 no. 1 (1994): 30.

McCoy, Martha, Phyllis Emigh, Matt Leighninger, and Molly Barrett. *Planning Community-wide Study Circle Programs: A Step-by-step Guide*. Pomfret, CT: Topsfield Foundation, Inc., 1996.

Murphy, D. J., N. E. Kiernan, and L. J. Chapman, "An Occupational Health and Safety Intervention Research Agenda for Production Agriculture: Does Safety Education Work?" *American Journal of Industrial Medicine* 29, no. 4 (1996): 392-396.

MVLA Directory, Schenectady, NY: Mohawk Valley Library Association, 2002.

National Safety Council, *Injury Facts, 2002 Edition*. Itasca, IL: National Safety Council, 2002.

Robinson, Jo, *Why Grassfed Is Best: The Surprising Benefits of Grassfed Meat, Eggs, and Dairy Products*. Vashon, WA: Vashon Island Press, 2000.

Saccardi, M. C. "Can We Read You Our Story?: The Tale of a School-Public Library Partnership." *The Reading Teacher* 51, no. 5 (1998): 445-448.

Salatin, Joel, *You Can Farm: The Entrepreneur's Guide to Start and Succeed in a Farming Enterprise*. Swoope, VA: Polyface, 1998.

Tomasulo-Mariano, Mary. "Libraries and the Many Faces of Reading: Reading Around the Block." *Library Talk*, 13, no. 2 (2000): 10-12.

Wiese, William H. "Green Acres: Small-Farm Resources" *Library Journal Online*. May 2001. Accessed 7 November 2002; available from http://libraryjournal. reviewnews.com/index.asp?layout=articleArchive&articleid=CA154504.

United Nations. "Rio Declaration on Environment and Development." *Report of the United States Conference on Environment and Development*. 12 August 1992. Accessed 11 November 2002; available from http://www.un.org/documents/ga/conf151/aconf15126-1annex1.htm.

Building a Collaborative AgNIC Site as an Outreach Model: Rangelands of the Western U.S.

Douglas Jones
George Ruyle
Barbara Hutchinson

SUMMARY. Construction of the *Rangelands of the Western U.S.* web site provides a dynamic model for information outreach. Central to its success is the collaboration between librarians, other information professionals, and rangeland experts committed to working together for a common goal: a selective, centralized, web-based resource designed to help meet the information needs of rangeland scientists, range professionals, students, faculty, ranchers, environmentalists, librarians, and other stake-

Douglas Jones is Librarian, Science-Engineering Library, University of Arizona Library, University of Arizona, Tucson, AZ 85721 (E-mail: jonesd@u.library.arizona. edu). He is a founding member of the Arizona AgNIC team and served as first Chair of the national AgNIC Executive Board. George Ruyle is Program Chair, Professor and Extension Specialist in Rangeland and Forest Resources, 301 Biological Sciences East, University of Arizona, Tucson, AZ 85721 (E-mail: gruyle@ag.arizona.edu). He is also an active member in the Society for Range Management. Barbara Hutchinson is Director and Librarian, Arid Lands Information Center, Office of Arid Lands Studies, 1955 East Sixth Street, University of Arizona, Tucson, AZ 85719 (E-mail: barbarah@ ag.arizona.edu). She is also a founding member of the Arizona AgNIC team.

The authors wish to thank Mel George and Mike Haddock who graciously provided detailed updates on their site development for incorporation into this article.

[Haworth co-indexing entry note]: "Building a Collaborative AgNIC Site as an Outreach Model: Rangelands of the Western U.S." Jones, Douglas, George Ruyle, and Barbara Hutchinson. Co-published simultaneously in *The Reference Librarian* (The Haworth Information Press, an imprint of The Haworth Press, Inc.) No. 82, 2003, pp. 125-140; and: *Outreach Services in Academic and Special Libraries* (ed: Paul Kelsey, and Sigrid Kelsey) The Haworth Information Press, an imprint of The Haworth Press, Inc., 2003, pp. 125-140. Single or multiple copies of this article are available for a fee from The Haworth Document Delivery Service [1-800-HAWORTH, 9:00 a.m. - 5:00 p.m. (EST). E-mail address: docdelivery@haworthpress.com].

http://www.haworthpress.com/store/product.asp?sku=J120
© 2003 by The Haworth Press, Inc. All rights reserved.
Digital Object Identifier: 10.1300/J120v39n82_08

holders. Begun over eight years ago by a University of Arizona AgNIC Project team, the effort is extending to include participation of range and information professionals from the other Western states. In addition to linking to existing digital content, the project seeks to create or support the creation of critical electronic information resources through an integrated user interface. *[Article copies available for a fee from The Haworth Document Delivery Service: 1-800-HAWORTH. E-mail address: <docdelivery@ haworthpress.com> Website: <http://www.HaworthPress.com> © 2003 by The Haworth Press, Inc. All rights reserved.]*

KEYWORDS. AgNIC, rangelands, collaboration, *Rangelands of the Western U.S.*, extension service, web-based outreach, partnerships

INTRODUCTION

Rangelands–including grasslands, shrublands, and savannas–represent approximately 60 percent of the total area in the Western United States. The multiple use and diverse ownership of these vast lands represent a complex environment from both a scientific and public policy perspective. Information needed to preserve and manage rangelands is critical for all stakeholders, including ranchers, environmentalists, rangeland professionals, policy makers, students, and researchers, as well as the general public. The *Rangelands of the Western U.S.* web site <http://rangelandswest.org/>, part of the national Agriculture Network Information Center (AgNIC) Alliance, provides accurate, evaluated information to a diverse community of users.

The Agriculture Network Information Center (AgNIC) <http://www.agnic. org> is a voluntary alliance of the National Agricultural Library (NAL), land-grant universities and other agricultural organizations, cooperating with citizen groups and government agencies to provide agricultural information over the World Wide Web. In addition to rangelands, current AgNIC subjects include agricultural economics, statistics, law, geospatial data, soybeans, corn, forestry, turfgrass, aquaculture, entomology, water quality, and viticulture. AgNIC users range from K-12 students to farmers and ranchers, and from professionals to scholars.

BACKGROUND AND CONTEXT

In 1995, the AgNIC Alliance was formed as an initial partnership between the National Agriculture Library (NAL), the University of Arizona College of Agriculture, and the following four land-grant libraries: Cornell University's Albert R.

Mann Library, Iowa State University Library, University of Arizona Library, and the University of Nebraska Library. The goal was to move the vast agricultural information system into the twenty-first century (AgNIC 2000). From the initial five institutions affiliated with the United States land-grant system, AgNIC has grown to include twenty-six partners and eleven supporting partners, listed on the web site <http://www.central.agnic.org/agnic/partners/index. html>. University of Arizona participation in AgNIC has always been a collaboration between the Library, the Arid Lands Information Center, and the Rangeland & Forest Resources Program of the College of Agriculture and Life Sciences. The AgNIC initiative provides a framework to leverage the historical strengths of the land-grant system with new technologies to better link people with information. Historical strengths include the body of knowledge created by the land-grant universities and the United States Department of Agriculture (USDA), the libraries collecting and providing access to publications, and the extensive network of professionals committed to providing information to the agricultural community. New technologies include the availability of powerful, relatively inexpensive computers coupled with high-speed telecommunication providing the capability to create, store, and disseminate information independent of the traditional barriers of space and time.

Each AgNIC partner develops, collects, and organizes an in-depth collection of electronic resources and references for a relatively narrow subject area. This "vertical" approach to development encourages institutions to build on existing strengths while the Alliance provides coordination of the different subject areas and a technical infrastructure, enabling the component parts to function as an organic system. The result is a rich resource network available to all, developed by institutions with unique expertise, with the ultimate goal to cover all areas of agriculture and related subjects.

Each topical area–for example food and nutrition, viticulture, or bees and pollination–has a web site with basic information, full-text documents, links to other sites, and sometimes datasets including extensive collections of images, interactive programs, or geographic information systems (GIS) information. Distinguishing AgNIC from other sites is a commitment to providing information evaluated by professionals. A reference component is provided for information needs not satisfied by the content on the web site. Those seeking information may submit a query to any of the primary AgNIC participant sites that then provide either a factual response, reference (or links) to resources, or referral to appropriate individuals or agencies.

For a more in-depth description of AgNIC, see "Partnering for Improved Access to Agricultural Information: The Agriculture Network Information Center (AgNIC) Initiative" by Melanie Gardner et al., published in the *ARL Bimonthly Report* 223, available at http://www.arl.org/newsltr/223/agnic.html.

UNIVERSITY OF ARIZONA INVOLVEMENT IN AgNIC:
A COLLABORATIVE MODEL

The University of Arizona (UA) became involved in the AgNIC initiative almost from the start. Interest by outgoing Arizona Senator Dennis Deconcini in the concept of a national agricultural information system led to the first official contacts between NAL and the UA Library. The senator saw AgNIC as an opportunity to involve Arizona in a national effort to push forward information technology for the benefit of his local constituencies. Senator Deconcini ensured that one of his departing legacies would be a collaboration between Arizona, NAL, and other institutions to build the AgNIC system. Once NAL began discussions with the UA Library, the process moved forward quickly.

The agricultural librarian at the UA Library began a series of meetings with key individuals from the College of Agriculture and Life Sciences (CALS) to determine the viability for AgNIC participation. Eventually this led to the selection of rangeland management as a "center of excellence" disciplinary area on which to focus web site development. These early meetings brought together the core interdisciplinary team that still remains the center of UA AgNIC activities, including representatives from the UA Library and various units in CALS (the Rangeland and Forest Resources Program in the School of Renewable Natural Resources, the CALS Network Support Group, and the Arid Lands Information Center in the Office of Arid Lands Studies).

Rangeland management was chosen as the topic due to its relevance to Arizona as well as the entire Western U.S., and because there was strong interest and expertise in the subject across campus. In Arizona, approximately 75 percent of the state can be considered rangelands, which are primarily deserts, grasslands, shrublands, and savannas. Rangelands offer a variety of products and values, including wildlife habitat, forage for livestock, recreational opportunities, open space, and watersheds. Because of their extent in the Western U.S., they are particularly important to local economies and lifestyles.

The first AgNIC funding came in 1995 through a Government Services Administration (GSA) grant given to NAL. Providing the funds necessary to create the technical and administrative foundation for AgNIC at NAL, it also provided seed money to begin UA AgNIC activities through a one-year cooperative agreement between the UA and NAL. The purpose of the agreement was three-fold: (a) to begin development of the Managing Rangelands web site; (b) to offer online reference services through the web site; and (c) to work with the Society for Range Management to digitize and bring the back volumes of their journal to the Web. Based on the results of this first effort, the UA again applied for and received another grant in the fall of 1996 from the CSREES Telecommunications program to further develop the Managing Rangelands web site.

Since that time, the interdisciplinary AgNIC team at the UA has worked to continually add content to the site and improve its navigation and design, moving through several iterations before settling on the current look and structure (Hutchinson and Ruyle 2000). As part of the reconfiguration of the site in conjunction with other Western states described below, the site name changed from "Managing Rangelands" to "Rangelands of the Western U.S." <http://rangelandswest.org/aboutsite.html>, and the Arizona component is now called "Arizona Rangelands" <http://rangelandswest.org/az/index.html> (see Figure 1). The positive feedback received from a variety of users, particularly from agency land managers, along with their ideas for improvements and enhancements, have been instrumental in guiding the development of the site. In particular, user participation has led to a variety of external partnerships resulting in the development of specific information modules and decision-making tools (Hutchinson and Ruyle in press).

These outside collaborations have been instrumental in the development of the site. For example, the Arizona Common Ground Roundtable approached the UA AgNIC team early on. This group, made up largely of

FIGURE 1. Arizona Rangelands Home Page

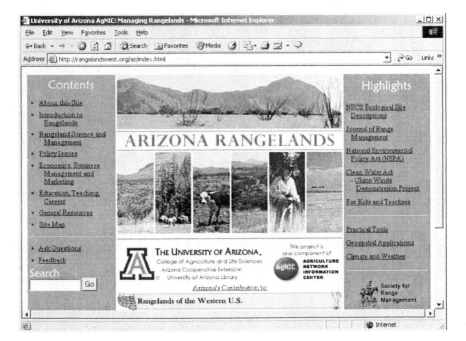

ranchers, environmentalists, academics, and agency land managers, works to support efforts to maintain ranchers' livelihoods and to preserve rangelands as open space. After attending a demonstration of the Managing Rangelands web site, members of the Roundtable expressed interest in working with the AgNIC team to add a more practical module of information for private land managers. Now called the Practical Tools section, this module provides diverse information related primarily to the economic aspects of ranch management targeted to the increasing number of people moving to small farms and ranches (often called 'ranchettes'), as well as for larger enterprises. In this instance, most of the content developed for the site was compiled and written by a graduate student working with the Roundtable and with the UA range extension specialist AgNIC team member. The connections made at the web site demonstration stress the importance of outreach to potential users and collaborators.

Another collaboration, this time with the Arizona Office of the Natural Resources Conservation Service (NRCS), brought a land management tool to the Web for Arizona land managers. Ecological Site Guides, produced by NRCS and used for planning purposes throughout the Western U.S, provide extensive descriptions of land resources, including soils, vegetation, hydrology, climate, and interpretations of wildlife, recreation, and grazing. Previously only available in paper format, the Arizona State Range Conservationist at NRCS had been working for three years to put the Arizona Guides into a database format. When the UA range extension specialist approached the conservationist with an idea to make them available through the AgNIC Rangelands web site, he willingly turned the database over to the UA AgNIC team. Cooperative Extension provided funding for a geographic information systems (GIS) specialist from the UA's Arizona Remote Sensing Center (ARSC). Drawing on the programming capabilities of a UA AgNIC web design team member, a prototype Ecological Site Guide module was developed for the rangelands web site including both a map and textual attribute interface to the database. Again, outreach to form a collaboration was the basis of the success of this project. Although all the Guides are not yet available at the mapping scale desired by most land managers, there is a demonstration of this level of accessibility for the Tohono O'Odham Nation lands. The entry point is at http://rangelandswest. org/az/siteguides/guides.html.

Another opportunity to work with ARSC soon followed, building on the UA AgNIC team's first foray into geospatial applications with the Ecological Site Guides. Through a NASA-funded Raytheon project, ARSC had been exploring the potential for developing applications of satellite remote sensing for rangeland management. As ARSC approached their proposal for a second year of project funding, they contacted members of the UA AgNIC team about tying the remote sensing products to the broader rangelands context presented through the AgNIC Managing Rangelands web site. When the project was funded, members of the UA AgNIC team worked with ARSC, creating an interim web page between the actual remote sensing applications and the Arizona Rangelands home page. A UA AgNIC web designer also developed a unique web site where the remote sensing applications reside. The Arizona Rangelands home page provides users with a "Geospatial Applications" link, taking them to the interim page <http://rangelandswest.org/az/geospatial.html> (see Figure 2). Besides providing explanations of remote sensing technology and its potential as a tool for rangeland management, the page links to RangeView <http://rangeview.arizona.edu> and other related sites. RangeView, a NASA/Raytheon funded project, has continued to develop during the past few years and the UA AgNIC team has remained involved. By working with ARSC, UA AgNIC team members have become more knowledgeable about bringing databases, animations, and interactive tools to the Web. Furthermore, their expertise in design, navigation, and web site structure has been sought out on a regular basis by ARSC collaborators.

FIGURE 2. Interim Page to Geospatial Applications

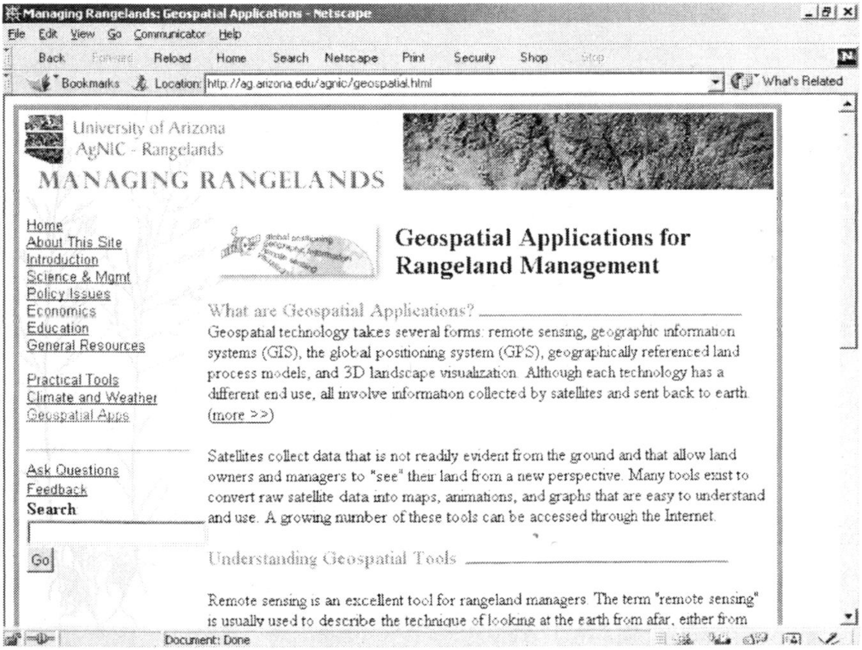

BUILDING A WESTERN REGIONAL AgNIC RANGELANDS COLLABORATION

For a number of years, the UA AgNIC team discussed expanding the Arizona AgNIC rangelands effort to include other land-grant universities representing all of the states in the Western region. In large part, this new direction recognized that the issues surrounding the understanding and management of Western rangelands do not stop and start at political borders. For such topics as invasive species, grazing systems, and endangered species, an ecosystem approach was considered a more appropriate means for informing users about the management of the West's extensive rangelands.

An outreach effort to other regions began with the UA AgNIC team making a series of presentations to determine if there might be broad support for such a collaboration. In the winter of 2001, the team made a presentation to the administrative members of the UA Library and College of Agriculture and Life Sciences, outlining the idea for a regional collaboration. This presentation and the subsequent discussion resulted in an invitation to demonstrate this concept to the administrators attending the Land Grant Colleges of Agriculture Western Regional Joint Summer Meeting in July 2001 at Keystone, Colorado. The positive feedback from various land-grant representatives at the meeting, including the Western Council for Agricultural Research, Extension, and Teaching (WCARET), subsequently led to another presentation given in the fall of 2001 to the Executive Committee of the Policy Analysis Center for the Analysis of Western Public Lands (PACWPL). The Western College of Agriculture Deans established this center a few years before to look particularly at rangeland economic issues.

Based on the strong expressions of interest and support by these groups, especially WCARET and the Deans, the UA AgNIC team made plans to host a workshop in March of 2002, with the goal of bringing key library and rangeland specialists together to discuss establishing a Western Regional AgNIC Rangelands group. Letters were sent to both Library and College of Agriculture Directors, and where appropriate, to Colleges of Natural Resources, requesting their participation in the effort by selecting representatives to attend the workshop. At the same time, letters were sent to designated library and rangelands contacts at many of the Western land-grant universities. Through this process, twenty-four people from twelve land-grant universities were identified as potential participants, including representatives from PACWPL, the Society for Range Management, and the AgNIC Coordinator from the National Agricultural Library. Funds obtained by the UA AgNIC team, leveraged through a related grant and through support by both the CALS and UA Library Deans, covered hotel and meal costs for the participants; however, individual institutions were responsible for travel expenses.

The basis for the workshop was to explore the possibility of forming a Western rangelands consortium to develop a comprehensive web-based resource on current issues and knowledge related to U.S. Western rangelands. The working goal was to unite and integrate the various land-grant university rangeland web activities through a Western rangelands gateway. An ambitious agenda included presentations by all states on rangelands-related web activities, a demonstration of a prototype regional rangelands home page, and discussions on potential organizational structure, content and metadata issues, and funding opportunities. The workshop resulted in a unanimous decision to pursue a common agenda including the development of a regional web site and closely-linked state sites, with the UA taking the lead on initial development activities.

Except for the governing board, the contributions outlined in the workshop to be provided by the UA have all been accomplished since the workshop was held. They include:

- establishing a listserv to facilitate participant communication
- making the workshop PowerPoint presentations available via the web
- transcribing and distributing notes from the workshop
- compiling a short summary of the workshop results
- creating templates for each state's interim rangelands web sites
- creating a regional home page and web site incorporating workshop suggestions
- appointing the first governing board and assigning task groups

The organizational structure is still being developed and how to organize for sustainability was addressed at the second regional meeting in March 2003. Under consideration is an Executive Board/Coordinating Committee to guide decisions about web site content and other issues. Task groups will potentially focus on such areas as content development, metadata issues, organizational structure, funding options, and planning for annual meetings. Participants at the workshop suggested that a liaison be designated to the national AgNIC Coordinating Committee, and further outreach should be conducted in the form of invitations for participation, sent to other Western state institutions including the Dakotas, Nebraska, Oklahoma, Alaska, and Hawaii. Similarly, participants expressed interest in having representation from the Society for Range Management and the national AgNIC organization at future meetings.

As a follow-up to the meeting, the Arizona team created a new regional home page titled "Rangelands of the Western U.S." which is now the entry page into the regional system <http://rangelandswest.org/> (see Figure 3). Taking the more general and regional-specific resources from the old Managing Rangelands web site, the major categories on the home page include: de-

FIGURE 3. Rangelandswest Home Page

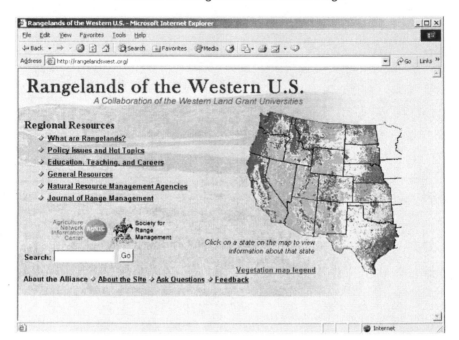

scriptions of rangelands, policy issues and hot topics, education and teaching, general resources, natural resource management agencies, and a link to the *Journal of Range Management (JRM)*. A clickable map including both political boundaries and vegetation cover provides access to the state-specific sites. A simple search capability ties the pages together, facilitating greater access for users to specific information. A separate search capability for *JRM* content is under development.

The original "Managing Rangelands" web site has been reorganized, focusing more on Arizona resources. Now called "Arizona Rangelands," the site has kept its basic structure and content with only a few modifications (see again Figure 1). Although some of the resources reside within the regional home page, they are still linked from the state page. Using the Arizona home page design as a foundation, collaborators are developing their own state-specific web sites on rangelands. Currently, Kansas State University, New Mexico State University, and the University of California, Davis, along with Arizona, have active AgNIC rangelands web sites linked from the regional page.

REGIONAL WEB PAGE HIGHLIGHTS

Two aspects of the Rangelands of the Western U.S. site that have proven very popular and useful for visitors include the *Journal of Range Management* and Policy Issues, both highlighted below.

Journal of Range Management *Digitization*

In 1995, the Society for Range Management (SRM) contacted the National Agriculture Library about the possibility of digitizing the back files of its premier publication, the *Journal of Range Management (JRM)*. This serendipitous inquiry occurred just as the University of Arizona was beginning development of its Managing Rangelands web site. A three-way agreement was negotiated in 1996 in which the SRM would provide copies of back files that the UA Library would digitize and mount for public access via the World Wide Web. NAL agreed to fund the digitization in return for unlimited use of the data and inclusion in networked databases.

The *JRM*–a refereed journal–is the oldest and one of the most respected publications dealing with the ecological management of rangeland resources. Beginning in January 1948, it has been published on a bi-monthly basis for over fifty years, providing a rich information resource as well as a unique record of the developing science and issues of rangelands. The SRM is an excellent partner not only because of the subject focus of the society, but because the over five thousand members represent the same variety of interests as AgNIC: scientists, educators, students, technicians, conservationists, administrators, ranchers, and commercial enterprises.

The agreement with SRM provided that the UA Library would digitize back files including volumes 1-47, covering 1948-1994, with access for current years limited to subscribers. This project gave the UA Library the opportunity to make a significant contribution to the online availability of rangeland information, as well as to develop technical expertise for future digitization projects. A project team developed timelines, specifications, and purchased software and equipment. The team unbound the paper issues, scanned them at 400 dpi using Avatar's EnMasse Software, and converted the text to PDF using Adobe Acrobat Capture. The PDF files were run against the Acrobat optical character recognition software, creating searchable text. Finally, graphic images were scanned and enhanced using Adobe Photoshop. For additional details about this project see http://jrm.library.arizona.edu/aboutjrm.htm#about.

Following this initial effort at the UA Library to digitize and mount the back files up to 1994, SRM also agreed to work with Cornell University to digitize additional back files through 1998 as part of The Essential Electronic Agricultural Library (TEEAL) project <http://teeal.cornell.edu/>. These additional years have been added to the earlier back files to provide access to 1948-1998 in a single location, http://jrm.library.arizona.edu/. The tables of contents and abstracts for more recent issues are available online at the SRM home page housed at Texas A&M University <http://uvalde.tamu.edu/jrm/jrmrecen.htm>.

The next enhancement to the *JRM* component will be a searchable database of the articles by author and keyword. Using bibliographic records downloaded from the AGRICOLA database (with permission of NAL), a searchable file utilizing the OCLC SiteSearch software is being created by the UA Library to enable users to identify articles from any issues of the fifty years of the full-text back file. Bibliographic records have been linked to corresponding text records. A prototype of this database is currently in beta-test and expected to be available soon.

Policy Issues

One of the web site sections of most interest to Colleges of Agriculture administrators has focused on policy issues related to rangelands <http://rangelandswest.org/policy/policy.html> (see Figure 4). Initially created as a module for news items about hot topics and controversial issues within the Arizona rangelands web site, it quickly outgrew its original design and became a

FIGURE 4. Rangeland Policy Issues Web Resource

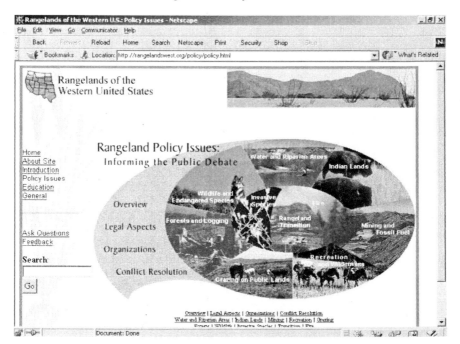

sub-project of its own which fit better into the regional concept and home page. Rangelands issues in the Western U.S. are unique in many respects due to the mix of public and private land management needs and interests. Involved are social, economic, political, and ecological influences that vie for priority in the establishment of policies and regulations. To better understand these viewpoints, the Policy Issues section now includes overview summaries of issues including grazing, water, forests, mining, recreation, urbanization, wildlife, invasive species, fire, and Indian lands. In addition, issues have been broken down into major aspects including further summaries and links to additional resources. The summaries and links have been prepared largely by graduate students from the Rangeland and Forest Resources program and the School of Information Resources and Library Science, under the guidance of the UA Range Extension Specialist.

OUTREACH TO THE RANGELANDS AUDIENCE

Because the intended audience for rangeland information is so varied, many different approaches are taken to reach potential users who include faculty and students at the university level, range scientists and professional range managers, as well as ranchers, farmers, and environmentalists. Perhaps the most basic technique for reaching a wide audience is appropriate registration of the site with the most popular search engines. It is also important to provide well-chosen metadata so that web crawlers will find the site. Being a part of the larger AgNIC community increases our availability to many users, especially librarians, who are familiar with agriculture-related web sources.

In addition, the UA AgNIC team regularly makes presentations and contributes poster sessions at meetings of various stakeholder organizations. These have included campus presentations to deans, department heads and faculty, and state level meetings such as the V-bar-V Ranch Explorers, the Arizona Farm Bureau, the Arizona Agribusiness Council, Arizona AgDay, and the Arizona Extension Conference. At a broader level, the team has presented at meetings such as the 9th U.S/Mexico Border States Conference, Professional Range Managers Update (Utah), Society for Range Management meetings, United States Agriculture Information Network (USAIN) Annual meeting, and the National Extension Technology Conference. For a more complete listing of presentations and poster sessions see <http://ag.arizona.edu/agnic/az/presentations.html>.

CONTRIBUTIONS TO WESTERN RANGELANDS
FOLLOWING THE REGIONAL MEETING, MARCH 2002

Participants from the Western states are beginning to explore ways to make unique contributions from their special or localized expertise and experience.

California and Kansas represent excellent examples of efforts currently underway.

Dr. Mel George, Extension Range Specialist at the University of California-Davis, has revamped the California Rangelands web site and is preparing additional changes to make it similar to the Western Rangelands template (http://agronomy.ucdavis.edu/calrng/range1.htm). Currently, the California site provides links to the AgNIC home page and the Western Rangelands site. Dr. George also prepared a set of rangeland water quality links that soon will be added to the web page making them more accessible to all participants and visitors to the site. Several publications are being added to the web site including useful but out-of-print materials as well as new web-based materials.

Mike Haddock, Agriculture Librarian at Kansas State University, began a state rangelands web site for Kansas in April 2002, after receiving templates to get the project started. Haddock first met with the rangeland specialists in KSU Department of Agronomy to discuss information to include on the site. Following this face-to-face discussion, numerous e-mail communications shaped the content development. The "look" of the original templates were changed and the content categories customized for Kansas information and needs. The site incorporates various photographs of Kansas rangeland scenes as well as other state-specific content. Reference questions submitted via the site go directly to the range specialists in the KSU Department of Agronomy. Feedback and technical questions go to Mike at KSU Libraries, where the site is maintained.

"Kansas Rangelands" (http://www.lib.ksu.edu/ksrange/kshome.html) went live in May 2002 (see Figure 5). The site receives approximately 160 hits per month and this number is expected to grow considerably as more people become aware of the site. Adding links on the web page of the Kansas Section of the Society for Range Management and elsewhere might help to increase exposure. The site itself would benefit from a search feature, but due to limited technical support this has not yet been possible. Additional content will be added to the site as it becomes available.

FUTURE PLANS FOR THE WESTERN REGIONAL AgNIC EFFORT

As has been demonstrated by the regional AgNIC collaborators, the development of the AgNIC Rangelands of the Western U.S. gateway is well underway. During the past nine months, the UA AgNIC team has spearheaded the effort to create new web pages and reconfigure existing web pages, and has looked to the future need to obtain funding to support the regional effort. A dialog continues with WCARET and PACWPL for developing more formal and potentially supportive ties to those groups. In addition, the team applied for

FIGURE 5. Kansas Rangelands Home Page

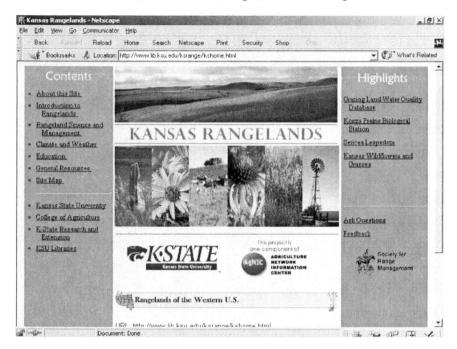

and received in July 2002 a grant from the Agricultural Telecommunications Program, which is administered by the Agricultural Distance Education Consortium (ADEC) and Cornell University. This grant funded a second workshop in March 2003, to bring together the regional collaborators again. It will also help support the development of the technical foundation for the regional gateway, which will be established through a regional metadata database to interface with the national AgNIC database system. Plans were to provide metadata training for all regional collaborators during the 2003 workshop. At the same time, the workshop will be used as a forum for demonstrating state-specific accomplishments and plans, and for discussing next steps in the development of the regional collaboration.

Although much progress has been made during the past seven years of the University of Arizona's involvement with AgNIC, and in the past year as the regional collaboration has begun, the UA AgNIC team recognizes there is still much to do. New web technologies offer possibilities for dynamic and user-driven web sites, and these capabilities should be integral to the delivery of rangeland information resources. Content needs to be repackaged to better facilitate learning and decision-making, and to make current information more readily available through thoughtful summaries representing a synthesis of knowledge. The future success of the regional AgNIC effort will rely on the continuing challenge to establish financial sustainability for the project. By continuing to take a pragmatic and enterprising approach, the UA AgNIC team hopes to keep the momentum moving forward on the AgNIC Rangelands of the Western U.S. initiative. Ultimately, the goal is for the gateway to become the most authoritative and comprehensive web site for rangeland management information.

REFERENCES

Agriculture Network Information Center. 2000. AgNIC Alliance Governance Document. http://www.central.agnic.org/agnic/about/index.html.

Hutchinson, B. and G. Ruyle. 2000. "Wired Without the Barbs: Using the Web for Rangeland Information." *Rangelands* 22(6): 19-22.

Hutchinson, B. and G. Ruyle. "Partnering for Better Management of Western Rangelands: Using Web Technologies to Get the Word Out." Submitted to the *Journal of Agricultural and Food Literature* (in press).

Bilingual Outreach: "Research for Teens" on an Academic Web Site

Awilda Reyes
Naomi Lederer

SUMMARY. The bilingual "Research for Teens" Web site was developed by academic research librarians as an outreach tool that teaches library research skills to teens. Connecting with a teenage audience can be difficult. Universities and businesses with Web sites should not ignore this difficult to please population and potential audience. The site's emphasis is on practicality and evaluation, and the research strategies apply to any library. This article will discuss the creation of "Research for Teens" and the surprising problems and unexpected rewards. *[Article copies available for a fee from The Haworth Document Delivery Service: 1-800-HAWORTH. E-mail address: <docdelivery@haworthpress.com> Website: <http://www.HaworthPress.com> © 2003 by The Haworth Press, Inc. All rights reserved.]*

KEYWORDS. Web sites–design, young adults' library services–Web sites, research techniques, Internet–evaluation, Internet–college and university libraries, research techniques, bilingualism

Awilda Reyes (E-mail: areyes@manta.colostate.edu) is Associate Professor and Business Librarian, and Naomi Lederer (E-mail: naomi.lederer@colostate.edu) is Reference Librarian and Associate Professor, both at Morgan Library, Colorado State University, 501 University Avenue, Fort Collins, CO 80523-1019.

[Haworth co-indexing entry note]: "Bilingual Outreach: 'Research for Teens' on an Academic Web Site." Reyes, Awilda, and Naomi Lederer. Co-published simultaneously in *The Reference Librarian* (The Haworth Information Press, an imprint of The Haworth Press, Inc.) No. 82, 2003, pp. 141-155; and: *Outreach Services in Academic and Special Libraries* (ed: Paul Kelsey, and Sigrid Kelsey) The Haworth Information Press, an imprint of The Haworth Press, Inc., 2003, pp. 141-155. Single or multiple copies of this article are available for a fee from The Haworth Document Delivery Service [1-800-HAWORTH, 9:00 a.m. - 5:00 p.m. (EST). E-mail address: docdelivery@haworthpress.com].

http://www.haworthpress.com/store/product.asp?sku=J120
© 2003 by The Haworth Press, Inc. All rights reserved.
Digital Object Identifier: 10.1300/J120v39n82_09

INTRODUCTION

When the "Research for Teens" Web site (http://lib.colostate.edu/teen_research/) was created as an outreach mechanism for the Colorado State University Libraries, the authors had already been working with students in grades six through twelve in various ways. For example, the librarians offer instruction sessions to junior and high school classes upon request and read Spanish language books during story time at the public library. These activities, while worthwhile and successful, do not reach a large number of students. Promoting the Libraries to potential students is one of the purposes for this type of outreach, and a wider audience was desirable.

A Web page aimed at teens is unusual for academic research libraries, but it can be a very valuable outreach and teaching tool. The recent wider accessibility of the Web in Colorado schools (and across the United States) has created opportunities available to all academic and public libraries with Web pages who want to conduct outreach to K-12 schools. At Colorado State University, the Assistant Dean for Public Services of the Libraries suggested taking advantage of this new opportunity to reach students in grades six through twelve. The authors accepted the challenge as an opportunity to expand their outreach activities without being labor-intensive and time-consuming, problems often connected to other forms of outreach. A Web site can reach every teenager in the state who has access to a computer linked to the Web, yet the librarians conducting the outreach do not have to leave the library.

In early 2000, before embarking on the creation of the "Research for Teens" Web site, the authors looked at academic library Web sites to find pages aimed at teens, with no success. Furthermore, no articles identified or described university library sites for teens in the library literature. Research libraries all over the country mostly assist college students, who often find research a difficult and discouraging experience. However, teaching high school students about research would enable them to arrive at college with basic knowledge about research strategies. With this knowledge already in hand, they could focus on evaluating and synthesizing their materials, instead of spending the bulk of their time looking for resources. Keeping this in mind when creating the "Research for Teens" Web site, the authors included basic research steps to familiarize teens with research strategies. These steps and strategies are relevant not only for preparing teens for college-level work towards a degree, but also to help teens with non-academic research needs, such as creating a resume or finding information about activities in their community. Thus, Research for Teens is relevant for college-bound teens as well as those who join the workforce or have other plans after high school (see Figures 1 and 2).

FIGURE 1. Introduction Page (in English)

Introduction

These Web Pages are designed to develop research skills using:

- Library resources
  - books
  - articles
  - other materials
- Web resources

With
  - a research strategy
  - examples
  - hints/tips

Start with the Research Strategy

Colorado State University
Libraries

© Colorado State University. Used with permission.

FIGURE 2. Introduction Page (in Spanish)

Introducción

Estas páginas del web están diseñadas para desarrollar destrezas de investigación utilizando:

- Recursos de la biblioteca
  - libros
  - artículos
  - otros recursos
- Recursos del Internet

A través de
  - estategias de búsquedas
  - ejemplos
  - ideas/sugerencias

Comienza con las Estrategias de búsquedas

Colorado State University
Libraries

© Colorado State University. Used with permission.

A REVIEW OF LITERATURE/WEB SITES

Determining the content of these research pages involved difficult decisions. And there was another component to address: the bilingual aspect. While information about teens is widely available, the research component related to bilingual instruction for this age group is fairly limited. A search of traditional library and information science literature fails to yield any articles specifically addressing the research needs of bilingual teens. An in-depth review of literature on teen research reveals only a few articles addressing either bilingual concerns or the teens themselves, without the combination of both.

The content of the Web sites we reviewed varies, as does their scope. We examined The New York Public Library's web site, because it serves a large and diverse population. Its site "TeenLink" (http://www2.nypl.org/home/branch/teen/index.cfm) lets teens submit creative writing to its electronic library magazine called "Wordsmiths." The Web site, which is English only, is open to teens everywhere, and also includes information about "TeenLife" in New York, TV and movies, and art links, homework help, and booklists that highlight titles.

The local public library to Colorado State University, the Fort Collins Public Library, serves a population that includes a significant number of Spanish-speaking patrons. It maintains a Web site that includes community information, homework help, history, biography, movies and music, and teen hangouts. Like the New York Public Library Web site, it offers the teens an opportunity to submit creative writing by linking the page to another Web site not maintained by the library. The teen site is also only in English.

The Web does contain bilingual tutorials for teens, but we did not find any hosted by libraries. For example, a tutorial called *Learn the Net*, translated into Spanish, French, German, and Italian, is available at http://learnthenet.com/english/index.html and in Spanish at http://learnthenet.com/spanish/index.html. This commercial site offers the opportunity to learn how to surf the Web and learn about the Internet. Teens can enroll in an interactive class, play games, learn how e-mail and search engines work, and study other related topics.

Some universities, but again, not their libraries, have created teen-oriented Web pages in English. These function as outreach and informational sites for teens. Indiana University has "Teens Only!" at http://education.indiana.edu/cas/adol/teen.html, part of the "Adolescence Directory On-Line (ADOL)," an electronic guide to information about adolescent issues, a service of the Center for Adolescent Studies at Indiana University. "Teens Only!" has some interesting links such as "Ask Dr. Math" and "CollegeEdge," which were not included on the public libraries Web sites mentioned previously. Iowa State University Extension has a site on "Healthy Teen Development": http://www.extension.iastate.edu/teen/inside/additional_web.htm. The University of

Virginia Health System has the "Teen Health Center" at http://www.healthsystem. virginia.edu/internet/teen-health/. These two preceding Web sites have content related to health. The University of Illinois Extension Website "Teen Research," http://www.urbanext.uiuc.edu/teenreach/gallery.html, is a mentoring program designed to offer youth ages ten through seventeen after-school activities to assist them in and out of school. University of Wisconsin River Falls offers "Teen University," a program providing academic enrichment classes at the University of Wisconsin-River Falls to students who show high academic potential, motivation, and talent. They also have "College for Kids," http://www.uwrf.edu/ogs/teenu/welcome.html, a program offering classes designed for students entering grades four through six.

WHY ARE TEENS IMPORTANT?

A significant percentage of the population, teens are traditionally young people aged thirteen to nineteen, hence the term "teenager." The U.S. Bureau of the Census International Database 2000 tallied 20.2 million of the United States' population between the ages of fifteen and nineteen.[1] Worldwide, one in six people is between fifteen and nineteen; these numbers do not even include thirteen and fourteen year olds. The teen population will continue to expand until the year 2010 as the children of Baby Boomers swell the ranks of twelve to nineteen year olds. In addition, the teens are on the Web: " 'about 17 million youth ages 12 through 17' use the net–that's 73 percent of teens in that age group."[2] Therefore, a good way to reach this large and growing audience is via the Web.

Teens are an important population for libraries to market to. They are future and current taxpayers whose taxes will support their community libraries. Furthermore, marketing research reveals that teens who form loyalties to brands will continue to do so throughout their lives:

> Teens throughout the world who become interested in a brand today have a much greater chance of having a relationship with it throughout adulthood . . . It is more efficient to retain a satisfied user than to pay expensive start-up costs to convert users of competing products.[3]

If this is true for brand loyalty, perhaps teenagers who become loyal to their libraries will remain library users throughout their lives, using libraries when they are parents needing guidance in raising their children, adult children needing information on tending elderly parents, and consumers wanting new products and services such as cars, washing machines, or vacation arrangements. All of these needs require a basic level of research skills and familiarity with library materials.

BILINGUAL CHOICE: SPANISH AND ENGLISH

In March 2000, 32.8 million Hispanics lived in the United States, making up 12% of the U.S. population. Moreover, the Hispanic population is younger than the non-Hispanic white population, with 35.7% of Hispanics under age eighteen.[4] This is an important part of the population targeted by the "Research for Teens" site. Our primary geographical target, Colorado residents, includes a greater number of Hispanics than many other areas of the country. Hispanics are more geographically concentrated than non-Hispanic whites, more likely than non-Hispanic whites to reside in the West and less likely in the Northeast and the Midwest.[5] Colorado has a large concentration of this special student population, with 132,084 Hispanic/Latinos between the ages of ten and nineteen.[6] With this statistical data on hand and the language skills to translate the information, Spanish was chosen as the second language for the Web site.

UNIVERSITY OUTREACH TO TEENS

In addition to the large numbers of teenagers, one might ask, why have a Web site aimed at them on an academic library site? A Web site serves as a marketing and recruitment tool for the university: teens familiar with an exceptional Web site might consider attending the university sponsoring it. "Research for Teens" increases the visibility of the university, with links to the university library's Web site, which links to the university Web site. Additionally, Colorado State University is the land-grant school with the responsibility to provide services and information to citizens in the state. This includes young adults, whether or not they will attend post-secondary education. Finally, in terms of availability of material, many sites on the Web are aimed at "kids," which is not necessarily appealing to a teen audience. Teens are sensitive about their position in the community, and to do anything "uncool" is anathema to them. Kids' sites, populated with cartoon figures, bright graphics, and large fonts, might not be the sort of thing a teenager wants his/her friends to see them viewing. The authors saw a need for a Web site that would appeal to the older teens, who are more likely considering higher education possibilities than younger students.

DEVELOPMENT OF THE WEB SITE

"Research for Teens" developed as an extension of the outreach program at Colorado State University Libraries. The site distinguishes itself from other information available on the Web by teaching generic research strategies in two languages. The pages provide parallel text, serving as a way for Spanish readers to get acquainted with English and English readers to Spanish, reaching out in yet another way. For example, most libraries in the United States have signs and materials in English. The parallel text throughout "Research for Teens" provides Spanish speakers with examples of library terms and jargon they might encounter in libraries, making libraries a little less intimidating to these users.

The Web site was deliberately written to be different from existing sites for teenagers. The generic research strategies described are designed to work for a variety of topics, varying widely from the content-based sites dominating the Web. This is critical because the site is available to a worldwide audience. The teenager in a small library will be able to use the strategies as well as a contemporary in a large library. The research techniques are applicable to junior/middle, high school, and college-level work. Furthermore, because of the content, the site does not require regular updates. The few links to outside pages are checked regularly, but the universal research strategies and examples will stay current and relevant.

Another concern regarding the site was the address itself. Often, Web sites change URLs, which can be frustrating for those who link to it or have it bookmarked in their browsers. Several of the sites the authors read about for their initial research have moved, some in less than a year. While the authors cannot vouch for the future, they discussed this concern with the Web librarian at Colorado State University, and the address that was selected should remain stable: http://lib.colostate.edu/teen_research/.

The research strategies used for the site are based on Lederer's "How to Do Library Research" Web site (http://lib.colostate.edu/howto/), a site for college students. Created with first-year college composition students in mind, the strategies and evaluation tools are nevertheless appropriate for any subject and age group. The site is described in Lederer's article, "New Form(at): Using the Web to Teach Research and Critical Thinking Skills."[7] "Research for Teens" uses the same strategies, reworded and simplified for a younger audience. Ties to the college-level site are available throughout "Research for Teens" in the form of links, enabling users to navigate to more information, in both Spanish and English, located on the "How to Do Library Research."

When the site was in its earliest stages, two groups of sixth-graders and their teachers were asked for input. This was overall positive and encouraging. One recommendation that came up more than once was that they wanted information on celebrities. Consequently, the authors added a section they had not considered including themselves on the current topics page, for latest news on celebrities.

ATTRACTING TEENS: APPEALING TO WHAT THEY LIKE

The authors wanted the Web site content to market itself to teen interests and expectations. Eighty-six percent of worldwide teens expect to complete their education, 82% expect to have jobs they like, and 81% expect to succeed in their career, the top three expectations they have for the future. Of the top ten advertising techniques for teens mentioned by Moses in *The $100 Billion Allowance*, "Research for Teens" uses four of them:

- Be realistic (Number 4)
- Use young actors (male and female) (Number 5)
- Use contemporary colors and graphics (Number 6)
- Show that the company [library/librarian] cares (Number 10).[8]

By emphasizing the practical, the site is being as realistic as it possibly can. The digital images are of young adults of both sexes. The site has self-generated images: the menu with rollovers, next, and previous buttons, along with the imported contemporary graphics of teens and animals. Referring teen researchers to their librarian reminds them of the availability of additional help at their own library. The research strategy examples have upbeat closings on purpose to suggest success in the teen researchers' own endeavors.

The music used on the site partially conforms to marketing strategy Number 3: Use popular music.[9] However, most libraries lack the funds to pay for a recognizable sound. Also, since the popularity of celebrities changes rapidly, recognizable sounds would require change on a regular basis. The strategy to stay away from the limelight has already paid off. Other libraries with links to contemporary stars have to keep updating their information; "Research for Teens" avoids that necessity (see Figure 3).

ATTRACTING TEENS: DESIGN/LOOK

Several considerations, and a great deal of time and thought, were put into the graphic, technical, and organizational design of the site. Designed to be easily navigable, computer users and libraries with low-end computers and/or slower modems should be able to access the site at a reasonable speed. "DON'T use the latest and greatest graphical and audio bells and whistles in an attempt to attract teens" is a piece of Web site advice taken to heart.[10] The site needs to be accessible and appealing to both teens and the adults recommending the site to their students. Teens may not seek out Web sites describing how to do library research, but the adult educators in their lives might recommend such sites. Teachers likely prefer reading text without moving objects constantly in front of them. Consequently, every time "Research for Teens" has an option for a flash sequence, there is notification to the user ("flash presentation" or "flash welcome" on the link). Anecdotally, this notification tactic has been approved in loud and emphatic terms by every librarian and teacher asked about it! Youth librarians in Colorado, our primary promoters, expressed a

FIGURE 3

Research for Teens
Library Research

English version

versión en Español

Flash Welcome

Bienvenida en Español con Flash

by Naomi Lederer & Awilda Reyes webmaster
Disclaimer & Copyright Statement

Colorado State University
Libraries

© Colorado State University. Used with permission.

strong preference for a warning when there is going to be a flash action sequence (see Figures 4 and 5). The descriptions in each section are clear, simple, and brief. Quick-loading images that are graphically straightforward speed the time for each page to display. The fact that some people are colorblind, and some like to browse the Web with the images turned off, was also taken into consideration.

Nevertheless, coolness is a factor. Some obviously up-to-date and interesting items on the site include a graphic of a cutting edge flat screen computer monitor, used as a basis for the top of the menu found on every page. Menu buttons running down the side change color when the cursor goes over them, while the words on the monitor screen change to that button's section. For example, when the cursor is over the menu's "careers" button, the monitor at the top has the word "careers" in it. This makes the navigation and the look of the web site cutting edge and appealing to teens (see Figure 6). The menu was created as a way to make sure users could easily locate other parts of the site. It is always be possible to return to the beginning of a section or to the opening page. If one avenue of exploration proves uninteresting to the user, it is easy to jump to another section.

ATTRACTING TEENS: WHAT IS PHAT OR RAD WITH IMAGES

The images for the page were carefully chosen. CD-ROMs with royalty-free photographic images of real teens were purchased, as opposed to cartoons, with the hope that realistic images of teens are more appealing to an older and more sophisticated audience. The images of teens are multicultural,

FIGURE 4

for Teachers

These web pages are targeted at students in grades 6 through 12. Emphasis is on practicality and on using the best resources possible. We simplified the vocabulary of library research. Comments and suggestion are welcome.

Awilda Reyes · versión Español/English version
Naomi Lederer - English version

Español
Introduction
Research Strategy
Some examples
    sports
    animals
    US History
    careers
Current topics
Hints/Tips
for Teachers

Research for Teens

© Colorado State University. Used with permission.

FIGURE 5

Para Maestros

Estas páginas del Web tienen como objetivo alcanzar estudiantes entre el 6to y 12mo grado. Hacemos énfasis en la utilidad práctica y en la utilización de los mejores recursos disponibles. Para las estrategias de búsqueda utilizamos vocabulario simple y fácil de entender. Comentarios y sugerencias son bienvenidos.

Awilda Reyes - versión Español/English version
Naomi Lederer - English version

Jóvenes Investigadores

English
Introducción
Estrategias de búsqueda
Algunos ejemplos
    deportes
    animales
    Historia EU
    carreras
Temas de actualidad
Ideas/Sugerencias
Para Maestros

© Colorado State University. Used with permission.

FIGURE 6

to make the site appeal to as many teens as possible. While the authors tried to have a good mix of images on the site, in the early stages it was observed at a session showing the site that there were a lot more girls than boys on the site. This was an unexpected, but a welcome commentary. The images for the pages had been mostly chosen by the Web developer, a student; for the next batch of pages it was suggested that they have more boys than girls in them. In addition to purchasing digital images of contemporary, multicultural teens, a CD-ROM with royalty-free music sequences was also purchased. These upbeat sounds were added to the flash sequences to liven them up and make it more attractive to the users.

ATTRACTING TEENS: CONTENT: BRIEF, RELEVANT, PRACTICAL, AND INTERESTING

The content of the site has an emphasis on practicality. Teen researchers often have little time or patience to cover all of their bases, and librarians are aware of due dates and other constraints upon students' schedules. Therefore, the strategy recommends changing topics in the early stages if there are no resources to support it. The site never suggests or encourages ferreting out hard-to-find items. However, it does encourage finding more items than are required for an assignment. Also, if a student has not selected a subject to research yet, a flash and then rollover sequence gives hints for choosing a topic. The topic selection tips include a recommendation regarding the amount of time the student has to devote to the project. Furthermore, the site encourages evaluating research sources, a critical component of library research.

The example research strategies also include some of the frustrations of research. Some indexes are more helpful than others. Some topics do not lend themselves to books or articles or Web pages. The examples on the site provide three scenarios: two rather straightforward research topics, one topic that starts broad and is narrowed down, and one topic starts narrow and gets broadened until there is enough information for it.

The straightforward topics are "U.S. History → Colorado → Gold rush" and "Animals → Service Dogs." The topic that starts broad and got narrowed is "Sports → Baseball → Balk → New balk rule in 1988," and the topic that starts narrow and gets broadened is "Fashion → Bell Bottoms → Pants/Trousers → Popular Clothing → Fashion Trends of the 1960s." The strategies demonstrate unsuccessful searches and methods that do not work, just like real-life searches. All too frequently, examples used in the library world show research as a smooth process. This site shows examples of things that are difficult and demonstrates that at times a user needs to try another direction.

After examining the site as a whole, an additional section on careers was added to the "Research for Teens" site. Many teens go directly from high school to the workforce, so career options are an important part of their lives that needs to be addressed by the library. Once again, practicality is emphasized on the Web pages. The career section has proportionally more links to other Web locations than other parts of the site, but the concepts still apply.

ATTRACTING TEENS: BEING REALISTIC

One point the site emphasizes is the need to allow time for research. Many students tend to be surprised and frustrated when a research session in the library takes longer than they think it should. Students are often unrealistic about the actual amount of time it takes to identify, locate, and examine sources, and the site tries to get the point across that research, when done properly, is going to take some effort. Knowing and following the research strategy will save, but not eliminate, time spent doing research. If students are aware that the process is not instantaneous it may ease in the long run some of their frustrations and make them more realistic and productive.

CHALLENGES AND PLUSES

The most difficult part of the project was translating certain idioms. The translator/author has tried using the proper Spanish by using dictionaries and thesauri. The author of the Spanish part, a native speaker, has attempted to avoid words with different meanings in different countries. Occasionally it was difficult to find a definition that can be properly understood by Spanish speakers from different countries; when this happened, the authors went back to the English Language versions of the pages and revised them to ensure that the site would remain parallel.

Another difficulty that had to be overcome was that the Web developer, a college student, was unfamiliar with Spanish and took much more time working with the text than was anticipated. Many typos needed correcting, and an additional problem was the software incompatibility between the authors and the developer. This generated numerous errors in both English and Spanish; the authors had worked in Word 97 and the developer had Word 2000. Files opened into Word 2000 manifested errors that had not existed in the other format; it was a frustrating experience to have to correct text that had already been carefully checked.

One of the major difficulties in producing the site is that the authors have many other commitments and responsibilities, and were not able to give undivided attention to its creation. Fortunately, the authors had the opportunity to work with a Library and Information Science student who had a practicum to complete as part of her degree from the University of Illinois at Urbana-Champaign. Susan K. Smith designed the careers sequence and wrote and designed the fashion research example section. She also looked at the entire site, making valuable suggestions that were integrated into the site. Her contributions helped make for a more cohesive site.

OUTREACH/MARKETING/USE OF THE SITE

The initial title for the site was "Teen Research," as reflected in the Web address, but the name changed after the authors received feedback. "Research for Teens" more closely reflects the idea that the site teaches research skills, rather than containing information about teens, like the initial name suggested. During the initial year of development there were no direct links available to the site; after that, an indirect link was established from the "How to Do Library Research" page. Users can now reach the site from Colorado State University Libraries' A-Z Index (see Table 1).

Once the site neared completion, the authors promoted it across Colorado, mailing approximately 1,000 letters to school principals and headmasters, and roughly 200 to school superintendents and district supervisors. The letter included a picture of the initial page of the site, the URL, and a short informational narrative about the site. In addition, the site was demonstrated at a state

TABLE 1. Individual Pages Viewed on "Research for Teens" Site

2003	Pages viewed	Average per day
January	48950	1398
February	18569	714
March	47161	1684

library conference and to young adult librarians from around the state at one of their meetings. They gave us positive and encouraging feedback on what we showed them.

Schools, libraries, and government agencies, including the Colorado Department of Education, are beginning to link to the site, and list it on bibliographies. The Libraries started gathering use statistics for the site in 2003 (see Table 1). The data collected also show that while the majority of the users of the site are from the United States, multiple users from Mexico and Spain visit weekly, as well as users from other countries. Argentina, Dominican Republic, Peru, Uruguay, Costa Rica, Columbia, and Japan all have users making regular visits. It is encouraging to see that the intended audience is finding a use for "Research for Teens."

NOTES

1. "Census International Database" U.S. Bureau Census, < http://blue.census.gov/cgi-bin/ipc/idbsum?cty=US> (25 November 2002).

2. Linda Beck, "Beyond Proms: Teen Psychology Today," *Library Journal* 126, 1 October 2001, 69. Internal quote from Pew Internet & American Life Project <http://www.pweinternet.org>.

3. Elissa Moses, *The $100 Billion Allowance: Accessing the Global Teen Market* (New York: Wiley, 2000), 10.

4. Roberto R. Ramírez, "U.S. Hispanic Population 2000," Ethnic and Hispanic Statistics Branch, March 2000, PGP-4, U.S. Census Bureau, <http://www.census.gov/population/socdemo/hispanic/p20-535/00show.ppt> (24 November 2002).

5. Melissa Therrien and Roberto R. Ramírez, "The Hispanic Population in the United States," U.S. Census Bureau 2000, <http://www.census.gov/population/socdemo/hispanic/p20-535/p20-535.pdf > (24 November 2000).

6. "P12H. Sex by Age (Hispanic or Latino) [49]–Universe: People who are Hispanic or Latino," *Data Set: Census 2000 Summary File 1 (SF 1) 100-Percent Data*, U.S. Census Bureau 2000, <http://factfinder.census.gov/servlet/BasicFactsServlet> (23 November 2002).

7. Naomi Lederer, "New Form (at): Using the Web to Teach Research and Critical Thinking Skills," *Reference Services Review* 28, no. 2 (2000): 130-153.

8. Moses, *$100 Billion*, 182.

9. Ibid. 182.

10. Sara Ryan, "It's Hip to Be Square," *School Library Journal* 46, no. 3 (March 2000): 138-41.

Taking Library Recruitment a Step Closer: Recruiting the Next Generation of Librarians

Ira Revels
LeRoy J. LaFleur
Ida T. Martinez

SUMMARY. During the summer of 2002, Cornell University Library implemented the Cornell University Library Junior Fellows Program–an initiative aimed at introducing high school students of color to academic libraries and librarianship. The six-week program was developed in response to the need for innovative approaches to the recruitment and retention of people of color to the academic library profession. Additionally, the program sought to support the academic achievement of minority students through involvement in research and technology training opportunities. This paper outlines the program's curriculum, performance out-

Ira Revels is Librarian for Educational Technologies and Library Fellow, Department of Instruction Teaching and Learning, Instruction Research and Information Services, Cornell University, 220 Olin Library, Ithaca, NY 14853 (E-mail: ir33@cornell.edu). LeRoy (Lee) J. LaFleur is Social Sciences Bibliographer, Albert R. Mann Library, Cornell University, Ithaca, NY 14853 (E-mail: ljl26@cornell.edu). Ida T. Martinez is Reference and Instruction Librarian and Library Fellow, Cornell University, 106 Olin Library, Ithaca, NY 14853 (E-mail: im58@cornell.edu).

· [Haworth co-indexing entry note]: "Taking Library Recruitment a Step Closer: Recruiting the Next Generation of Librarians." Revels, Ira, LeRoy J. LaFleur, and Ida T. Martinez. Co-published simultaneously in *The Reference Librarian* (The Haworth Information Press, an imprint of The Haworth Press, Inc.) No. 82, 2003, pp. 157-169; and: *Outreach Services in Academic and Special Libraries* (ed: Paul Kelsey, and Sigrid Kelsey) The Haworth Information Press, an imprint of The Haworth Press, Inc., 2003, pp. 157-169. Single or multiple copies of this article are available for a fee from The Haworth Document Delivery Service [1-800-HAWORTH, 9:00 a.m. - 5:00 p.m. (EST). E-mail address: docdelivery@haworthpress.com].

http://www.haworthpress.com/store/product.asp?sku=J120
© 2003 by The Haworth Press, Inc. All rights reserved.
Digital Object Identifier: 10.1300/J120v39n82_10

comes, and challenges, and includes discussion of the need for similar programs or initiatives to be designed and implemented at other libraries. *[Article copies available for a fee from The Haworth Document Delivery Service: 1-800-HAWORTH. E-mail address: <docdelivery@haworthpress.com> Website: <http://www.HaworthPress.com> © 2003 by The Haworth Press, Inc. All rights reserved.]*

KEYWORDS. Outreach, recruitment, minority recruitment, high school students, secondary school students, students of color, young adult programs, partnerships, initiatives, academic libraries, Cornell University

BACKGROUND AND INTRODUCTION

In recent years there has been a notable increase in the number of university library initiatives to recruit and retain minorities to the profession of academic librarianship, most prominently through residency programs for recent library school minority graduates. Traditional means of hiring new staff have proven ineffective in generating applicant pools representative of the user populations academic libraries serve. Oftentimes, minority recruitment efforts are also thwarted by factors that cannot be controlled, such as demographics. In a 2002 newsletter, DeEtta Jones, then the Director of Diversity Initiatives at the Association of Research Libraries, noted, "Even though our best energy is devoted to developing strong recruitment processes, the reality is that more than 75% of U.S. counties have a greater proportion of White residents."[1] As such, academic institutions have had to become more aggressive, innovative, and committed to improving the diversity of candidate pools for academic librarian positions across the spectrum of services.

By designing minority residency programs, academic libraries seek to increase the appeal of academic librarianship for minorities and to aid in training a new and growing body of librarians for the future. With faculty and student bodies on college campuses rapidly becoming more diverse, attracting more representative professional staff to the library is of valid concern. Likewise, with many librarians retiring over the course of the next decade, recruitment at all levels is of significant importance.

In January of 2002, with the support of Cornell University Librarian, Sarah Thomas, an advisory committee made up of Cornell University librarians was assembled for the purpose of designing a unique program to address these concerns. The group convened under the direction of Ira Revels, Cornell University Library Fellow and Librarian for Educational Technologies, and included representatives from a range of library divisions including reference and instruction, collection development, preservation, and information technology.

Constructive discussion led to a consensus to pilot the Junior Fellows Program, an initiative that would seek to recruit a small group of minority students from area high schools to receive training and experience working in the library. Since the fall of 2000, Cornell University Library (CUL) has hosted the Library Fellowship Program–a program with a primary objective of recruiting and retaining recently graduated professional librarians of color to CUL. The CUL Junior Fellows Program emerged from the same concept. However, the main purpose of the program was to proactively introduce local high school students of color to the library profession.

Early discussions envisioned the program as hosting four to six students for a period of six weeks during the summer of 2002. The main goal was to expose them to the various aspects of academic librarianship. While it would be years before these students would realistically be eligible to apply for professional library positions, the program model centered on the idea that familiarizing young students of color with academic libraries might lead them to pursue careers in academic librarianship in the future. The committee also noted that by taking steps to support the academic success of high school students of color, libraries can play a critical role in encouraging them to realize their full potential.

The program was designed to meet a number of other goals as well. Among these were opportunities providing library learning, technology training, college preparatory and admissions counseling, interaction with academic faculty and staff, and affirmation that a university environment could be both a welcoming and inviting atmosphere for young people of color. The committee also envisioned addressing a variety of challenges associated with the digital divide. It called for a curriculum with particular attention to technologies and information literacy.

RECRUITMENT AND SELECTION

Whereas adults might clearly see the benefits of such a program, there was agreement that to ensure success, the program had to be an appealing alternative to more traditional summer activities and job opportunities aimed at high school students. Furthermore, the program would need to combat the usual stereotypes about libraries and librarians as well as confront long-held sentiments about the division between the university and city populations. These concerns were in line with the challenges faced by the Ohio Library Council's (OLC) production of two minority-recruitment videos aimed at young audiences. In the August, 2002 issue of *American Libraries*, Carol Verny reports that during production development, collaborators on the project "faced daunting challenges such as how to portray libraries as exciting places to work [and] how to persuade young adults to consider a career in library and information science."[2] She notes of the project's focus groups, "In overwhelming numbers, teens revealed that they held the traditional stereotypes that have plagued librarianship for years."[3]

Anticipating that recruitment would be challenging, the CUL group sought the input and involvement of a variety of prominent university and local community members. By early February, 2002, CUL had begun to form partnerships with area non-profit organizations and Cornell outreach offices, some of which contributed financial support to the project. Discussions led to the development of several incentives that would attract the participation of students, including wages, a summer bus-pass, free lunch until the first paycheck, and a free refurbished computer for each student upon their successful completion of the program.

Throughout the spring, members of the advisory committee promoted the program to parents, students, and high school personnel through personal contacts and public forums, including the high school's career day fair. High school administration and staff, including those from the library/media center, played key roles as on-site contacts for referrals and recommendations. Additionally, administrators from two local community centers assisted in the effort by distributing promotional materials and program applications. Naturally, the program was marketed to minority students. The committee took into account several factors that affect individuals' decisions on selecting a career. In *College & Research Libraries*, Mark Winston reports that several researchers of "Recruitment Theory" have found that some factors that influence peoples' career decisions are " 'interesting' academic courses and curricula, extracurricular activities, work experience, and ethnicity."[4] The committee kept these factors in mind while recruiting participants and while designing the curriculum.

Approximately fifteen applications were submitted by the deadline in late May. The pool was narrowed to ten, and interviews were scheduled for June at the main high school in Ithaca. Students were asked about their academic studies, extra-curricular activities, academic and career goals, library awareness, and interest in the Junior Fellows Program. Letters of recommendation from teachers and community leaders were also considered in the selection process. Ultimately, eight students were invited to participate in the program. Table 1 illustrates select information about the 2002 CUL Junior Library Fellows.

PROGRAM AND CURRICULUM

Beyond developing a model recruitment and information literacy program for high school students, it was important to design a program that could be easily implemented by other research libraries interested in developing similar

TABLE 1. 2002 Cornell University Library Junior Fellows–Select Information

Race/Ethnicity*	
African American	4
Afro Caribbean	1
Muslim American	1
Cambodian Émigré	1
Kenyan Émigré	1
Gender	
Female	6
Male	2
High School	
Ithaca High School	6
Alternative Community School	2
Grade Level	
Entering Sophomore	2
Entering Junior	4
Entering Senior	2

*self-reported

initiatives. Furthermore, the program was envisioned as a service to the community, where CUL would provide beneficial job and learning opportunities not available elsewhere in the community. Of equal importance, the program served as a mechanism to foster partnerships between the research library and community-based civic and youth organizations. Regarding the OLC's aforementioned recruitment videos, Verny reports that their effectiveness hinged on the people who would be filmed. She notes that the production team "wanted 21st-century library and information professionals–people as comfortable with community partnerships as they are with technology and people who understand the changing role of the library in the community and the changing nature of information needs."[5] In designing the curriculum for the CUL Junior Fellows Program, the advisory committee looked for the same qualities in the librarians who would be working closely with the students. It was vital to the CUL committee, as it was to the OLC production team, "to place the profession at the heart of the Information Age and to capture the diversity of people and career opportunities."[6]

The Junior Fellows Program ran for six weeks in the summer of 2002. The weekly schedule was Monday through Thursday from 9:00 a.m. to 3:00 p.m. The curriculum was designed to meet a number of goals, but the three most salient were (1) to introduce the students to careers in academic librarianship, (2) to introduce the students to the principles and methods of academic research and project development, and (3) to introduce the students to an academic library system. Special interest sessions and field trips were arranged to supplement and enhance the students' experience as junior fellows. The program was divided into two phases, where the first phase provided emphasis on teaching and learning objectives and the second phase allowed for more time to meet research project goals.

Phase One, Weeks 1-4. Emphasis on Library Orientation and Instruction

First, students needed a well-guided and interactive approach to learning about the libraries where they would be attending classes, conducting research, using technologies, job-shadowing librarians, and interacting with Cornell students and staff. The junior fellows received guided tours at nearly half of Cornell's nineteen Ithaca-campus libraries, plus several tours of special collections and departments within those libraries. The libraries where students would spend most of their time, naturally, were toured during the first week.

The students were introduced to the research component of the program on the first day of the program. They were instructed to choose a topic of interest to them and over the course of the six weeks they were to research the topic using CUL resources. The final projects would be multi-media presentations of their findings. During phase one, the curriculum placed particular emphasis on introducing the students to starting and developing the research process. Early sessions included topics such as brainstorming, constructing search statements using Boolean operators, using the library catalog to find print resources, evaluating content on web sites, and evaluating print sources (scholarly vs. popular, primary vs. secondary, etc.). The latter stage of phase one also included instruction on the use of technologies for their research projects. Students received hands-on instruction using scanners, video and still digital cameras, and desktop publishing programs. Throughout the program, students were allowed full access to Uris Library's Creation Station, an up-to-date suite of desktop and portable computing equipment, sophisticated design and multimedia composition software, and communication and collaboration tools useful for teamwork.

It was also essential to the mission of the program that students gain an awareness of and appreciation for the library profession. All instruction sessions and tours were lead by Cornell University librarians who volunteered to participate in the program. Their support and enthusiasm for the program greatly enhanced the curriculum. These instructors/leaders were encouraged to share information about their duties and experiences in libraries with the students. The specific nature of a librarian's work was most prominent when students visited areas like the map collection in the university's main library, central technical services, or The Kheel Center labor archive located in the School of Industrial and Labor Relation's Catherwood Library. Students also participated in job-shadowing where they received overviews on the nature of a librarian's work and hands-on experience. Departments that hosted some of these sessions included Conservation and Preservation and Access Services. One session that the students particularly enjoyed was an informational overview of special libraries led by a librarian from the university's Nestlé Library, which serves the School of Hotel Administration and houses one of the largest and best hospitality collections in the world. These opportunities contributed to the students' awareness of career opportunities in academic libraries.

In summary, during phase one, the daily curriculum generally consisted of a combination of library or department tours, research strategy information sessions, technology demonstrations, and job-shadowing. Some time was also allotted for students to work on their research projects during phase one, but more time was allowed for project development during phase two, the last two weeks of the program.

Phase Two, Weeks 5-6. Emphasis on Completing Research Projects

After immersion courses in librarianship, research, libraries, resources, and technologies, students spent the final two weeks of the program concentrating primarily on fully developing their research projects and finalizing them for presentation to the Cornell community on the final day of the program. During this phase, students were given one to two hours at the beginning and end of the day to work independently on their research projects. They were allowed to work at any of the libraries on campus, use the technologies in the Creation Station, use the library computer labs, or sit at a table to compose longhand. Program staff members were always available to them during these independent-study periods. Staff assisted by proofreading drafts of papers, recommending sources of information, and developing technical components for the final products.

Table 2 illustrates four days of the curriculum and the trend from instruction to research development over the course of the six-week program.

FIELD TRIPS AND SPECIAL INTEREST SESSIONS

Three day-trips were planned to enhance the students' awareness of how the roles of academic interests and libraries extend prominently into communities and important cultural attractions. Visits to the DeWitt Historical Society of Tompkins County, the Harriet Tubman Home, and the Corning Museum of Glass encapsulated how effective research, collection, organization, and presentation of information fulfill important educational interests and needs for

TABLE 2. Sample Days from Cornell University Library's 2002 Junior Fellows Summer Program

Sample Day and Time	Activity
Sample Day During Week 1	
9:00 a.m.-10:30 a.m.	Locating print resources using the online library catalog
10:30 a.m.-11:45 a.m.	Tour of Mann Library
12:00 noon-1:00 p.m.	Lunch
1:00 p.m.-2:00 p.m.	Introduction to Library of Congress Classification
2:00 p.m.-3:00 p.m.	Research Project Discussion/Brainstorming
Sample Day During Week 2	
9:00 a.m.-10:30 a.m.	Content and Context: Popular vs. Scholarly Literature
10:30 a.m.-11:45 a.m.	Key Technologies: Scanning/Graphics
12:00 noon-1:00 p.m.	Lunch
1:00 p.m.-2:00 p.m.	Introduction to Archival Research: Primary Sources
2:00 p.m.-3:00 p.m.	Archives Tour
Sample Day During Week 4	
9:00 a.m.-10:30 a.m.	Research Project Development
10:45 a.m.-12:00 noon	CAVE/Server Farm Tour*
12:00 noon-1:00 p.m.	Lunch
1:00 p.m.-1:45 p.m.	Engineering & Physical Sciences Library Tour
2:00 p.m.-3:00 p.m.	Digital Libraries & Information Technologies/Desktop Services Tour
Sample Day During Week 6	
9:00 a.m.-10:30 a.m.	Research Project Development
10:30 a.m.-12:00 noon	College Preparation Information and Discussion
12:00 noon-1:00 p.m.	Lunch
1:00 p.m.-3:00 p.m.	Research Project Development and Presentation Test Run

*Cornell Theory Center's CAVE provides a three-dimensional, stereo immersive virtual reality environment for viewing scientific, engineering, architectural and art applications (http://www.tc.cornell.edu/Services/Docs/Cave/).

both immediate and extended communities. At each of these cultural centers, docents and librarians led guided tours of the exhibition spaces and the libraries, and included information on their roles and experiences as information specialists.

It was vital to include time in the curriculum for discussion about general college preparation activities, career exploration, feedback about the program, and special receptions. A Cornell librarian with experience in college admissions and career counseling facilitated two information sessions covering topics such as selecting a college, preparing for college, and applying to college. She also led a discussion session on careers in librarianship and the need for more librarians of color. The discussion followed the viewing of the OLC's ten-minute recruitment video, *Looking for Leaders in the Information Age*, which features enthusiastic librarians from richly diverse backgrounds and specialties offering their perspectives on the exciting and rewarding nature of their careers. Hopefully, the issues discussed in this session will remain with the junior fellows for many years. Winston believes that positive recruitment results are possible "if the profession can be 'marketed' by highlighting its strengths with a focus on the desired populations of potential new professionals."[7]

Also, students were invited to share their opinions on various aspects of the program. This was done through written evaluations, group discussions, daily journal entries, and in individual meetings. Finally, it was important to make the students feel welcome at the university. Winston reports on the "apparent perception that academia may not be a welcoming environment for minorities" and, therefore, "recruitment efforts should . . . highlight organizational and administrative support for diversity."[8] Students and their families were invited to meet and socialize with the Cornell community, from administrators to faculty to staff, at two functions: one at the very beginning of the program–a welcoming reception opened by the University Librarian–and the other the annual library picnic held the last day of the program, just before the students presented their final research projects. Everyone in the Cornell University Library system was invited to attend both of these events.

PERFORMANCE OUTCOMES

The Advisory and Planning Committee for the Junior Fellows Program met in mid-August to discuss the successes and lessons learned from the program. Written evaluations and feedback from the students and librarians reflected favorable opinions and confidence that goals and objectives were met.

Substantive feedback from students was gathered mainly from their program journals, in which they were asked to write regularly about the daily activities and programming. Also, a nine-page program survey provided ample opportunity for students to offer both objective and subjective feedback. The survey asked them to indicate their satisfaction with instructors, sessions, tours, assignments, expectations, and tasks. Students were also asked to reflect upon their own performance and identify their strengths and the areas in which they needed improvement. They were asked if they might consider careers in the library profession. These data currently are being quantified, summarized, and analyzed for future papers and reports.

More than thirty-five Cornell librarians and staff members had participated in the summer program. Their perceptions about recruiting high school students of color, their ability to instruct these students, and their knowledge of diversity and recruitment issues were also measured. In a survey and during formal group discussion, most staff members indicated that they did not believe the junior fellows had learned how to conduct good, sustained, and effective library research. However, after discussing the benefits of the program and offering ideas for changes in the curriculum, most agreed that the program should be offered again in the summer of 2003.

One immediate outcome of the Junior Library Fellows Initiative was that students produced a multimedia project or research paper on a topic of their choice and were required to present their work to library and campus staff, as well as to members of the community. This activity allowed them to discuss their research, disseminate information about a topic of concern or interest to them, and develop their presentation skills. An intermediate outcome was the resulting dialogue between the library and the community and the potential for forming new partnerships with non-profit organizations. Long-term outcomes include revealing librarian attitudes about working with high school students of color and developing effective and measurable diversity and recruitment initiatives.

CHALLENGES

There were several challenges in preparing students for their work environment. While most of the students had held jobs before, the Junior Library Fellows Program was the first job for some of the participants. Two students were hired through the Ithaca Youth Bureau after they had received some guidance in employer/employee relations and behavior. The Youth Bureau assigns social workers to assist employers in managing students with little or no workplace experience. Their assistance was valuable, as they provided useful techniques for interacting with all of the students, and not just those under their purview.

During the course of the program, some students demonstrated short attention spans, disruptive behavior, and tardiness. On more than one occasion, it was necessary for the program director to convene key committee members to address concerns over students' behavior. The advisory committee worked to develop practical solutions as such issues arose. One solution was to implement previously unscheduled reflection hours for the students to offer candid and immediate feedback. During one of these sessions, students revealed they were very interested in doing more job-shadowing activities and less classroom work. They also identified particular challenges the program presented for them individually and they offered good ideas for future programming. Some were unsure about their ability to complete their research projects in the time allotted and this concern often manifested itself in their dissatisfaction with other tasks that they perceived to be unrelated, such as library tours or special collection information sessions.

It was noted that the application and interview process for acceptance to the program should be revisited and redesigned to ensure the participants' interests and the program's objectives were a good-fit for each other. The behavioral issues that some students presented were those commonly exhibited by teenagers; still, the committee conjectured that coupled with a more exploratory application process, perhaps the program should be limited to students entering their junior or senior year in high school. There was also discussion of limiting the number of participants to six or less.

There was consensus that changes should be made in the curriculum as well. Feedback from both committee members and students called for more structure in the day-to-day schedule and clearer definitions of expectations, especially in the job-shadowing and academic assignment components of the program. In designing a program for 2003, the committee discussed the possibilities of having written job descriptions, performance contracts, and syllabi with clearly defined assignments, objectives, and due-dates.

CONCLUSIONS

Approximately $8,000 was spent designing and implementing this program. Students participated twenty-four hours per week in instruction and other sessions. Of the 144 total hours, approximately twenty-six hours were spent in instruction sessions, twenty-two hours in tours and on field trips, and twenty hours in mentoring and job-shadowing activities. The remaining seventy-six hours were spent in preparing their multimedia research project or paper.

All eight students completed the program. Their research projects demonstrated that they had learned how to use an academic library's information, technological, and human resources to gather, organize, and present their findings creatively and effectively. Research topics included (1) comparing Harlem Renaissance and modern Hip Hop dress fashions, (2) describing the effects of drug and alcohol abuse on teens, (3) relating a personal account of a family's experiences as Cambodian refugees, (4) encapsulating a brief history of Cornell libraries and the individuals for whom they are named, (5) designing a personal web portfolio using Macromedia's™ Flash technology, (6) discovering how to break into the music and entertainment industry, and (7) examining the societal impact of African American women in rap music videos.

Overall, the program served an important function in exposing high school students to the academic library. As indicated by their final projects, verbal feedback, and through surveys, student confidence and skills in information technology increased and some agreed that they would consider careers in librarianship. Moreover, committee members felt that the majority of the students had gained a greater appreciation for and awareness of libraries, librarians, and librarianship. As evidence of this, members cited the students' stated interests in returning to the program next summer; the students' familiarity and comfortable rapport with a number of librarians whom they shadowed and sought advice from; and the students' enthusiasm for bringing information and technology together in creative ways. To further encourage the students' interests in librarianship, the committee discussed ways of engaging the junior fellows in library activities throughout the regular school year.

In general, the program received favorable comments from the Cornell University Library community and local presses. Advisory committee members and library staff who participated as tour guides, instructors, and job-shadow hosts have expressed support and interest in continuing this initiative.

As a result of CUL implementing the Junior Fellows Initiative, significant qualitative data has been gathered on student and staff attitudes towards diversity and recruitment in an academic research library. Data collection on this topic continues at CUL. It is hoped that the results of these and other studies will help to foster a broader knowledge of the issues related to serving diverse populations in libraries.

The effects of diversity and recruitment programs are critical for students of library and information science, faculty in library schools, research libraries, and members of the information community. Ensuring equitable access to information resources requires the efforts of everyone in the library profession. To ensure that academic research libraries can improve the quality of their staff and services, all librarians must assume responsibility for educating the next generation of library professionals, especially those of color. Efforts may require a lot of hard work, time commitment, and innovation, but they are essential to the future of the profession. Cornell University Library is doing its part through the Junior Fellows Program Initiative.

NOTES

1. DeEtta Jones, "North American Demographic Shifts and the Implications for Minority Library Recruitment," *Bimonthly Report on Research Issues and Actions from ARL: Cultural Diversity and Minority Recruitment* 208-209 (February/April 2000).

2. Carol Verny, "Ohio Goes Recruiting for Minority Librarians," *American Libraries* 33, no. 7 (2002): 52-55.

3. Ibid.

4. Mark Winston, "The Role of Recruitment in Achieving Goals Related to Diversity," *College & Research Libraries* 59, no. 3 (1998): 240-247.

5. Carol Verny, "Ohio Goes Recruiting for Minority Librarians, *American Libraries* 33, no. 7 (2002): 52-55.

6. Ibid.

7. Mark Winston, "The Role of Recruitment in Achieving Goals Related to Diversity," *College & Research Libraries* 59, no. 3 (1998): 240-247.

8. Ibid.

REFERENCES

Jones, DeEtta. "North American Demographic Shifts and the Implications for Minority Library Recruitment." *Bimonthly Report on Research Issues and Actions from ARL: Cultural Diversity and Minority Recruitment* 208-209 (February/April 2000).

Verny, Carol. "Ohio Goes Recruiting for Minority Librarians." *American Libraries* 33, no. 7 (2002): 52-55.

Winston, Mark. "The Role of Recruitment in Achieving Goals Related to Diversity." *College & Research Libraries* 59, no. 3 (1998): 240-247.

Internet Access and Training for African-American Churches: Reducing Disparities in Health Information Access

Julia Sollenberger
Christine DeGolyer
Marilyn Rosen

SUMMARY. Edward G. Miner Library, the health sciences library at the University of Rochester Medical Center, is reaching out beyond its usual user group to improve health knowledge of members of six inner-city African-American churches and one community center. With the Congregation Healthy Heart Action Partnership (CHHAP) and the Rochester Public Library as partners, and with funding from the National Library of Medicine, Miner is providing Internet access at the churches

Julia Sollenberger (E-mail: Julia_Sollenberger@URMC.Rochester.edu) is Director, Health Science Libraries and Technologies; Christine DeGolyer (E-mail: Christine_Degolyer@urmc.rochester.edu) is Outreach Librarian, Edward G. Miner Library; and Marilyn Rosen (E-mail: Marilyn_Rosen@urmc.rochester.edu) is Reference Librarian, Edward G. Miner Library, all at University of Rochester Medical Center, 601 Elmwood Avenue, Rochester, NY 14642.

This article is supported in part by the National Network of Libraries of Medicine (NNLM), and by NIH/NLM, Award Number 467-MZ-102245.

The views expressed are not endorsed by the sponsor.

[Haworth co-indexing entry note]: "Internet Access and Training for African-American Churches: Reducing Disparities in Health Information Access." Sollenberger, Julia, Christine DeGolyer, and Marilyn Rosen. Co-published simultaneously in *The Reference Librarian* (The Haworth Information Press, an imprint of The Haworth Press, Inc.) No. 82, 2003, pp. 171-182; and: *Outreach Services in Academic and Special Libraries* (ed: Paul Kelsey, and Sigrid Kelsey) The Haworth Information Press, an imprint of The Haworth Press, Inc., 2003, pp. 171-182. Single or multiple copies of this article are available for a fee from The Haworth Document Delivery Service [1-800-HAWORTH, 9:00 a.m. - 5:00 p.m. (EST). E-mail address: docdelivery@haworthpress.com].

http://www.haworthpress.com/store/product.asp?sku=J120
© 2003 by The Haworth Press, Inc. All rights reserved.
Digital Object Identifier: 10.1300/J120v39n82_11

and training church and community members to use reliable health Web sites such as MedlinePlus. A train-the-trainer approach and follow-up meetings empower church members to carry the information to others. In addition to trainees learning about reliable health Web resources and Rochester Public Library's health resources, new relationships between libraries and churches have resulted. It is hoped that this program will help reduce health disparities between Rochester's inner-city minorities and residents of the surrounding suburbs. *[Article copies available for a fee from The Haworth Document Delivery Service: 1-800-HAWORTH. E-mail address: <docdelivery@haworthpress.com> Website: <http://www.HaworthPress. com>* © 2003 by The Haworth Press, Inc. All rights reserved.]

KEYWORDS. African-American churches, inner city, community centers, Internet access, training, train-the-trainer, consumer health information, health information literacy, outreach, partnerships, medical libraries, public libraries, health and information disparities

INTRODUCTION

In recent years the terms "digital divide" and "health gap" have been used to describe two different aspects of a disparity that exist for African-Americans in our society. Two studies, "Health Information, the Internet, and the Digital Divide" (Brodie et al., 2000), and the Pew Report entitled "African-Americans and the Internet" (Spooner et al., 2000), indicate that access to the Internet relates directly to income and education, and African-Americans are behind in both areas. Regarding the "health gap," various U.S. government agencies have taken steps to address the "continuing disparities in the burden of illness and death experienced by African-Americans, . . . as compared to the nation's population as a whole" (Protecting the Health . . . , 2002, par. 1). In fact, the Department of Health and Human Services has responded with a multifaceted plan through its Office of Minority Health, a plan called "Closing the Health Gap," which partners with the ABC Radio Network and includes a variety of local health initiatives, as well as a national Web site of health information (Closing the Health Gap, 2002).

Recognizing disparities in the health status of African-Americans, as well as in their access to and use of computers and the Internet for finding health information, health sciences librarians also have reached out within their communities, looking for ways to help close the gap and to narrow the divide. Librarians that serve in urban areas with significant African-American populations are developing programs to help these individuals gain the knowledge they need to make good health care choices. As stated in *Healthy People 2010*, the nation's health agenda for the current decade, "the greatest opportunities for reducing health disparities are in empowering individuals to make informed health care decisions . . ." (Healthy People 2010, 16). Librarians can help by providing access to high-quality health information on the Web and by teaching individuals how to find and evaluate this information.

Funding for librarian-directed programs that seek to improve access to Web-based health information for minority groups has come primarily from the National Library of Medicine. Several national and regional "calls" have generated new ideas and fostered community collaborations. One such successful funding proposal set in motion a collaboration between the Edward G. Miner Library at the University of Rochester Medical Center, the Rochester Public Library, and the Congregation Healthy Heart Action Partnership (CHHAP), a coalition of thirty-seven African-American churches and one community center in inner-city Rochester.

In 2000 and 2001, Miner Library received funds from the National Library of Medicine to conduct a pilot and then a follow-up program that enabled the placement of a computer and an Internet connection in each of six CHHAP-affiliated African-American churches and the one community center. Using a train-the-trainer model, librarians instructed members of the churches and clients of the center in the basics of using computers and the Internet and in finding high-quality health information on the Web. By facilitating access to information, the project is working toward "closing the health gap" that exists for African-Americans today.

BACKGROUND

There is a long history of social action and outreach centered in black churches (Baskin et al., 2001, 823). Efforts to disseminate health information and conduct health programs continue today through the avenue of these strong religious/community centers. For example, in Atlanta there is the "Eat for Life" program, as well as the Go Girls project targeted at adolescent girls (Baskin et al., 2001, 825-827). The Health Care Revival in Boston, modeled after religious revival meetings, is aimed towards health knowledge and assessment (Lawson et al., 2002, 177).

Many local, regional, and national initiatives promote the reduction of the digital divide. The Community Technology Centers Network, dedicated to "providing low cost access to computers and computer-related technology, such as the Internet, together with learning opportunities that encourage exploration and discovery . . . ," (Community Technology Centers' Network, n.d.) has played an active role in nurturing and supporting the development of community computing centers across the country, with support from the National

Science Foundation and many for-profit and non-profit organizations. There are at least twenty-seven agencies in the Rochester area alone affiliated with this group, according to their membership directory (Community Technology Center's Network: New York, n.d.). Movements also exist to place computers and to extend the World Wide Web into the homes of low-income families. For example, a national non-profit group called One Economy Corporation, has partnered with other organizations and public housing authorities to achieve this end. One Economy has also established a Web site, www.thebeehive.org, which helps meet the literacy, health information, and economic needs of low income individuals (Hecht, 2001, 16).

Promoting access to Internet-based health information and training consumers in its use seems to be largely the domain of libraries. The National Library of Medicine alone has awarded more than one hundred Internet Connection Grants to health-related organizations since 1996 (NLM Funds 34 Internet . . . , 2001). In response to the public's ever-growing need for quality health information, NLM also has created a new grant program entitled "Internet Access to Digital Libraries," a funding initiative that will benefit hundreds of communities with its fifty-two recently funded grants. Recipients range from health centers, to school health clinics, to housing authorities, usually in partnership with university libraries and hospitals (NLM Funds 52 Grants . . . , 2002). In September 2002, NLM awarded fifteen new grants for "AIDS Information Community Outreach" projects, as part of a continuing commitment to AIDS education. These initiatives bring libraries together with such entities as patient advocacy groups, faith-based organizations, and departments of health (NLM Funds 15 AIDS . . . , 2002).

HISTORY

The progression of this church/library partnership in Rochester–from idea to reality–demonstrates that sometimes circumstances and events just fit into place, as *good* ideas become *great* projects. The initial impetus came from the Deputy Director of the Monroe County Department of Health, in an e-mail to the Director of the Edward G. Miner Library, University of Rochester Medical Center. "Had an idea . . . What about applying for a grant (to somewhere?) to provide Internet access to the 35 African-American churches that are part of our heart disease prevention project?" (Bennett 2000).

Investigation uncovered the Congregation Healthy Heart Action Partnership (CHHAP) coalition, a group that began in 1987 as a panel of African-American pastors that worked with the Health Department to increase the rate of influenza immunization in the African-American community. Over the years, as CHHAP has evolved, it has provided some kind of health education or screening service to practically every one of the more than 20,000 African-American adults that the coalition represents. CHHAP is administratively supported by a unique community-academic partnership, the Center for the Study of Rochester's Health. Founded in 1997, the Center's mission is to improve the health of Monroe County residents through health research, project design and evaluation. These are critical functions for advancing the local health agenda.

Partnering with the CHHAP coalition is the key element that has made this project a success, since the church is the core of African-American socialization and interaction. Often adults participate in programs three to five days a week in the church, volunteering for a variety of health and well-being ministries, food distributions, and community programs. Churches provide transportation, lunches, and fellowship to facilitate participation. While considering the best model for CHHAP, church pastors voiced the opinion that there is a general sense of mistrust of outsiders or public health officials. Therefore, the coalition uses a "train-the-trainer" model to implement programs (e.g., nutrition education and physical activity programs) in participating sites. Each participating church selects a Healthy Heart lay health advisor who is responsible for developing a Healthy Heart ministry or committee in his/her congregation. CHHAP program staff facilitate a monthly education/training program for these coordinators. In turn, the coordinators are responsible for replicating the education session at their location and reporting their activities to CHHAP program staff.

Prior to this project, an informal survey of the lay health advisors revealed that over 75% of them knew very little about computers. Typical comments were: "my grandkids know more about them than I do," or "I am embarrassed that I don't know how to use the computer." This project allowed participants to learn about computers and the Internet with others who are at the same point in the learning curve and with the support of fellow congregation members.

Working with the lay health advisors in the CHHAP train-the-trainer mode appeared to be the ideal paradigm for this project. With the church coalition and lay health advisors already in place, the National Network of Libraries of Medicine was eager to fund a pilot to install a computer and provide Internet access for one CHHAP congregation. This pilot was extended when the National Library of Medicine provided monies over two years for five more churches and one community center to receive access and training through its "Consumer Health Information Outreach for Minority Organizations" program.

THE PROGRAM

Pilot Project

The NNLM-funded pilot project in the spring and summer of 2001 involved just one church, Memorial AME Zion. This congregation is the oldest African-American church in Rochester and is a founding member of CHHAP. The church actively provides services to the community and is also a leader in this project.

In the spring of 2001, Memorial's minister and lay health advisor, the CHHAP coordinator, and two Miner librarians met to discuss the pilot and agreed to offer three 1.5-hour hands-on training sessions to church members. Seniors would be trained in the afternoon and others in the evening. The first class would cover computer basics, including turning on a computer and shutting it down; exploring the desktop; opening and closing programs; using windows, the mouse, and the keyboard; and a bit about troubleshooting. The second class would introduce the World Wide Web, including using the Internet Explorer browser; exploring sites such as the Healthy Heart homepage, which the librarians developed for the class; and using an Internet search engine. The third class would focus on MedlinePlus and other reliable Health Web sites, such as Healthfinder and NOAH, as well as how to evaluate other health Web sites.

Miner Library bought the computer and the CHHAP director arranged for a local information technology company to install it and provide ongoing technical support. Dial-up Internet access was also provided by the grant. Miner's outreach librarian and the AME Zion lay health advisor worked together to plan the classes. The lay health advisor advertised the classes by posting announcements in church newsletters and on church bulletin boards, and she made announcements during church services. Before the first class, the outreach librarian spent time with the lay health advisor to acquaint her with the computer and the class content.

Providing training in the church itself proved to be difficult. The computer room was too small to hold all registrants, so the church library was the training site. Since the library had no phone line for Internet access, the two librarians brought in laptops with Web pages available offline to simulate a Web experience. Also, the church library had no good viewing area for projecting the instructor's computer screen or the planned slide show. The eight church members who attended the first class found the laptops more difficult to use than the church's desktop computer. In addition, some other concurrent activities at the church were distracting to the class. After this not-so-successful first class, everyone agreed to hold future sessions in one of Miner Library's computer classrooms so that each participant could use a desktop computer with an Internet connection. The church provided transportation to Miner Library for the remaining classes, and participants stated that they strongly preferred the Miner Library classroom.

After all initial training was completed, the librarians and four of the participants met for a structured evaluation interview. Participants reported that they enjoyed the project, found it helpful, and would like to continue. One commented: "I think the computer will be an enhancement to the church community. People with no access have the opportunity to have access. People who are a little older . . . will have the opportunity to try the computer, make some mistakes and recover without incident." Participants suggested holding two-hour classes in the evening or on Saturday, with more time to practice. They also felt that serving snacks would be viewed positively. When tested for knowledge, the participants seemed comfortable with using the computer and the Internet, but confused the health Web sites with the Internet search engines. Librarians expressed concern about having people with a wide range of skills in the same class, but participants with more advanced computer skills said they enjoyed helping the beginners or surfing the Internet while waiting for beginners to complete the exercises.

The Full Project

In July 2001, CHHAP and Miner Library applied to the National Library of Medicine's Consumer Health Information Outreach for Minorities program and received a two-year contract to expand the project to six more churches. Interested churches applied to participate in the project, and CHHAP selected the sites. The requirements for participation were: (1) to provide a coordinator who would oversee the project at the church and serve as a liaison with the outreach librarian; (2) to provide a secure room for the computer that would be accessible to participants; (3) to select ten members to attend training sessions at Miner Library and to provide transportation for the participants, if necessary; and (4) to ask the participants to each train three other people. Two churches built rooms to house a computer so that they could participate. Computers were ordered and installed, and Internet access was provided using the model that was used in the pilot program.

To extend the concept to churches that had no appropriate space for a computer, a partnership was developed that would pair one of these sites with a nearby branch of the Rochester Public Library. The public library computers would be used for the training and ongoing access. Webster Avenue Community Center, a member of CHHAP, was chosen as that site, rather than a church, because of its proximity to the Sully Branch Library and because of the enthusiasm of staff of both the community center and the neighborhood library.

Training

The first group of trainees included all the church coordinators; they could then act as facilitators during the training sessions for their own churches. As in the pilot project, the training included three sessions: Computer Basics, Web Basics, and Researching Health Information on the Web. The instructors implemented suggestions from the pilot project by expanding the sessions to two hours, scheduling them for evenings or Saturdays, and serving healthy snacks.

The Healthy Heart web site (http://www.healthaction.org/healthyheart/), developed by the librarian instructors, served as a basis for the teaching. This site expanded to become the CHHAP Web site and now includes a tutorials page and copies of the slideshows used in the training sessions, as well as links to useful Web sites. The training sessions for each church followed the same structure. Classes began and ended with brief pre-tests and post-tests. Instruction consisted of ten-minute segments of slideshow and demonstration followed by ten minutes of hands-on exercises. Each participant received four copies of the handouts, one for his/her own use, and three to use when training others. Handouts included pre-tests and post-tests, printouts of the slideshow, exercise sheets, a reference sheet for skills taught in the session, definitions of terms, and an evaluation sheet.

The participants' knowledge of computers and the Internet ranged from "none" to daily use of computers and the Internet. The instructors reminded more experienced people at the beginning of sessions that they may already know much of the information, but to think of the session as a way they could learn to convey the concepts and skills to their friends and family. Those who completed the exercises quickly were encouraged to help less experienced participants or to spend time exploring suggested Web sites in more depth. This strategy seemed to work well.

As in the pilot project, more people registered than actually attended the training. As of May 2003, however, fifty-five people have attended at least one session, thirty-six of these have completed all three classes, and four sites have trained twenty-nine others in a train-the-trainer mode. Most class participants were women, who often searched for health information for their families as well as for themselves. A few men, teenagers, and even children (for lack of babysitters) also participated. Even though classes had only four to ten people, two instructors seemed necessary since the participants interacted with them frequently while doing the exercises. A common comment on evaluation forms was appreciation for the instructors' and facilitators' patience and help.

As mentioned earlier, Webster Avenue Community Center partnered with Sully Branch Library for the project. After meeting with Miner's outreach librarian, the Sully Library director and the Community Center director adapted the training materials for their situation. Webster Avenue Community Center staff attended the initial training at Sully, and then trained members of the community. Sully's director and the Community Center director also directly trained additional community members. Trainees had varying levels of knowledge, so Webster Avenue Community Center grouped people with similar knowledge levels together. The initial trainees suggested two sessions instead of three, so Sully's director shortened subsequent training to two 2 1/2 hour sessions.

Follow-Up Activities

In Fall 2002, the outreach librarian, the church coordinator, and at least three participants from each church held midpoint evaluation meetings to: (1) assess the participants' knowledge of Web health resources, (2) evaluate their progress with training others, and (3) identify and remove any barriers preventing each church from meeting the goal of at least ten church members knowing and using reliable consumer health Web sites. Almost all participants reported using health Web sites since the training, although not necessarily the sites most recommended by the instructors. The participants generally rated the Internet search engines among the most useful tools they learned.

With the exception of two sites, trained church members have been slow to train others. Success in extending the instruction beyond those initially trained appears to depend on these factors: (1) prior knowledge of computers and the Internet, or frequent practice after the training; (2) easy access to the church's computer room; (3) a ready supply of trainees; and (4) an enthusiastic church coordinator. One of the most successful trainers is a church coordinator who had minimal computer experience and no Internet experience before the project. She learned quickly, used the church computer frequently, and eagerly trained fellow members of the congregation. Other beginners felt much less comfortable about training their friends and family; six hours of class time and occasional use of the church computer does not provide enough experience to be a confident trainer. The church coordinators, having completed the classes twice, generally were the most successful trainers.

The most successful church combined its training program with its free lunch program. Since the church's computer room is next to the dining hall, church members use the Web to provide information for people who attend the lunch program; they have also trained a number of these individuals. Some participating churches are inviting members from other CHHAP congregations who were not selected for the program to attend training. Two churches participated at health fairs in neighborhood public libraries to advertise the program and to register people for training. Unfortunately, some churches' training programs have faltered because the churches are still working out how to provide access to their computer rooms while at the same time providing some level of security.

At each church the project coordinator and the Miner outreach librarian continue to meet monthly or confer by phone to discuss any problems with the computer and progress with training. The other Miner instructor sends monthly e-mails called "CHHAP Chats" to inform church coordinators about new Web sites of interest. In March 2003, Rochester Public Library held a workshop about other consumer health information resources available through the library. The Miner librarians plan to hold an update and review session in the final months of the program. At the end of the project, the churches will keep the computer equipment and will begin paying for Internet access.

CONCLUSIONS

The following comments indicate that participants find the program useful:

- "You have really awakened my curiosity and have broaden[ed] my horizon . . . very-very-very useful."
- "We're finding it exciting. We're having a lot of fun with it."
- "I just thank CHHAP for including us in the computer [project], because we can go in and I find that anytime day or night, sometime if I have a question sometime later even when everything is closed, I get up and come to the computer. It's very convenient and I really appreciate CHHAP very much for including us."
- "I'm a nurse so I come across a lot of situations where I would like to . . . find out more information about helping or treating."
- "It's informative, not only for ourselves, but to help someone else when they have a question. Then you can go and pull up the information. Even if they're not computer literate, you can, like, read it and go through it with them."

The project was enlightening not only for the participants, but for the coordinators and instructors. The initial pilot project proved worthwhile because it determined which strategies and logistics worked and which needed to be changed before doing a larger project. Frequent contact between the trainers and the church coordinators has helped to keep the coordinators' knowledge fresh. Contracting with an information technology company for technical support prevented a number of problems, although need for the company's services has been infrequent.

Participants generally arrived fifteen minutes to half an hour late for the workshops. It may help to provide a social focus activity before starting the class to encourage interaction, help people to focus on the class, and allow time for stragglers to arrive. Interspersing ten minutes of lecture, slideshow, or demonstration with ten minutes of practice was very successful, and held trainees' interest. Miner Library plans to use this training approach in future projects with its outreach clients. The approach used for teaching people of varying skill levels in the same class was useful and necessary, such as including optional extra activities and providing tips for more experienced participants. It became clear that it was necessary to have different expectations for beginners than for more advanced participants in a train-the-trainer situation. The sites that were most successful in training others were churches that are open many hours and have accessible computer rooms. The church coordinator's attitude and approach are also crucial to the success of the training.

It was great fun to work with the individuals from these congregations. Participants are lively, they interact often with the instructors and each other, they provide plenty of feedback, and they are most appreciative. Many of the participants are very dedicated to helping others and are concerned about health. This project introduced the Miner librarians to a population they wouldn't ordinarily serve and has opened new possibilities for both the library and the churches.

Librarians at the Edward G. Miner Library consider this project to be the first of many future projects that will reach out to Rochester's minority populations with Internet access and with training in finding reliable health information on the Web. These modest initial efforts have informed us and provided a set of strategies and instructional content that can be carried forward as we partner with additional groups in an attempt to close the health gap and narrow the digital divide.

REFERENCES

Baskin, Monica L., Ken Resnicow, and Marci K. Campbell. 2001. "Conducting Health Interventions in Black Churches: A Model for Building Effective Partnerships." *Ethnicity & Disease* 11:823-833.

Bennett, Nancy. E-mail message to Julia Sollenberger, October 16, 2000.

Brodie, Molyann et al., 2000. "Health Information, the Internet, and the Digital Divide." *Health Affairs* 19(6):255-65.

Closing the Health Gap. (2002, November 26). [Internet]. U.S. Office of Minority Health. Retrieved November 26, 2002 from http://www.healthgap.omhrc.gov.

Community Technology Centers' Network (CTCNet). (n.d.) [Internet]. Community Technology Centers' Network. Retrieved November 21, 2002 from http://www.ctcnet.org.

Community Technology Centers' Network: New York. (n.d.) [Internet]. Community Technology Centers' Network. Retrieved November 21, 2002 from http://www2.ctcnet.org/ctc.asp?co=&setting=&st=NY&cat=.

Healthy People 2010. (2000 November). [Internet]. U.S. Department of Health and Human Services. 2nd ed. With Understanding and Improving Health and Objectives for Improving Health. Retrieved November 21, 2000 from http://www.healthypeople.gov/Document/pdf/uih/uih.pdf.

Hecht, Ben, 2001. "Bridging the Digital Divide." *Journal of Housing and Community Development* 58(2):14-17,45.

Lawson, Emma and Azzie Young, 2002. "Health Care Revival Renews, Rekindles, and Revives." *American Journal of Public Health* 92(2):177-179.

NLM Funds 34 Internet Connection Grants to Health-Related Organizations. (2001, November 14). [Internet]. U.S. National Library of Medicine. Retrieved November 21, 2002 from http://www.nlm.nih.gov/news/grantstohealth01.html.

NLM Funds 52 Grants for Internet Access to Digital Libraries. (2002, November 21). [Internet]. U.S. National Library of Medicine. Retrieved November 21, 2002 from http://www.nlm.nih.gov/news/Internetgrants02.html.

NLM Funds 15 AIDS Information Community Outreach Projects in September 2002 in the 9th Round of the Program. (2002, November 4). [Internet]. U.S. National Library of Medicine. Retrieved November 21, 2002 from http://www.nlm.nih.gov/news/aidsprojs02.html.

Protecting the Health of Minority Communities. (September 24, 2002). [Internet]. U.S. Department of Health and Human Services, Office of Minority Health. Retrieved November 21, 2002 from http://www.healthgap.omhrc.gov/factsheet2.htm.

Spooner, Tom et al. (2000, October 22). African-Americans and the Internet. [Internet]. Washington, D.C.: Pew Internet & American Life Project. Retrieved November 25, 2002 from http://www.pewinternet.org/reports/pdfs/PIP_African_Americans_Report.pdf.

If You Build It Will They Come?
Using a New Library Building
to Establish a Culture of Marketing

Karen Brodsky

SUMMARY. While most college campuses have strong support for the libraries, as competition on university campuses for limited financial resources gets tougher, support for libraries can be more theoretical than actual. Library users are unaware of the complexity of and expense required for library services. Not only must libraries compete for limited financial resources, they must also compete in a complex information marketplace. Today, libraries must market themselves to their constituents to ensure that services are utilized and appropriate resources are allocated for all formats of library materials. By committing to a strong marketing program, the University Library at Sonoma State University developed strategic plans to gain broader support from faculty, students, administrators and greater use of services. Libraries wishing to explore the possibility of integrating marketing efforts or libraries in the process of a move can adopt and/or adapt some of these techniques. *[Article copies available for a fee from The Haworth Document Delivery Service: 1-800-HAWORTH. E-mail address: <docdelivery@haworthpress.com> Website: <http://www.HaworthPress.com> © 2003 by The Haworth Press, Inc. All rights reserved.]*

Karen Brodsky is Senior Assistant Librarian, University Library, Sonoma State University, 1801 East Cotati Avenue, Rohnert Park, CA 94928 (E-mail: karen. brodsky@sonoma.edu).

[Haworth co-indexing entry note]: "If You Build It Will They Come? Using a New Library Building to Establish a Culture of Marketing." Brodsky, Karen. Co-published simultaneously in *The Reference Librarian* (The Haworth Information Press, an imprint of The Haworth Press, Inc.) No. 82, 2003, pp. 183-197; and: *Outreach Services in Academic and Special Libraries* (ed: Paul Kelsey, and Sigrid Kelsey) The Haworth Information Press, an imprint of The Haworth Press, Inc., 2003, pp. 183-197. Single or multiple copies of this article are available for a fee from The Haworth Document Delivery Service [1-800-HAWORTH, 9:00 a.m. - 5:00 p.m. (EST). E-mail address: docdelivery@haworthpress.com].

http://www.haworthpress.com/store/product.asp?sku=J120
© 2003 by The Haworth Press, Inc. All rights reserved.
Digital Object Identifier: 10.1300/J120v39n82_12

KEYWORDS. Marketing, public relations, outreach, new building projects, building projects

I once asked an administrator on my campus for advice about how the library could gain more resources and support for information competence initiatives. Her response was: "Of course there is support for the library, the library is like mom and apple pie." In essence, she was telling me that libraries epitomize the notion of a democratic society and, in theory, there is great support for what we do. Well, of course people support libraries! Libraries are the storehouse of information. They are the great equalizer by providing access to the world's recorded knowledge. People working in libraries are there for the sole purpose of assisting others in their pursuit of knowledge, with no judgment. Librarians, and others who work in libraries, facilitate the discovery of information and the wonder of learning. How could anyone NOT support the notion of libraries and librarians; and, in this day and age, it is easy to argue that libraries are more important than ever. Our society is inundated with information daily (some of it cited, some of it not). The Web has made so much information more easily accessible than ever before in history. A librarian's ability to assist people in weeding through the morass of information in order to make informed, intelligent decisions is more crucial than ever. However, with a lack of resources in most academic institutions, and the exponentially rising costs of running a library, support can often be only of the philosophical kind. Many library budgets have remained flat (or worse, decreased) over the past several years, while operational costs have risen.

Further, students constantly tell us they prefer using the Web because it is easier and more convenient than using complex library resources; and of course, as many students might say, everything they would ever need is available on the Web anyway. According to the recent Pew Internet and American Life Project "nearly three quarters (73%) of college students say they use the Internet more than the library, while only 9% said they use the library more than the Internet for information searching."

In addition to the changing information environment, the information marketplace has changed. In the past, libraries did not have to compete with such information services as Google and Amazon.com. A library could simply send out a flier or newsletter about upcoming activities or changes in a collection because users were very limited in where they could go to find information. Ellen Dodsworth states "it is easy for an academic library to become complacent because it has no natural information competitors on campus to stimulate the business instincts to market within an institutional structure" (320). This is not the case today. If libraries believe they have a valuable product, it is essential for them to compete. Libraries can learn from Theodore Levitt's heavily cited article "Marketing Myopia (With Retrospective Commentary)" in which he states, "There are only companies organized and operated to create and capitalize on growth opportunities. Industries that assume themselves to be riding some automatic growth escalator invariably descend into stagnation" (30). Of the four conditions Levitt claims can lead a company into a downward spiral, the one that resonates most directly for libraries is "The belief that there is no competitive substitute for the industry's major product" (30).

It is easy for people in this evolving profession to bemoan a lack of understanding and actual support by administrators and faculty of what we do and what it takes to operate a library, and it is easy to "tsk tsk" the students who "are less aware of a pre-Internet world than they are of one in which the Net is central to their communication" (Pew). However, it can be argued that a lack of marketing naturally causes users to not know about the rich offerings of libraries. It is astounding that librarians of all ranks continue to belittle the need for marketing. While librarians' understanding of and commitment to marketing is changing, some in this profession believe it is the users' responsibility to find out about the challenges we face, the complexity and costs of the services we provide, and that it is NOT our responsibility to tell them what we do. Some librarians are of the opinion that resources are too precious to be spent on marketing initiatives like newsletters. Ironically, this logic actually contradicts what it means to be a librarian; that is, it is our professional responsibility to assist people in their pursuits of becoming more informed–so why not help them become more informed about libraries by committing to marketing initiatives?

Throughout the literature, there are pleas for libraries to move marketing efforts from the philosophical to the tangible. As recently as November 2002, articles in library journals continue to impress upon librarians the need to promote library benefits to their campus. W. Lee Hisle writes:

> We must find ways to promote the values, expertise, and leadership of the profession throughout the campus to ensure appreciation for the roles librarians do and can play. Though access to information is increasingly decentralized, and computer labs now compete with libraries as campus gathering points, librarians must demonstrate to the campus community that the library remains central to academic effort. (715)

E. L. Morgan states, "There are many more people and institutions providing information services today than even five years ago . . . We have to do more to improve our services and convince people that they should use libraries instead of other information providers" (qtd. in Jackson 50). Anne Lipow declares, "If we don't act, we will not only witness the disappearance of reference service by librarians but will also see commercial interests like Microsoft step in and fill the vacuum, furthering the privatization of library functions" (50). Rudi Denham says:

> In the past 10 years there have been tremendous changes in society that affect the entire concept of what a library is and does. Libraries are under threat. They face critical issues that threaten their very existence. The same issues face all types of libraries: university, research, public, school, and special. Libraries face increased cost and expansion in the variety of materials. They face increased competition and the impact of new technologies. But these threats may also be challenges. They give libraries the opportunity to redesign their own future. (qtd. in Dodsworth 320)

However, some librarians *are* responding to the call of their colleagues. Maureen Jackson states, "In an increasingly competitive world, Library and Information Services have come to realize that they too must promote and publicize the services and products they offer" (43).

Developing an effective culture of marketing to stay competitive is often the biggest challenge. The marketing program of the University Library at Sonoma State University was a proactive response developed to reposition the library from what had been a small and rather traditional academic library into a lively, energetic, rejuvenated, and welcoming resource for the entire community. By committing to a strong marketing program, the University Library was able to develop strategic plans in order to gain broader support from faculty, students, administrators, and greater use of services. Libraries examining the possibility of integrating marketing efforts or libraries in the process of a move can adopt and/or adapt some of these techniques.

For the University Library at Sonoma State University (SSU), a new building afforded a unique opportunity to begin a marketing program enabling us to examine the role of the library on the campus and in the community, as well as incorporate marketing activities into daily operations, thus developing a culture of marketing.

THE SETTING AND THE IMPETUS

SSU is a public liberal arts institution, one of twenty-three campuses in the California State University system, approximately one hour north of San Francisco. Established in 1961, SSU grew up during the free-spirited and turbulent '60s and '70s. Staff and faculty, many still employed at the university, came from the radical Bay Area during those early years, looking for a place where the true expression of ideas could flourish. In the rural tranquility of Sonoma County, a unique sense of community developed. The library was part of this charming family, doing what libraries did in those days–building and managing collections in order to help whomever came through the door. Throughout the years, the library sent occasional fliers informing the campus of various services. As the years moved forward, the university maintained its small size while remaining largely isolated from the larger community.

During the early 1990s, campus budget cuts forced the library to drastically reduce periodical holdings. Many faculty have never recovered their faith in the library; they are unaware that many titles were reinstated later either in print or electronically. At approximately the same time, a bond measure was passed to build a new university library. This new facility was to be truly cutting edge, not a typical library. In fact, much to the chagrin of many on campus, it was to be called an information center, not a library. One of the cutting edge features was to be an Automated Storage and Retrieval System in which books and bound periodicals could be stored and quickly retrieved via requests from the online catalog. Because some items would be in storage, more space would be available for group study, computers, and other developing student needs. There was such negative reaction from faculty about the concept of storing library items, i.e., not having materials on the open shelves, the library management decided to drop the term "Storage" and call it the Automated Retrieval System (ARS).

As the initial plans for the new building were developing, society entered the information age, and the electronic era took control of libraries. The world of information was changing, and libraries had to change with it. Also during this time, the local environment of Sonoma County was changing. People began moving to the area in record numbers in order to avoid rising housing costs in San Francisco and Berkeley, the telecommunications industry moved to the area with fervor, and the wine industry became as strong a voice as traditional Sonoma County agricultural products such as apples and poultry.

An interim dean took over in 1999, just as the final phases of planning and construction began for what was to be the Jean and Charles Schulz Information Center, named after the famed Peanuts cartoonist. Under the direction of this new dean and with the support of the library faculty, a commitment to undertaking marketing initiatives was agreed upon *despite* limited resources and strong resistance from some in the library. An extensive marketing/public relations campaign was developed to inform the campus about the new building, any moving plans that would impact library services, library services in general, and to dispel some of the rumors that had been circulating for years, such as the library has no current materials, and the new library would have closed stacks.

DEVELOPING THE PLAN: ASSESSING STRENGTHS AND WEAKNESSES

In developing marketing efforts, the library adhered to such standard marketing principles as assessing strengths and weaknesses and clearly identifying clientele. To begin, the library faculty and dean had many discussions examining the patron base, goals for the library, and the library's resources. It was not always easy to honestly look at strengths and weaknesses in an open collegial exchange. A facilitator was hired to help to ensure discussions were productive. It was clear to all that many obstacles were ahead–the new building was surrounded by great controversy because of the ARS and the name, for example. Further obstacles included a growing traditional-aged student population, a newly integrated library system, enormous misunderstandings about library resources and services, and developing plans for working in a new building twice as large with the same number of staff.

Through these discussions, it was agreed upon that educating the entire SSU community about the library's vital role should be the ultimate marketing goal. Specific issues related to the new building also needed to be addressed, and through honest dialogue, the group realized we also wanted to change the image of the library, use of the library, and support for the library. Truly becoming "student-centered" and being perceived as such was another agreed-upon goal. Yet another goal was for the library to become a cultural hub for the campus where all members of the community could come together to share and discover ideas. While we knew that a shiny new building would do much to help our image, there was no denying the new building offered us a limited opportunity to reposition the library on campus–both academically and politically.

A good marketing plan addresses external and internal customers. It was important to educate not only our users about the library, but to educate library employees about the need for marketing. Initially, it was difficult to get many of the library staff to understand the importance of pursuing marketing efforts. Because marketing seemed to be a four-letter word, the dean termed our marketing initiatives "outreach," thus initiating the Outreach Program, with a librarian put in charge. On the surface, some people seemed to understand the importance of outreach activities, but behind the scenes, there was not unanimous support. Often people appeared to support marketing initiatives, but did not think about marketing when planning new services or developing informational tools. It is easy to understand the apprehension and ambivalence about marketing–people fear the impact from an increased use of services; there can be a fear of loss of control, autonomy and, in an academic environment, loss of what can inaccurately be labeled academic freedom. In the University Library, the process of educating library employees about the need for marketing began with discussions in department meetings and special library-wide meetings on a variety of marketing topics. Often guest speakers were invited to library-wide meetings to discuss changing SSU demographics, student expectations, changing campus initiatives, and other topics that impact marketing decisions.

All library employees were encouraged to participate in marketing initiatives, share ideas, and provide feedback.

DEVELOPING THE PLAN: A MARKET ANALYSIS

Through many discussions, the library faculty and dean looked very closely at whom we served and what services they needed. SSU is an undergraduate liberal arts institution with changing student demographics and a substantially increasing residential population. There was an increase of newly hired faculty, as many of the original faculty retired, thus a changing curriculum. In addition to SSU students, faculty, and staff users, commitments for service in the new building had been made to the local school district. And, the University has spent the past few years reaching out to the greater community. User needs were also changing throughout the library world, as an early survey conducted by the Digital Library Federation finds: "84 percent of survey respondents indicated that the Internet had changed the way they use their own institution's library" (Greenstein and Healy 16). It was clear that not only were patron demographics changing since SSU's inception, but user needs were changing as well.

DEVELOPING THE PLAN: RESOURCES NEEDED

Once the library better understood who our users were becoming and how our services would need to change to better meet these users' needs, the library dean and library faculty looked at available resources for marketing. In order to develop a culture of marketing that would thrive beyond the move, the largest resource allocation would need to be staff time. The library did not have a history of marketing in a professional manner, nor had staff time ever been dedicated to marketing efforts. It was agreed that 50% of a librarian's time was to be allocated to directing a marketing program. Because marketing initiatives were to be more strategic than simply creating a few brochures or a newsletter, success would be dependent on someone having time to develop a program. Initially, student assistant time was also allocated to marketing efforts. The library's financial resources were extremely limited, thus innovation was essential to achieving marketing goals inexpensively and/or collaboratively with other units on campus or members of the community.

THE MARKETING MISSION

With a general sense of direction, planning the outreach program began by adopting a marketing mission statement:

The mission of the University Library's Outreach Program is to provide the Sonoma State University community with the knowledge that the Jean and Charles Schulz Information Center is the county's most vital resource for the discovery of information. We strive to promote the unique features and services available in the Jean and Charles Schulz Information Center by integrating the library, whenever possible, into the larger campus and local community. (Brodsky)

The goals for the program were twofold. First, we wanted to inform library users, especially students, of services and resources available. Second, we wished to garner the greatest support for library activities and initiatives on campus and in the community. Marketing efforts were designed to present an integrated, unified image of the library, in which each department's unique aspects combined to create a cohesive, student-centered organization. There was a constant need to combat the negative impressions of the library on campus and in the community, especially towards collections. Initially, it was also imperative to address a multitude of concerns surrounding the new facility.

THE PROMOTIONAL CAMPAIGNS

Two campaigns were developed, one to inform users of library services, and one to inform users about the new building. The strategy reasoned that by instituting a marketing plan for the new building, a culture of marketing would develop within the library to ensure future outreach efforts. Following is a brief description of the two campaigns.

Your University Library Campaign

As previously stated, this campaign was designed to inform the campus about library services and resources. Beginning in 1999, the marketing department systematically began highlighting services and collections using a variety of venues (the weekly campus newsletter, an internal library digest, the student newspaper, the library website, residence halls newsletter, and other appropriate venues). The "News from the Reference Desk" flier distributed each new semester was changed to "News from the University Library" in order to present a cohesive message from a seemingly unified organization. A "New Book" display was added in the main lobby, intended to combat the impression that new materials were not added to the collection. This was more difficult than expected; some in the library believed the display would be a disservice, because patrons would need to look in several locations for materials. After much discussion, it was agreed that having a new book display was an important service to patrons. This is now a favorite browsing area for patrons. A lively display, "50 Things You Can Do in YOUR Library," was created for the main lobby with a corresponding link on the website. Everyone in the library was asked to participate and submit ideas, generating a great deal of fun for those who participated. It is currently updated once or twice a year and is available at <http://libweb.sonoma.edu/about/50things.html>.

The Jean and Charles Schulz Information Center Campaign

Simultaneous to the "Your University Library" campaign, an exhaustive PR campaign began ten months prior to the move date. This campaign, which targeted the campus, was broken into three components:

1. Not Business as Usual–conducted prior to the move. The goal was to keep the campus informed of "move-related" issues and to educate patrons about features of the new building. An information campaign, titled "Library Move Alerts," disseminated timely updates through various venues such as the weekly campus newsletter, memos signed by the library dean and distributed to all employees, an easily accessible link from the library home page, an e-mail list, a bulletin board in the library lobby, "town hall" meetings, outgoing messages on all of the library public phones, and regular visits to campus departments.

Developing a graphic identity and graphic standards for the new facility was also necessary. This involved a new name, a logo for all letterheads, business cards, brochures, and a new web site. In so doing, the marketing coordinator worked closely with the Development Office, the President's Office, and the University Affairs Office. Aesthetic principles and standards were developed for maintaining the interior of the new facility. For example, templates were designed for signage, especially temporary signage, such as when the copiers were out of order.

2. We're Moving–conducted during the move. The library was closed only three weeks for moving from the old building to the new one. During this time, the University Affairs Office provided the marketing coordinator with an office to answer patrons' questions and field press queries. Temporary signs were posted across campus warning people of the moving trucks, and temporary signage was placed on both buildings informing people of the anticipated opening date, the first day of classes for the Fall 2000 semester.

3. Some Services Might Not Be Fully Operational–conducted after the move. While it only took three weeks to move and unpack the collection, the library was not fully operational on opening day. It was important to inform library users of the phase-in plan. To aid in this, the VP for Academic Affairs included information, supplied by the library dean, in his convocation speech, informing faculty and staff that the library would be open but not fully operational on the first day of classes. Most users were quite sympathetic to the "unpacking," and the library was able to bring services up fairly quickly. To inform users when services were fully operational, communication venues established before the move (campus newspapers, e-mail, and the library web site, to name a few) were again used. In addition, a variety of dedication events throughout the first year and a half aimed to bring people into the library and inform them of services and collections. Dedication events included a grand dedication, featuring students from the theater department singing songs from "You're A Good Man Charlie Brown," an appearance by Snoopy, and a special poem written for the library by the Sonoma County Poet Laureate.

The library also co-hosted a unique, mid-semester party with the Alumni Association titled "A Cook's Tour of the Information Center." Using recipes from a famed local chef's recently released book, *A Cook's Tour of Sonoma County*, guests had the opportunity to visit all three floors of the library while sampling different foods from the cookbook in each area. Dedication events were also held for the clock tower and carillon, a unique room built for the gift of a Jack London collection, and an outside plaza area named for one of the founders of the university.

NO LONGER THE NEW KID ON THE BLOCK:
A RETURN TO PROMOTING SERVICES AND COLLECTIONS

The library was aware that at some point the novelty of the new building would wear off, and the work of simply marketing library services and resources would begin. After the first year in the Jean and Charles Schulz Information Center, marketing efforts began to shift. Rather than focusing on the building, the efforts concentrated on informing users about library services, promoting the image of the library as student-centered, and gaining political support for library initiatives.

One of the visions for the new library building was to be a campus cultural center, or as our president refers to the library, the campus living room (to this end, we allow food and drink in the building). Thus, a variety of activities were developed as part of the Jean and Charles Schulz Information Center, all directly relating to the marketing goals. What follows is a brief list of some of the ongoing outreach activities. While each activity has a variety of unique goals, the common denominator is the intention to bring people into the building, with the assumption that once inside, they will become aware of other services.

Murder in the Stack

As a part of the campus Welcome Week activities, the library collaborates with other campus entities, such as the Residential Life Office and the Alumni Association, to create "Murder in the Stacks." A fun, educational event, "Murder in the Stacks" introduces incoming freshmen (although any student can attend) to the University Library's many features and services. Professional actor "suspects," hired through a murder mystery theater company, are stationed at various locations throughout the library, providing clues while highlighting library features and services. Teams of students explore the building, questioning the suspects and gathering clues to solve the murder mystery, as well as unlocking the mysteries of the library. This event is held the Friday before Labor Day (for students who stay on campus that weekend) and has a lively, party atmosphere with a dj, dancing, and food. The first year, over eighty students attended; the second over 200. The University is committed to continuing this successful program. More details about it are found at http://libweb.sonoma. edu/whatsnew/murder/index.htm.

Arts and Lectures Program

The design of the new facility provided space for hosting a variety of cultural activities. The Arts and Lectures Program in the University Library strives to enrich the intellectual, educational, and cultural life of the Sonoma State community. The program provides a venue for people to come together to share ideas through art, lectures, and discussions. Activities are designed to explore a diversity of ideas, values, and intellectual and artistic expressions. Emphasis is placed on exposure to library collections, research interests of SSU faculty, staff, and students, and regional issues including the support of local cultural initiatives. The program consists of an art gallery, which is approximately 1,200 square feet, a beautiful meeting room for hosting lectures and discussions that can accommodate nearly 100 people, and display cases positioned throughout the building. The Arts and Lectures Program is designed to host five exhibits per year, two of which exhibit student work or are student-curated; the fall semester lecture series is centered on a theme and the spring lecture series highlights faculty and student research and interests. This program, while coordinated through the library, is becoming a campus-wide collaborative endeavor. Faculty and students present ideas for lecture series and art exhibits. Long-established campus lecture series have begun looking to this program as a resource. During the first two years of this program, the University Library hosted eleven art exhibits, over 5,000 people attended a lecture or reading, and twenty displays highlighting library collections were created.

Schulz Unplugged

Premiering in the fall 2002 semester, this unique program brings live music into the library on Friday afternoons for one hour. Held in the multimedia area, Schulz Unplugged was developed to address the needs of a growing residential campus by furthering the role of the library as an activity center for the campus.

New Faculty Lunch

As a way to introduce the library and library faculty to new instructional faculty, an annual New Faculty Lunch takes place during the spring semester. During the lunch, sponsored by the Friends of the University Library, new faculty are provided with a library handbook, questions are answered about the collections, the librarians inform them of the instructional programs, and offer suggestions on how librarians can be important partners in meeting curricular goals, such as consulting in the development of library-related assignments.

Newsletter

The 2002/2003 academic year began with the first issue of the library news-letter–*Access*. This newsletter targets supporters and potential supporters (administrators, faculty, donors, and potential donors). The editorial content informs readers of services and collections (new and ongoing) and provides a glimpse into the intricacies of an academic library in this day and age.

Presentations

Information about the library is presented at every opportunity possible, such as the new and transfer student orientations, Life Long Learning orientations (a university program for the "over 50 crowd"), and parents weekend. Tours are provided to whomever may request one–from visiting librarians planning their own new facility, to retirement community members wanting an afternoon outing, to VIPs visiting the campus, to grade school students.

One-Time Events

Opportunities often present themselves for one-time "events," usually focusing on a new resource or change in a database system. For example, when eBooks were added to the library collection, an "eBook Signing (Up) Party" provided faculty the hands-on opportunity to learn about this new resource. While the turnout for this particular event was small, every faculty member on campus received information about the eBook collection through both print and electronic invitations. Publicity also appeared in the campus newsletter and a request was sent to all deans asking them to encourage faculty to attend.

Community Events

Whenever possible, the University Library participates in appropriate community events such as the annual Sonoma County Book Fair and the Sonoma County Reads project.

GETTING THE WORD OUT AND HOW IT LOOKS

Disseminating Information–Informing clientele of services available is one of the foundations of any marketing campaign. The library continues to use all possible avenues to disseminate information. Regular campus mailings occur to faculty, staff, residence halls, and student clubs, informing them of new services. These mailings consist of over 3,000 fliers distributed to all campus mailboxes. This requires a good relationship with campus mail services to ensure updated lists. Press releases are sent to campus newsletters, the student newspaper, residence hall newsletters, community newsletters, and all media venues in Sonoma County, large and small. A variety of e-mail lists have been created for weekly updates such as readings/lectures for the coming week. The librarians continue to regularly visit schools and departments at least once a semester, and liaison activities have taken on greater meaning. The library "tables" at campus and community fairs, and the library faculty and dean are actively involved with campus initiatives and regularly attend campus meetings, events, and participate on committees.

Materials–Another important marketing principle is the concept of brand identity, which is taken very seriously at the University Library. Every information item created for dissemination to the public includes the library name and logo (or a variation if space is an issue). Those in the library who understand the need for marketing have come to realize that the library web site is not only an important tool for accessing information, it is one of the most important marketing tools; thus resources are put into assessing the usability of the site. The web site is also heavily used to promote library activities, events, and initiatives. All informational and instructional handouts, orientation materials, and temporary signs have a standardized format making it easy for people to identify materials from the University Library. Even the handouts the librarians create for one-shot sessions include the library name and logo.

FRIENDS AND PARTNERS

Part of the success of the library's marketing program is due to the partnerships developed. Because of the implications of the new building for the University, exceptional working relationships were forged with the University Affairs Office and the President's Office. The dean and the marketing coordinator worked closely with the Development Office in finalizing building details such as donor plaques and dedication events. Through the library's ongoing commitment to students, close working relationships have developed with the residence halls, dining services, and other student focused organizations. Through the Arts and Lectures program, strong working relationships with departments on campus such as the art and theater department now exist. Finally, one of the most unique collaborations has been with the Alumni Office. The library is able to organize, promote and host lectures by the Distinguished Alumni as well as highlight the achievements of these individuals through displays in the building. The Alumni Association, in turn, is often one of the first organizations to support library initiatives with financial resources such as co-sponsoring "Murder in the Stacks."

WHAT IT TAKES

Developing a marketing program requires first and foremost a strong commitment from the library dean. Without leadership from the top, it would have been very difficult to successfully undertake most of these initiatives. Following the dedication of the dean is support of the other librarians and staff. While not everyone was on board from the start, critical mass has developed over time in support of marketing.

Marketing is a constant balance of opportunities and challenges. It is important to understand that marketing opportunities exist everywhere; it is simply a matter of seeking them out and realizing that ideas come from anywhere. Looking at everything as an opportunity implies the need for ingenuity–in imagining what can be accomplished and in learning how to get projects completed. Some things work magnificently the first time and fail miserably the second time. It is important to have patience and remain optimistic.

The costs for maintaining a marketing program can vary as widely as the variety of academic libraries. For the program at the University Library at SSU, 50% of a librarian's time is now dedicated to outreach initiatives. When the program began, student assistants provided help. The student hours have since been replaced by 50% of a staff person's time. This library was fortunate to have in-house design capabilities and through the many relationships developed on campus, campus "friends" often provide assistance. Most printing is done in-house with copy machines on quality paper. There is not a line item in the library budget for any of these activities; financial support comes from the Friends of the University Library, the Alumni Association, partnering with other campus entities, and others.

CONCLUSION: SUCCESS OR FAILURE

Have we meet our goals of (1) informing library users, especially students, of services and resources available; and (2) garnering the support for library activities and initiatives on campus and in the community? In assessing this program over the past two and a half years, there have been both successes and failures. Students feel comfortable in the library building, visit librarian office hours, ask questions at the reference desk, use various services in ways not seen prior to the move or since instituting an outreach program. Building use statistics have increased by 40%. While some of the increase is easily attributed to a beautiful new facility, two and a half years after opening, with ongoing outreach activities, these statistics continue to increase. The library now presents a cohesive, unified organization to the entire campus community. A culture of marketing has developed within the library (although not everyone is yet on board). The library is now included in most important discussions on campus, especially concerning the academic curriculum. Students, faculty, and administrators report that the library is the most vital entity on the campus. The library has become a magnet for campus initiatives as colleagues now look to us for leadership, support, and input. However, as we will no doubt continue to experience downturns in the economy, changes in the academic environment, and technological advances impacting the world of information, threats to the library budget will continue to be a reality. While the University Library at SSU has changed its image and the use of services and collections, it seems that not all support is tangible yet. Much remains philosophical–an important reason to continue marketing.

WORKS CITED

Brodsky, Karen. "Marketing Plan Jean and Charles Schulz Information Center, 1999." Internal Document.

Dodsworth, Ellen. "Marketing Academic Libraries: A Necessary Plan." *The Journal of Academic Librarianship* 24:4 (1998): 320-322.

Greenstein, Daniel and Leigh Watson Healy. "Print and Electronic Information: Shedding New Light on Campus Use." *Educase Review* September/October 2002: 16-17.

Hisle, W. Lee. "Top Issues Facing Academic Libraries." *College & Research Libraries News* 63:10 (Nov 2002): 714-15, 730.

Jackson, Maureen. "Marketing the HyLiFe Project." *Library Management* 22:1/2 (2001): 43-49.

Levitt, Theodore. "Marketing Myopia." *Harvard Business Review* 75 (1975): 26-48.

Lipow, Anne Grodzins. "In Your Face Reference Service." *Library Journal* 124 (August 1999): 50-52.

Pew Research Center. *The Internet Goes to College: How Students are Living in the Future with Today's Technology.* September 15, 02 <http://www.pewinternet.org/reports>.

Outreach:
Why, How and Who?
Academic Libraries and Their Involvement
in the Community

Tina Schneider

SUMMARY. Academic libraries have often participated in outreach to their surrounding communities. This article focuses on independent outreach efforts of academic libraries to move beyond their walls or traditional clientele. Academic libraries determine their interaction with their communities based on three factors: whether a need is expressed from outside the academy, whether they see their mission as an invitation to pursue an action on their own accord, or whether they construct a form of outreach in response to a specific problem or crisis. Most libraries, public and private, recognize outreach as part of their mission and obligation to the community. This article examines why libraries choose to initiate outreach programs. *[Article copies available for a fee from The Haworth Document Delivery Service: 1-800-HAWORTH. E-mail address: <docdelivery@ haworthpress.com> Website: <http://www.HaworthPress.com> © 2003 by The Haworth Press, Inc. All rights reserved.]*

KEYWORDS. Outreach, community involvement, academic libraries

---

Tina Schneider is Reference Librarian, Ohio State University at Lima, Lima, OH 45804 (E-mail: schneider.290@osu.edu).

[Haworth co-indexing entry note]: "Outreach: Why, How and Who? Academic Libraries and Their Involvement in the Community." Schneider, Tina. Co-published simultaneously in *The Reference Librarian* (The Haworth Information Press, an imprint of The Haworth Press, Inc.) No. 82, 2003, pp. 199-213; and: *Outreach Services in Academic and Special Libraries* (ed: Paul Kelsey, and Sigrid Kelsey) The Haworth Information Press, an imprint of The Haworth Press, Inc., 2003, pp. 199-213. Single or multiple copies of this article are available for a fee from The Haworth Document Delivery Service [1-800-HAWORTH, 9:00 a.m. - 5:00 p.m. (EST). E-mail address: docdelivery@haworthpress.com].

http://www.haworthpress.com/store/product.asp?sku=J120
© 2003 by The Haworth Press, Inc. All rights reserved.
Digital Object Identifier: 10.1300/J120v39n82_13

Academic libraries have often participated in outreach to their surrounding communities, but a comprehensive examination of why libraries choose to begin outreach programs has not yet been undertaken. What kinds of programs begin in response to different pressures, whether internal or external? How do academic libraries determine their level of interaction with the community? Is such interaction always a part of the libraries' mission? What are the actual levels of involvement? What types of libraries are more likely to begin outreach, and how do they define outreach? The present article examines why libraries choose to initiate outreach programs.

The term "outreach" appears in many different contexts. The working definition for "outreach" in this discussion will be partially borrowed from Ruth J. Person's survey of cooperative efforts of community college libraries, specifically (1) "inter-library cooperation (i.e., with all other types of libraries in the same geographic area)" and (2) "inter-agency cooperation (i.e., with non-library agencies such as museums, governmental units, and social service organizations)."[1] Outreach in this context focuses less on circulation policies and shared libraries, and more on independent efforts of academic libraries to move beyond their walls or traditional clientele to interact with their surrounding communities.

Libraries can determine how to interact with and reach out to their surrounding communities by studying existing library outreach programs. Each academic library is in a different position, whether public, private, big, small, rural, or urban. Nevertheless, every academic library needs to consider why and how to conduct outreach. The type and extent of an outreach program depends a great deal on the resources available to a library. For example, staffing, time, long-term commitment (if called for), and funding play large and practical roles in a library's endeavors. This discussion is meant to encourage libraries to reflect on their missions, opportunities, and commitments to move beyond their walls if their means and mission allow it.

Interest in outreach has been in the literature for at least forty-five years. *Library Trends* devoted an entire issue to library cooperation in January 1958, in an issue called "Building Library Resources through Cooperation," focusing not only on cooperation in academic libraries, but also cooperation among libraries of different types and cooperative efforts among libraries in Europe. Also among the first large studies of outreach, or serving those beyond traditional academic library clientele, is one from 1965, when the ACRL conducted a nationwide survey of 1,110 academic libraries.[2] The primary topics of interest include community users and their access to the library, how community users are defined, what borrowing privileges they have, and methods of safeguarding collections.[3] The study finds that ninety-four percent of academic libraries do provide some or all of the above services to most community members (i.e., non-affiliated users), although most impose restrictions.[4] The survey does not ask about endeavors in outreach beyond circulation policies, or what types of libraries are more likely to participate in outreach, or the impetus for such activities. However, the ACRL study is the first of its kind, and provides a baseline on which other studies can be founded.

A survey of the literature since then indicates that academic libraries determine their interaction with their communities based on three factors: whether a need is expressed from outside the academy, whether they see their mission as an invitation to pursue an action on their own accord, or whether they construct a form of outreach in response to a specific problem or crisis. Certainly, access issues over the past several years have changed significantly, especially with the introduction of the Internet; some issues, such as fee-based searching, are not as pertinent to libraries today as in the past. Even though technicalities may have changed, ideas about cooperative ventures have not. Partnerships with local libraries, innovative programming, and issues related to handling "public" patrons in the library, continue to appear in the literature. The principles of librarianship have endured over the years; issues of access to information, responsibility of the academy to the public, and creating useful partnerships continue to play a large role in our profession.

OUTSIDE INFLUENCES ON OUTREACH

When a need for library services is expressed from outside the library, from the public sphere, the library has a choice about how it will respond, based on its mission and resources. Some libraries, both public and private, undertake proposed projects to promote goodwill in the community, others because it is virtually mandated by their state legislature. For example, in 1988, the Hawaii State Legislature passed a Telecommunications and Information Act to promote the development of an information industry.[5] This legislation, which relied heavily on the University of Hawaii, resulted in the Library External Services Program, a product of the University of Hawaii Libraries and the university's Office of Technology Transfer and Economic Development.[6] This program was designed to provide information to businesses, government agencies, professional associations, and others. The program offered many services, including document delivery, lending of materials, and translation services.[7] This was not a casual arrangement for external services; it is unlike most other outreach services in that the state legislature provided the start-up funds, and its business plan, once approved, led to the "process for developing the necessary Board of Regents policy and State of Hawai'i Administrative Rules for implementation of the program."[8] As a result of this program, "there has been statewide recognition that the University Library resources are a statewide asset."[9] Today, the program's clientele includes not only non-university-affiliated individuals and businesses, but also libraries from the United States and abroad.[10]

Likewise, North Dakota State University (NDSU) faced pressure both from the business community and the state legislature to assist in a "major state-wide push for economic development."[11] The NDSU library, located in Fargo, a regional center for small and medium-sized businesses, already "routinely answered questions from businesspersons."[12] Due to increasing demands and the pressure to assist the state in its economic development, the University Libraries developed a successful fee-based information service for document delivery and research. Although this service originally targeted businesses, local "manufacturing firms, consulting firms, attorneys' offices, and health care management organizations" also expressed interest in document delivery and "scientific and technical information," thus expanding the level of outreach to the community.[13] Though the issue of a fee was resisted at first, it gradually lessened; the library also made an effort to guide users to less expensive options.[14]

External requests for outreach also include local public libraries, which occasionally begin the interaction with the academic libraries. In 1986, for example, the San Diego County Library noticed that "none of the nine institutions granting degrees in the San Diego area maintained any liaison with local public libraries. The result was a lack of library usage by students who eventually became teachers."[15] The resulting Project Intercept brought awareness of the public libraries into the education programs in the area, and also provided internships for students. Two of the schools eventually entered into a more formal internship agreement.[16]

Another example of public libraries taking the lead was a "scholar-led, library-based book discussion service" called *Let's Talk About It*, sponsored by the ALA with a grant from the National Endowment for the Humanities from 1983 to 1987.[17] The program invited a "scholar facilitator" to lead book discussions in public libraries. Although this program did not require the participation of academic libraries, nothing could have been more natural. In one example, the Southern Connecticut Library Council (a multitype organization, with membership favoring public and school libraries) adapted the idea and presented hundreds of discussion programs in public libraries across Connecticut.[18] Although it was the public libraries that were contacting members of academe through informal networking with local universities and colleges, this type of cooperation could and should be moving through the public and academic libraries in a community effort to bring scholarly discourse to the public. At present, other efforts initiated by public libraries have not made their way into the literature; public and academic librarians alike would benefit from learning about other such programs, if they exist.

At times, the idea can be a shared inspiration of both the public and local academic library. Ohio State University at Lima has a very small library with a staff of four. It serves both the Ohio State University regional campus in Lima, and also Rhodes State College, a two-year institution. The library conducts outreach in the form of a delivery agreement with the Lima Public Library. Students and faculty can request to have Lima Public's materials delivered to campus; likewise, members of the public, provided they have a courtesy card, can request materials from the Ohio State University library. Much as Ohio State considers this service outreach on its part, the Lima Public Library also can claim it as outreach on theirs. In the near future, the Lima Public Library will install a collection of popular reading materials at the Ohio State library, essentially creating a new branch location that will serve the recreational reading needs of students and faculty alike.

OUTREACH AS MISSION

The push to go beyond the campus does not always come from outside the library. More often than not, it comes from within the library. If a library acknowledges outreach as part of its mission, which is most commonly found in tax-supported schools, its outreach actions can take several forms, from circulation privileges to programs for youth. Even when it is part of the library's mission, the reasons for and implementations of outreach are many and varied. Likewise, outreach can "provide a linkage to members of the community who may never take a course in the university or send their children there and, as a result, is an important part of the effort to develop acceptance within the community for the university and to increase its political clout in the city and state."[19]

Most libraries, particularly at public universities, will provide cards to the public; this can be considered standard outreach, although the qualifications for obtaining such a card can vary widely.[20] The literature is expansive on both sides of this issue, and has been a common topic for some time. Suffice to say that the issue has not yet been fully resolved, and many librarians stand passionately on both sides. At times, the public's demand for access puts too much strain on the academic library, even if the library originally wanted to provide its services publicly. As a result, access can be restricted, especially when resources and personnel are stretched too thin for students and faculty.[21] Some also argue that the academic library, by providing too much access to the public, takes away from the support that should be going to the public library, or, in some cases, the school library. Ford and Likness of Trinity University, a private institution, state that "libraries cannot be all things to all people."[22] They rightly argue that grade-school students are best served by school and public libraries, and they also explain the restrictions their library has for high school students:

> Students under nineteen years of age are admitted to the library evenings and weekends only when accompanied by a parent, or with a referral form from their school librarian . . . The referral form has increased communication between high school students and their librarians who have found that the students don't always need Trinity's collection. In response to this policy, some high school libraries have opened in the evenings. While some high school librarians have found the Trinity policy an irritation, others strongly support it, arguing that it gives them greater opportunity to demonstrate the demand for their materials and services and to work with their own primary clientele. This supports our view that academic libraries that offer the general public what should be public library services endanger community commitment to the public library.[23]

Again, service to high school students can vary tremendously, depending on their needs. Conversely, others argue the oft-cited obligation of tax-supported schools to provide cards to the public, including high school students. In addition, authors McNamara and Williams state that it is vital to welcome high school students, because in some situations such an effort can "make first-generation college students feel that higher education is possible for them, and access to campus facilities, including libraries, can provide a bridge for potential students . . . This kind of access can also impress parents with the importance of having a university in their community, whether their children go to that university or not."[24] Clearly the issues of access go beyond public/private status, and get into thornier issues of the location of the library and clientele, both real and potential.

Many libraries see their mission as going well beyond providing basic access to library materials to the public. Many academic library programs provide outreach to the public domain, whether that means going into the community itself or by working with other libraries in the area. These programs demonstrate a library's (or librarian's) creativity, initiative, and sense of how best to present itself to those outside of an academic institution.

Among the most commonly reported outreach projects are services to local public health practitioners. The Texas Woman's School of Library and Information Studies, Department of Health Studies, and the University libraries provide a "Public Health Information Project" to local public health professionals "working at the state, county, city, and local levels in the Dallas, Denton, and Fort Worth region."[25] The Project assists those working in public health in navigating the many online resources available to them, and helps to show their applicability in their various fields. Likewise, but in the age before widespread access to the Internet, the Health Sciences Library at the State University of New York at Buffalo had a program to assist in online searching, document delivery, and referral services for local health professionals, administrators, researchers, lawyers, and faculty at other institutions.[26]

Self-initiated efforts mean sometimes simply making a connection among just a few people within a community. The connections eventually affect many others in the community, as with a concert series at the library of San Diego State University, North County. In 1986, a new librarian was hired there, and when the director of the campus noted her background in coordinating jazz festivals and her connections with local musicians, she was "charged with the responsibility to establish a tradition of cultural events at the fledgling university."[27] This charge grew into a noted concert series that drew hundreds of audience members into the library, helping to put the campus at the forefront of cultural activity in the community. Even more importantly, "several people commented that they didn't know we [the campus] existed before they heard about the concert . . . The concerts gave us a unique visibility that conventional university outreach did not."[28]

In other cases, the library will partner with existing outreach programs at the university to participate in its mission to serve the public. Among the examples of these partnerships is a "noncredit mini-course" class taught by an archivist at the University of Toledo, offered through its Division of Continuing Education.[29] The class covers the ever-popular interest in preserving personal documents and memorabilia, and takes place in the special collections and archives department of the university library. Through this class students are not only acquainted with methods of preservation, but also introduced to the existence of area archival institutions, thus widening the connections between the public and local academic institutions.[30]

Other examples of library outreach programs include partnerships with small business centers and the creation of a Grants Information Center. Central Missouri State University libraries partnered with a local Small Business Development Center (SBDC); the library staff and the staff of the SBDC "assisted new product developers by providing patent and trademark searches, and technology and market research."[31] The partnership began as a way for the library to assist the SBDC with researching patents; it was more cost-effective to have a librarian "to actually do the searching rather than rely on [SBDC personnel] to keep up with research techniques."[32] The library at Western Kentucky University created the Grants Information Center as a service for both academic and public patrons, with assistance from an organization called The Foundation Center and, later, government grants. In the 1980s, The Foundation Center provided discounts on annual publications, and in exchange a participating library "agree[d] to provide free public access to . . . sources of private funding information during regular hours of operation";[33] the director of the library at Western Kentucky submitted an application to become an "affiliate" of this program in 1983.[34] The Grants Information Center reported that "well over one-half of its contacts have been with non-university clientele," and have served both local government offices and other, independent, organizations.[35]

UNEXPECTED OUTREACH

The third category consists of a form of outreach in response to a specific problem or crisis. The library at Springfield College, a private institution, had developed into a popular hangout for local youths, who enjoyed using the computers with Internet access after school and during the summer.[36]

Springfield had developed a number of ties with the surrounding community, including the Parks and Recreation Department and the YMCA; it had also acknowledged as a priority "to undertake activities to build a community, both internally and with external neighbors."[37] With the growing numbers of youths in the library, library staff wrestled with issues of mission and their own conflicts; many did not want to work with young adults or children, but rather the college students attending Springfield College. Despite some of the misgivings, the library designed a training program on how to use the library; it also provided youth with a Youth Card identifying them as graduates of the program. This program grew, guiding these youths to other areas of campus as well, such as a tour of a dorm room and eating at the campus snack bar, and served to broaden their horizons in a way that was not anticipated.[38] As a result, the library resolved the initial problem with young adults and strengthened their relations with the community.

Once committed to outreach, a library must decide if and how to promote it. Daniel Savage notes that "small university libraries can passively serve their local communities in addition to their students and faculty by simply responding to requests from community patrons, or they can actively promote the library services available."[39] Before Springfield College began its program for youth, the concern was expressed that if by advertising this new programming for youth, they might exacerbate the problem by attracting more youths. Although this concern was legitimate, it was unwarranted.[40] The library had not planned on implementing a youth outreach program, but found that it was the most effective way for them to keep the situation under control and still expose youths to a positive view of higher education.[41]

With an understanding of the three major types of situations that produce outreach programs to the community, it is appropriate to look at the types of libraries that proceed with these services. As mentioned before, libraries at public universities are more likely to undertake these services due to the nature of their funding. But are they big, small, regional campuses, a departmental library, or a main library? It is also important not to stereotype public and private institutions based on their funding or classification.

A survey of libraries represented in the literature on outreach programs showed that most of the libraries were at very large public universities.[42] This is to be expected, since most if not all publicly-assisted schools are dedicated to public service at some level. It is of course possible that many library outreach services from private institutions simply have not been documented in the literature. As private institutions, however, they are not obligated to serve the public and may not feel pressured to being outreach. Again, the situation often depends on the resources available to the private library. At one British art library, librarian Derek Toyne believes he has an obligation to provide outreach, and suggests three reasons for doing so:

- The nature of art itself. Toyne states that the artist is "someone with a vision of things just beyond the perception of us non-artists," and that our society "desperately needs this deeper insight, this better understanding, this clearer view."
- The nature of education, "the training one needs to play a responsible and creative role in society."
- Local art. The art "of a community, particularly the less sophisticated art, is both a distillation and symbol of local character . . . [the library] could and should provide a contact point and clearing house for information on local collections."[43]

Toyne recognizes the primary clientele of a private library are the students and faculty of the institution, clearly stating that academic endeavors should not undermine those of public libraries, thus taking into consideration the objections of Ford and Likness to academic library outreach.[44] However, he makes an interesting case for the unique kinds of outreach available from private libraries that might not otherwise be available to the community. Likewise, St. Catherine College in St. Paul, Minnesota, partnered with the St. Paul Public Library system to provide the "Family Place." This program is aimed at both parents and children of the predominantly Somali and Hmong immigrant population, and encourages not only family literacy but also promotes the various community services available to them.[45] It is important to note that St. Catherine has four social justice centers of its own which address "real community problems and issues,"[46] and was actively seeking opportunities for its students to gain experience working with immigrant families and community resources. In response to a challenge from one of the justice centers, the Center for Women, Economic Justice, and Public Policy, St. Catherine began to explore the possibilities of collaborating with the St. Paul Public Library system;

ultimately, the Family Place developed into a joint venture that benefited immigrants and St. Catherine participants alike.

Even among public institutions, some debate exists about which types of libraries (research universities, four-year colleges, community colleges) do what kind of outreach, or which offer access to the public and which do not. Ruth J. Person's survey of "interlibrary cooperation" and "interagency cooperation" as discussed at the start of this article found that ninety-nine percent of community college libraries surveyed reported "some level of inter-library cooperation, and eighty percent reported interagency activities."[47] These numbers contrasted with David Bender's findings that seventy-five percent of community college libraries participate in these types of outreach, including "cooperative activities with other community groups and organizations through conferences and visits."[48] He goes on to say that, "approximately one-third of the colleges reported involvement through reports, bibliographies, program exchange, and several other methods, including consortia, workshops, union lists of resources, loans of resources, speaker's bureaus, and professional organizations."[49] While his numbers are still high, clearly they can vary from a very high ninety-nine to a relative low of thirty-three. Which is accurate? The problem in the literature is that the definition of outreach changes constantly; sometimes it encompasses a phone call to another library, and other times a definition requires out-of-the-ordinary action.

Person's analysis of her findings found that a library's location, enrollment size, or membership in state or regional community college systems had no effect on whether the library engaged in outreach. She did find that membership in a formal cooperative influenced the "variety of activities" in which libraries were engaged; libraries that did not join cooperatives refrained from doing so for the following reasons: strain on primary clientele, financial strain, and greater complexity of operation and organization.[50] Person's findings provide an interesting contrast to Blanche Judd's study of the public academic libraries of the State University of New York and the City University of New York. Each of these libraries was surveyed for its policies on community access to the library and borrowing privileges; all else being equal, it was the libraries in urban areas that most frequently denied borrowing privileges to community users.[51] This contrasts with Person's findings that location has no bearing on outreach, although the discrepancy may lie in the differing definitions on "outreach." Person focused on inter-agency cooperation; Judd on patron access. The example of Springfield College's program for youth would support Judd's argument in reflecting an initial reluctance to serve local youth (although this reluctance seemed to fade as the program developed), but has little bearing on how Springfield College relates professionally to other organizations in its area, which include longstanding partnerships with the local Parks and Recreation Department and the YMCA.[52]

McNamara and Williams raise an interesting point on the topic of location as well. They found that "while the evidence is not entirely consistent, it appears that the most successful programs of this kind [i.e., for high school students] tend to take place in smaller cities."[53] McNamara and Williams suspect that success in the smaller cities provides enough students to test a program without overwhelming it.[54]

Within public institutions, different libraries have different missions. Notably, regional campus libraries have a particular mission to serve their communities, because regional campuses typically have a stronger emphasis on community service than do main campuses.[55] They are often located in areas that have place-bound students, and are sometimes the only institution of higher learning in the region; as such, the campuses have a unique obligation in representing higher education. The mission statements of regional campus libraries, when available, do reflect a greater awareness of serving the public, but regional campus libraries have a varied history of such participation. Despite the difference in mission from main campuses, it is unclear whether regional campus libraries actually do proportionally more than main campus libraries. Some regional libraries have become heavily involved in outreach, and have helped to stimulate the local economy in some situations, and in others have assisted in providing employment for the elderly and storytime for preschoolers. Others have sponsored speakers and held conferences.[56] The sizes of these programs undoubtedly differ from programs found on main campuses, but proportionally may be more appropriate.

An academic library's participation in a regional library system can also be considered part of community service. Regional systems are usually local, multitype organizations that include academic, public, school, and special libraries, although many were originally intended for public libraries.[57] These systems typically offer opportunities for continuing education, interlibrary loan, and technical support, among other services.[58] Many academic libraries, even with sophisticated systems linking them together to form statewide consortia, still participate in their local multitype systems. Academic libraries remain members primarily to promote multitype library cooperation and to become more involved with their surrounding communities; their membership has prevented "isolation in the library community" and has led to "deep ties to public and school libraries."[59] Both public and private libraries maintain membership in these systems for similar reasons: to encourage local communication, to foster goodwill, and to be exposed to issues affecting all types of libraries.[60] In Ohio, thirty-eight libraries participate in one of seven regional library systems; nineteen libraries are public and nineteen are private. This proportion roughly estimates the fifty-fifty ratio of public and private campuses in Ohio; altogether, there are sixty-two public universities/community colleges in Ohio, including all of the regional campuses; there are fifty-eight private colleges. In this instance, then, the regional systems have equal numbers of public and private libraries participating; there is no distinction between the two.

CONCLUSION

Outreach can come in many forms. Although it would be easy to say with confidence that libraries at public universities and colleges are the most likely to perform outreach, it is clear that many private school libraries have engaged in innovative and thoughtful programs as well. Most libraries, public and private, recognize outreach as part of their mission and obligation to the community. Some find themselves responding to outside pressure ranging from community groups to the state government, and yet others find themselves in a situation that requires them to consider their level of commitment to outreach.

Most academic outreach programs deal with children or youth, local business interests, or local health services; many partner with programs already on campus. Some of the more original efforts depend upon one person, although large and small libraries both seem to be making efforts according to their resources. The libraries in urban settings seem to be a group that is more complex to study; some are more restrictive than most, yet others go out of their way to serve the public. What is encouraging are the many examples of "fourth-generation cooperation," where libraries have moved from the first generation of working in isolation, to the second generation of networking with libraries of the same type, to the third generation of cooperative systems of multitype libraries, to a fourth generation of "a cooperative combination of various types of libraries and non-library agencies engaged in related activities."[61] Many business, government, health, and school-related outreach programs are examples of reaching the fourth generation.

While it is difficult to pin down a universal agreement on what constitutes outreach, with few exceptions academic libraries accept the presence of the public. Making the effort to leave campus, or leave the library itself, is more remarkable, and the outcomes are frequently endeavors that serve as inspiration for those libraries looking for ideas. Each effort must be tempered with careful thought about the impact on staffing, funding, and resources for the library's primary clientele. But it may just be that your outreach efforts help to attract the primary clientele in the first place.

WORKS CITED

1. Ruth Person, "Community College LRC Cooperative Efforts: A National Study," *Community & Junior College Libraries* 3, no. 2 (1985): 55.

2. E.J. Josey, ed. "Community Use of Academic Libraries: A Symposium," *College & Research Libraries* 28, no. 3 (1967): 184-185.

3. Josey, 185-202.

4. Josey, 198.

5. John Haak, Helen B. Josephine, and Glenn Miyataki, "Information Services and Economic Development: New Opportunities for Collaboration," *Journal of Library Administration* 20, nos. 3/4 (1995): 59.

6. Haak et al., 60.

7. Haak et al., 65.

8. Haak et al., 68, 71.

9. Haak et al., 76.

10. DeeDee Acosta, External Services Program, University of Hawaii at Manoa, e-mail message to author, February 24, 2003.

11. Diane Richards, "Starting a Fee-Based Service in a Rural Area," *The Bottom Line* 5, no. 1 (1991): 15.

12. Richards, 15.

13. Richards, 16.

14. Richards, 15-17.

15. "Library Awareness is Goal of 'Project Intercept,'" *School Library Journal* 32 (February 1986): 11.

16. "Library Awareness is Goal of 'Project Intercept,'" 11.

17. Barbara A. Rader, "Humanities Programming in Public Libraries: The Connecticut Perspective," *Public Libraries* 29, no. 6 (1990): 342.

18. Rader, 343.

19. Delmus E. Williams, "Defining the Mission of the Urban University and Its Library: The Beginnings of a Typology," in *Academic Libraries in Urban and Metropolitan Areas: A Management Handbook*, ed. Gerard B. McCabe. (New York: Greenwood Press, 1992): 12.

20. Many articles on outreach discuss the varied requirements for cards for the public. For a recent, statewide survey, see Cinderella W. Hayes and Hal Mendelsohn, "Community Service in Louisiana Academic Libraries," *LLA Bulletin* 60, no. 3 (1998): 136-139.

21. Anne B. Piternick, "Problems of Resource Sharing with the Community: A Case Study," *Journal of Academic Librarianship* 5, no. 3 (1979): 154.

22. Barbara J. Ford and Craig S. Likness, "Varied Clientele, Service Objectives and Limited Resources: The Academic Library in Transition," *Urban Academic Librarian* 6-7 (fall 1989): 20.

23. Ford and Likness, 21.

24. Jay R. McNamara and Delmus E. Williams, "High School Students and Libraries in Public Universities," in *Academic Libraries in Urban and Metropolitan Areas: A Management Handbook*, ed. Gerard B. McCabe. (New York: Greenwood Press, 1992): 58.

25. Jeffrey T. Huber and Susan E. Ward, "Facilitating Information Access for Public Health Professionals in North Texas: The Public Health Information Project," *Texas Library Journal* 74, no. 4 (2000): 24.

26. Randy Wheeler, "Information Dissemination Service: Service for the Community from an Academic Health Sciences Library," *The Bookmark* 44 (fall 1985): 31.

27. Bonnie Biggs, "Quiet Study Area: No Applause Between Movements," *College & Research Libraries News* 52, no.1 (1991): 16.

28. Biggs, 17.

29. Joel Wurl, "Methodology as Outreach: A Public Mini-Course on Archival Principles and Techniques," *American Archivist* 49, no. 2 (1986): 184.

30. Wurl, 184, 186.

31. Linda Medaris and Mark Manley, "Building a Better Mousetrap: Networking with Community Business Resources," *The Reference Librarian* 58 (1997): 42.

32. Medaris and Manley, 43.

33. Marvin D. Leavy and Elaine E. Moore, "I&R in an Academic Library," *The Reference Librarian* 21 (1988): 110.

34. Leavy and Moore, 110.

35. Leavy and Moore, 112.

36. Robert Kudlay, "Orienting Neighborhood Youth to an Academic Library: Creating Campus-Community Connections," *The Reference Librarian* 67/68 (1999): 112.

37. Kudlay, 115.

38. Kudlay, 124.

39. Daniel Savage, "Town and Gown Re-Examined: The Role of the Small University Library in the Community," *Canadian Library Journal* 45, no. 5 (1988): 293.

40. Kudlay, 127.

41. Kudlay, 127.

42. *American Library Directory*, 38th-44th eds., 46th ed., 48th-51st eds., 53rd-54th eds. Libraries were compared on number of volumes held and size of staff.

43. Derek Toyne, "The Community Role of Academic Art Libraries," *Art Libraries Journal* 12, no. 3 (1987): 35-36.

44. Toyne, 37.

45. Carol P. Johnson, Ginny Brodeen, Helen Humeston, and Rebecca McGee, "Collaboration Generates Synergy," *Reference & User Services Quarterly* 41, no. 1 (2001): 21.

46. Johnson et al., 20.

47. Person, 57.

48. David R. Bender, *Learning Resources and the Instructional Program in Community Colleges*. (Hamden, Conn.: Library Professional Publications, 1980): 126.

49. Bender, 126.

50. Person, 60.

51. Blanche Judd, "Community Use of Public Academic Libraries in New York State: A SUNY/CUNY Survey," *The Bookmark* 42 (winter 1984): 129.

52. Kudlay, 114-115.

53. McNamara and Williams, 62.

54. McNamara and Williams, 62.

55. Tina Schneider, "The Regional Campus Library and Service to the Public," *Journal of Academic Librarianship* 27, no. 2 (2001): 122.

56. Schneider, "The Regional Campus Library," 125.

57. Sarah Ann Long, "Systems, Quo Vadis? An Examination of the History, Current Status, and Future Role of Regional Library Systems," *Advances in Librarianship* 19 (1995): 126, 135.

58. Tina Schneider, "Academic Libraries and Regional Library Systems: How Do They Stand Today?" *Journal of Academic Librarianship* 28, no. 3 (2002): 144.

59. Schneider, "Academic Libraries and Regional Library Systems," 144.

60. Schneider, "Academic Libraries and Regional Library Systems," 145.

61. Beverlee A. French, "The Fourth Generation: Research Libraries and Community Information," in *New Horizons for Academic Libraries*, ed. Robert D. Stueart and Richard D. Johnson (New York: K.G. Saur, 1979): 287.

Index

Page numbers followed by f indicate figures; those followed by t indicate tables.

© 2003 by The Haworth Press, Inc. All rights reserved.

SPECIAL 25%-OFF DISCOUNT!

Order a copy of this book with this form or online at:
http://www.haworthpress.com/store/product.asp?sku=5152
Use Sale Code BOF25 in the online bookshop to receive 25% off!

Outreach Services in Academic and Special Libraries

___ in softbound at $18.71 (regularly $24.95) (ISBN: 0-7890-2432-2)
___ in hardbound at $29.96 (regularly $39.95) (ISBN: 0-7890-2431-4)

COST OF BOOKS ___	**❏ BILL ME LATER:** ($5 service charge will be added)
Outside USA/ Canada/	Bill-me option is good on US/Canada/
Mexico: Add 20%. ___	Mexico orders only; not good to jobbers,
	wholesalers, or subscription agencies.
POSTAGE & HANDLING ___	
US: $4.00 for first book & $1.50	**❏ Signature** ___
for each additional book	
Outside US: $5.00 for first book	**❏ Payment Enclosed: $** ___
& $2.00 for each additional book.	
	❏ PLEASE CHARGE TO MY CREDIT CARD:
SUBTOTAL ___	❏ Visa ❏ MasterCard ❏ AmEx ❏ Discover
In Canada: add 7% GST. ___	❏ Diner's Club ❏ Eurocard ❏ JCB
STATE TAX ___	Account # ___
CA, IL, IN, MIN, NY, OH, & SD residents	
please add appropriate local sales tax.	Exp Date ___
FINAL TOTAL ___	
If paying in Canadian funds, convert	Signature ___
using the current exchange rate,	*(Prices in US dollars and subject to*
UNESCO coupons welcome.	*change without notice.)*

PLEASE PRINT ALL INFORMATION OR ATTACH YOUR BUSINESS CARD
Name
Address
City   State/Province   Zip/Postal Code
Country
Tel   Fax
E-Mail

May we use your e-mail address for confirmations and other types of information? ❏Yes❏ No
We appreciate receiving your e-mail address. Haworth would like to e-mail special discount
offers to you, as a preferred customer. **We will never share, rent, or exchange your e-mail
address.** We regard such actions as an invasion of your privacy.

Order From Your Local Bookstore or Directly From
The Haworth Press, Inc.
10 Alice Street, Binghamton, New York 13904-1580 • USA
Call Our toll-free number (1-800-429-6784) / Outside US/Canada: (607) 722-5857
Fax: 1-800-895-0582 / Outside US/Canada: (607) 771-0012
E-Mail your order to us: Orders@haworthpress.com

Please Photocopy this form for your personal use.
www.HaworthPress.com

BOF04